'The Great Patriotic War'

'Wait for me, and I'll return – only wait very hard;
Wait when you are filled with sorrow as you watch the yellow rain;
Wait when the wind sweeps the snowdrifts;
Wait in the sweltering heat;
Wait when others have stopped waiting, forgetting their yesterdays;
Wait even when from afar no letters come to you;
Wait even when others are tired of waiting;
Wait even when my mother and son think I am no more;
And when friends sit around the fire drinking to my memory,
Wait and do not hurry to drink to my memory too;
Wait for I'll return, defying every death;
And let those who do not wait say I was lucky;
They will never understand that in the midst of death,
You with your waiting saved me;
Only you and I will know how I survived –
It's because you waited as no one else did.'

The most famous Russian poem of the war,
by Konstantin Simonov, 1941,
memorized by countless thousands.

▼Savage fighting flared on the East Prussian border as 3rd Belorussian Front hammered at Third Panzer Army from 13 September to 30 October 1944. Here Guards Sergeant Samoilov commands the advancing 76mm anti-tank gun that has already accounted for five German tanks, one of which, a Panther, burns in the background.

'The Great Patriotic War'

Peter G. Tsouras

Consulting Editor: Vladimir Fiodorovich Grib
With an Introduction by David G. Chandler

BCA

LONDON · NEW YORK · SYDNEY · TORONTO

To my father, Theodore P. Tsouras, and all the other merchant mariners and naval gun crewmen of the SS Alcoa Pioneer *who braved the Kamikaze at Leyte Gulf in 1944.*

Acknowledgements
My thanks to Bruce Watson for his brotherly help, advice, and encouragement through the writing of this book, not to mention the loan of his fax machine. My appreciation to the professional staff at Planeta in Moscow for their beautiful initial editing and to David Gibbons, Anthony Evans and Michael Boxall in London for the high polish of the book; also to Albert D. McJoynt for creating the maps. My salute to Lionel Leventhal of Greenhill Books, who knows how to get the best from his authors and make it fun. And finally my love to my wife who indulges me with infinite patience and happy encouragement when I disappear into my basement office with my word processor. She also is the only one who really understands that machine, and I'd be lost without her.

Peter G. Tsouras

This edition published 1992 by BCA by arrangement with Greenhill Books, Lionel Leventhal Limited.

Photographs © Planeta Publishers, Moscow
Text and collective work © Lionel Leventhal Limited, 1992

CN 9531

British Library Cataloguing in Publication Data available

ISBN 1-85367-128-2

Library of Congress Cataloging-in-Publication Data available

Designed and edited by DAG Publications Ltd, London. Designed by David Gibbons; edited by Michael Boxall; layout by Anthony A. Evans; typesetting by Ronset Typesetters, Darwen, Lancashire.

Quality printing and binding by Colorcraft Ltd., 6A Victoria Centre, 15 Watson's Road, North Point, Hong Kong.

CONTENTS

◄Soviet infantry dismounting in the assault from a KV-1 heavy tank, Southwest Front, February 1943. Soviet motorized rifle troops actually had very few vehicles but would ride into battle aboard tanks, a practice called *tankoviy desant* or tank assault. Motorized rifle troops were the élite of the infantry; a motorized rifle company would have a high proportion of automatic weapons: 9 DP machine guns, 27 rifles, 57 machine-guns and 5 pistols.

▼Losses on both sides at Kursk were enormous. Zhukov claimed the Germans lost 1,500 tanks, 3,000 guns and 1,500 aircraft. Soviet losses are harder to gauge. Army Group South claimed to have taken 32,000 prisoners, inflicted 85,000 other losses, and destroyed about 2,000 tanks and an equal number of guns on Voronezh Front. After the Tank Battle at Prokhorovka, Soviet operational tanks may have fallen as low as 1,500 from the almost 4,000 when the battle began. But control of the battlefield is one of the great dividends of modern warfare. The Red Army was able to recover and repair large numbers of its tanks while depriving the Germans of that same opportunity. Two weeks later the number of Soviet operational tanks had climbed to 2,750.

INTRODUCTION
by David G. Chandler

'God of battles, was ever a battle like this in the world before?' – Alfred Lord Tennyson, *The Revenge*

When one studies the sheer scale of the Second World War on what was to Westerners the 'Eastern Front' (but which, by most Russians, understandably enough, was always referred to as their 'Western Front') it becomes evident that the Soviet Union's share in defeating the *Wehrmacht* was of the greatest significance to the winning of the overall struggle. It is true that the Molotov–Ribbentrop Pact of August 1939 was a major and un-anticipated strategic blow to England and France, permitting Hitler, after the conquest of Poland and the so-called 'Phoney War', to employ all his military power in the west – against Denmark and Norway, then the Low Countries and France – during the triumphant months of April to June 1940, and thereafter to threaten Great Britain with imminent invasion when these islands truly 'Stood Alone', effectively protected only by 'the Few' of RAF Fighter Command.

But as Winston Churchill once stated, 22 June 1941 – the opening of Operation 'Barbarossa' against the Soviet Union – was one of two* truly critical dates during the course of the whole war: 'On that date,' he asserted, 'I knew we would not lose the war.' The vast size of Russia and its huge if at first badly equipped (and somewhat indifferently led) Red Army, was likely to pose such grave logistical and strategic problems to the vaunted and seemingly unstoppable German war-machine that the invader at the very least would find all his attention absorbed by the immensity of the task in hand. The Germans might also come to share the ultimate fates of earlier would-be conquerors of Russia from the west – as illustrated by the martial and political cataclysms that befell Charles XII of Sweden in 1709 and Napoleon in 1812. And so, indeed, it was to prove. As Field Marshal Viscount Montgomery was to say with the advantage of post-war hindsight: 'Never march on Moscow.'

Not that Churchill was, or had ever been, a fervent admirer of Stalin or Soviet Communism. 'I cannot forecast to you the action of Russia,' he declared on 1 October 1939. 'It is a riddle wrapped in a mystery inside an enigma, but perhaps there is a key. That key is Russian national interest.' The Nazi–Soviet Pact was, he saw from the beginning, merely a matter of temporary mutual convenience between two politically and ideologically incompatible powers. Once they had come to blows, it was very much in Britain's 'national interest' – and that of all other enemies of the Third Reich – to support the Soviet Union in every way possible. Although not made much of by Soviet historians of the Stalinist and Brezhnev eras, the British arms, equipment and other material of war selflessly sent to Archangel in the gallant and costly North Cape convoys, or the even larger transfusions of Anglo–American aid transported by rail and lorry from the Middle East to the Caspian region, were vitally important to Russia's survival and war effort from 1941 to at least 1943.

Despite the romantic streak in his character, Churchill was a supreme realist where Soviet Russia was concerned. When a Labour MP once questioned the change in Churchill's attitude from his 'Red peril' warnings of the 1920s and 1930s to his declared support for 'Uncle Joe' and the gallant Russian people from late-June 1941, charging him with inconsistency, the great statesman and war leader responded to the effect that if Hitler and his denizens were to invade Hell itself he would not be able to prevent himself from making, in passing, at least one favourable reference to the Devil in the House. The defeat of Nazi Germany, Churchill well knew, was the greatest single priority, even though its achievement might necessitate the acceptance of some strange bed-fellows. As he informed the British Nation in a broadcast on the evening of 22 June 1941, 'No one has been a more consistent opponent of Communism than I have for the last twenty-five years. I will unsay no word that I have spoken about it. But all this fades away before the spectacle which is now unfolding. The past with its crimes, its follies, and its tragedies, flashes away. I see the Russian soldiers standing on the threshold of their native land, guarding the fields which their fathers have tilled from time immemorial. I see them guarding their homes where mothers and wives pray – ah yes, for there are times when all pray – for the safety of the loved ones, the return of the breadwinner, of their champion, of their protector.'

To defend 'Holy Russia' (for Stalin did not hesitate in 1941 to invoke the traditional patriotic and emotive rallying cry as used by Tsars Peter the Great, Alexander I and Nicholas II in 1708, 1812 and 1914 respectively – as superb historical films such as *Alexander Nevsky* (1938), and *Ivan the Terrible* (1944) produced to order by the great film-maker Sergei Eisenstein bear testimony), the Red Army's soldiers and the 100 separate peoples of the USSR bled themselves white. The price of, first, bare national survival, and second, of hard-won ultimate victory over Germany and its allies on the Russian Western Front was – it is now calculated – *twenty-eight million* Soviet dead, eight great cities, more than 500 towns and 2,000 villages being razed by ruthless attack from land and air. As Churchill had foreseen, no less than two-thirds of the *Wehrmacht*'s strength – more than 200 divisions in all – were tied-down in White Russia, the Baltic States, the Ukraine, the Crimea, and latterly, Eastern Europe as the 'Soviet steamroller' advanced remorselessly towards Warsaw, Breslau and, at last, Berlin, for practically all of four years. During the earlier stages of this titanic struggle the Germans fought to within sight of Moscow (but, unlike Napoleon, never occupied it); besieged Leningrad for 29 *months* (causing some 1,100,000 Russian military and civilian deaths in the process, many from starvation, but never captured it); occupied nine-tenths of Stalingrad on the River Volga, conquered the Crimea, gained the

---

* The second was 7 December 1942 (Pearl Harbor). 'On that date, I knew we would *win* the war,' Churchill concluded.

Caucasus with its coveted oilfields – but all ultimately proved in vain.

The staunch fighting qualities of the reorganized Red Armies under Marshal Zhukov, the harsh effects of 'General Winter', the stalwart efforts of Soviet partisans against enemy rear areas, and above all the heroic struggle for Stalingrad over the autumn months of 1942 and the winter months of 1942/3 – all led ineluctably to the last turning-point in the fortunes of the war on the Eastern Front. The verdict was made irrevocable by the great tank battle of Kursk in July 1943. Then, with the Anglo–American invasion of north-west Europe from 6 June 1944 and continuing struggles in Italy and Yugoslavia, time and good fortune at last ran out for Hitler's Germany, and on 2 May 1945 the Red Army occupied Berlin, having met the Americans on the Elbe near Torgau a few days earlier – and the war with the 'Thousand Year Reich' of Nazi Germany was at last over. 'Was ever a battle like this . . . before?'

Up to this point the USSR had avoided joining the other Allies in the war against Japan. Not until 8 August, two days after the dropping of the atomic bomb on Hiroshima, and the day before the dropping of the second (and last) such weapon on Nagasaki, did Stalin declare war on the Emperor Hirohito. There followed from 9–17 August the Campaign of Manchuria – rarely mentioned in English-language histories of the Second World War – which saw 1,500,000 Red Army soldiers pitted against an estimated 1,217,000 troops of the Japanese Kwangtung Imperial Army Group. For a cost of some 40,000 casualties, the Red Armies of the Trans-Baikal and First Far Eastern Fronts killed almost 84,000 Japanese and took another 594,000 prisoner. On 14 August Japan surrendered. The Second World War was at last over, and the world looked forward – somewhat optimistically – to a long and lasting period of peace.

The USSR's share in achieving victory over Hitler's Germany was immense by any standard if comparatively minuscule and belated in the defeat of Japan. But even this statement needs qualification. In the whole five years of war British military and civilian fatal casualties amounted to just 510,000; those of the USA to 295,000; the casualties of the whole United Nations' alliance against Hitler's Germany and Tojo's Japan (the USSR *excluded*) came to almost 22 million (to include horrific losses to Nationalist China, Poland and Yugoslavia). The losses of the Axis powers are generally put at *c.* 11,000,000. All these figures are horrendous enough by any standards, but need to be balanced against the USSR's total of *28 million dead* (perhaps 9 million military and 19 million civilian – the majority of both being Russians); which brings the Anti-Axis Coalition's total losses to some 51 million in all.

Small wonder that until just a few years ago the USSR feared a new large-scale war in general and a reunited Germany in particular. Many of the Soviet post-war attitudes and actions that appeared patently aggressive to the West at the time and indeed since (or at least until very recently), were chiefly regarded as defensive necessities in the Kremlin. The ideological, political, economic and physical strains of the long 40-year Cold War and its many crises, caused distortions and exaggerations on both sides – this has now to be freely admitted. 'If you would have Peace, prepare for War' was the cynical but realistic rule of the Roman Republic and Empire of some 2,000 years ago – and the great achievement of the Western Alliance and NATO has been based precisely upon that tenet – 'deterrence' in modern parlance. In the end, it was the opposing Warsaw Pact and the Soviet Union that was outfaced, cracked under the ceaseless strain – and imploded with results we still may only guess at. The present rush to disarm – or at least reduce the size of Western armaments for very understandable political and economic reasons – may possibly be being indulged in rather too fast for

◀Aircraft designer Sergei V. Ilyushin (1894–1977). Ilyushin was one of the younger, new men of talent whom the Soviet authorities allowed to flourish. He joined the Red Army in 1919 and fought in the Civil War, serving as commander of an aircraft maintenance unit. By 1931 his abilities had placed him in charge of the Central Design Office. Under his direction were produced the Il-4 and Il-28 bombers and the famed and dreaded Shturmovik ground-attack aircraft in its Il-2 and Il-10 variants. Known to the Germans as the 'Black Death', the Shturmovik was one of the most successful ground-attack aircraft in history. Soviet industry produced a phenomenal 41,159 Shturmoviks which the Red Army employed as flying artillery to reach ahead of conventional artillery and prepare the way for Soviet ground forces.

real comfort and true safety. A plethora of 'little wars' throughout the former Soviet Union, not to forget Yugoslavia and the Balkans, and other parts of the world may yet have to be faced – and History has often shown, alas, that one small thing can very easily lead to another – both larger and worse. We must earnestly hope this will not be the case. Or when will mankind ever learn?

But this is no time to be a Jeremiah. One great advantage of the present relatively cordial relations with Russia has been the unlocking of many Soviet Second World War documentary and pictorial archives, and their being made available to Western scholars and publishers. The result is the present stunning selection of Soviet Second World War photographs, culled from the 3,500 available, many of which have never been seen outside Russia before. The late Lieutenant-General Pavel Zhilin (1913–86), former Chief of the Historical Institute of the Soviet Army (whom the author of this Introduction was privileged to know as fellow military historian of the Napoleonic era and indeed as an esteemed friend for more than 15 years) achieved the immense feat of seeing through to publication the multi-volume Official Soviet Army History of the Great Patriotic War, which, for all its slants and biases in certain areas (for instance its somewhat overrated claims for the effectiveness of 'People's Partisans' in 1941-4 – as also in the histories relating to the defeat of Napoleon's invasion in 1812, sometimes called 'the First Great Patriotic War', or its underplaying of the significance of British and American aid to Russia already referred to earlier in this introduction) was a vitally important first step. His successor, General Dmitri Volkogonov, has recently written and published his very notable two-volume study of Josef Stalin, which is leading to a major reappraisal of that highly sinister yet indubitably impressive cruel dictator. Thus a more balanced account from what until very recently was a propaganda-dominated view of the events of 1941-5 from 'the other side of the (Allied) hill' is at last slowly becoming available to an eager world-wide audience. Perhaps Churchill's 'Russian riddle' is becoming a little more understandable and answerable. Or so we may now justly hope.

This impressive *'The Great Patriotic War: an Illustrated History of Total War: the Soviet Union and Germany, 1941–1945'* will indubitably be of further assistance in this ineluctable historical process. With the significant editorial assistance of Vladimir Fiodorovich Grib, and the first-rate scholarly linking text written by the American Peter Tsouras (author of the recent *Warriors' Words*, a fine compilation of military sayings drawn from the whole military history of mankind), this book represents an Anglo–Russo–American combined achievement of no little significance. 'History', claimed the great Dutch historian Pieter Geyl (1887–1966), 'is indeed an argument without end.' That is true, and always will continue to be so providing the rights to free expression of ideas and to unbiased analysis of established facts are jealously safeguarded against the perils of censorship and suppression. This book is surely a notable, if in itself small, step in the right direction.

This stunning and dramatic book presents a unique collection of hundreds of photographs with a strong text and valuable reference matter. It reveals, as never before, the titanic scale and cataclysmic struggle of the largest conflict ever seen on earth. *The Great Patriotic War* will be valued by anyone with an interest in twentieth century military history who wants to add an outstanding book to their shelves.

Sandhurst and Yateley.
22 June 1992 (51st Anniversary of
the German invasion of the USSR)

▶Rifle designer Fyoder V. Tokarev (1871–1968). Like so many others who saved the Soviet Union, Tokarev began his professional life in the service of the Tsar. He graduated from the Cossack Cadet School in 1900, and after the Revolution worked in the Tula Armoury where he designed a number of small arms including the MT light machine-gun (1925), the TT semi-automatic pistol (1930) and a number of automatic and semi-automatic rifles including the SVT semi-automatic rifle (1938).

THE BLOODY PRELUDE
Soviet Military Operations, 1936-40

The smell of war had been in the wind for five long years before Hitler unleashed the hurricane of 'Barbarossa' on the Soviet Union in June 1941. During those years the Red Army had acquired more experience and shed more blood than most armies do in generations. Beginning with the Spanish Civil War in 1936, those five years saw Stalin's massacre of the Red Army officer corps in 1937-8; the campaigns against the Japanese in the Far East, 1938-9; the occupation of eastern Poland and the Baltic States and Bessarabia in 1939-40; and the Russo-Finnish War of 1940-41.

By 1936 the Red Army had acquired the structure of a first-class military institution. The years since the Civil War had seen the diligent creation of a solid, well-trained officer corps and an effective general staff. The armed forces had been gradually increased in size and undergone considerable professional-ization. Beginning in 1929 the Soviet Union's rapid and brutal industrialization had been conducted with the chief aim of preparing for war. The Red Army had received the lion's share of production in almost every sphere. The Army's command echelons contained many men of ability if not brilliance, and the Red Army had led the world in innovation. It had, for example, been carrying out the first airborne operations in history at a time when American lieutenant colonels such as Patton and Stilwell were being reprimanded for even discussing such ideas at the US Army Command and General Staff College. Of greater significance was the development of the theories and techniques of armoured warfare. The mass output of the new Soviet arms industry transformed those ideas into realities while Liddell Hart in Britain and Charles de Gaulle in France were still considered to be annoying cranks by their own armies and governments. The Red Army was beginning to field tank and mechanized corps when western armies were grudging the cost of single battalions.

Apart from the Civil War and counter-insurgency operations in Central Asia, this new Red Army had acquired little operational experience since 1921. The outbreak of the Spanish Civil War in 1936 would begin to remedy that shortcoming. Soviet advisers, a small tank unit, artillery, and an air contingent were rushed to Spain to support the Loyalists against Franco's Fascists who were in turn reinforced by the Germans and Italians. It was Soviet aid, chiefly in training and organization of the Loyalist Forces, that staved off a rapid Franco victory. In three months the Soviets were able to convert what was essentially a mob into a military organization capable of effective defensive operations. The Soviet talent for creating military formations in short order would not be appreciated by the Germans until much later. The Soviet tank contingent under General Dmitri G. Pavlov gave a good account of itself though it was too small to be decisive. Soviet fighters helped even the odds in the air, and on one occasion in 1937 Soviet dive-bombers attacked and routed an Italian corps of two divisions. Soviet propaganda was able

◀There was a new Russian fighting man inside his Soviet uniform. Better-educated, trained, equipped, and motivated than the Japanese expected with their smug memories of 1904–5. The Japanese put unquestioning faith in the Spirit of Japan, *Yamato Damai*, that particular Japanese will to victory, and they too easily dismissed the changes that marked the Red Army. The Japanese manual entitled, *How to Fight the Soviets* characterized the Russian as submissive, docile, prone to blind obedience, susceptible to despair and depression, dull-witted, without initiative, and stolid. This caricature was not the soldier that would slug it out with his Japanese opponent with guts, cold steel, skill and superior material. And when the dust had settled, it was the *Russkaya Dusha* – the Russian Soul – that triumphed.

▶Tank Brigade Commander (general officer ranks were not introduced into the Red Army until 1940) Dmitri G. Pavlov reporting the situation in his sector to Largo Caballero (second from right), head of state and war minister of the Loyalist government of Spain in October 1936. Pavlov was awarded the decoration Hero of the Soviet Union for his aggressive use of tanks. He was one of the few senior officers to escape death or the camps on his return to the Soviet Union. That fate caught up with him in July 1941 when, as a general of the army, he was accused of lack of firmness and initiative in commanding the troops on the Soviet Western Front, demoted and shot.

to attract to the cause of the Loyalists perhaps as many as 50,000 Soviet and Communist-led volunteers such as the American Abraham Lincoln Brigade.

The reward for many of the Soviet participants in the Spanish Civil War was to perish in the convulsions of the purge of the Red Army's officer corps in 1937-8. With them also perished much of their painfully acquired experience of modern warfare. Having broken every other element of Soviet society to numb obedience, Stalin turned on the leadership of the Red Army in 1937. In two years he eliminated 35-40,000 of the Red Army's officers, half of the total and the upper and more experienced half at that. Three of five marshals perished including at least one certifiable military genius, Mikhail N. Tukhachevsky; the surviving two were certifiably incompetent. The list went on: 13 of 15 army commanders, 220 of 406 brigade commanders, 90 per cent of all generals and 80 per cent of all colonels. So relentless was the harvest that one division in the Soviet Far East found itself commanded by a first lieutenant. The surreal nature of this catastrophe is found in an exchange between one horrified general and Marshal Budenny, a Civil War crony of Stalin. 'Semyon, they're taking everyone!' 'Don't worry,' replied Budenny. 'They're only taking the smart ones.'

Stalin not only murdered the genius of the Red Army. He dismembered their creations and declared their principles anathema. The strong tank and mechanized corps were broken up into a number of smaller units meant to support infantry forces. Modern concepts of warfare were rejected in favour of 'Revolutionary' concepts that loosened discipline. At the same time the commissars were returned to the Red Army with such power that the principle of unity of command was destroyed.

The purge was only beginning to subside when the Red Army was faced with combat on its own border. On the poorly defined border where Manchuria, Korea and the Soviet Far East meet, the Japanese attempted but failed to dislodge Soviet forces from a position in the region of Lake Khasan near the mouth of the River Tuman in the late summer of 1938. The following year the Japanese tried again but this time on the border of Outer Mongolia then occupied by Soviet troops. Attacking

◀One hundred and forty Soviet volunteer pilots fought alongside the Loyalist forces in Spain. These pilots, at an airfield near Madrid in September 1936, are going over the results of the mission they have just completed. In the following year such Soviet pilots would rout an Italian corps in a precision dive-bomber attack.

◀Red Army war booty. The first trophies of combat with the Japanese being inventoried by Red Army troops after the fighting around Lake Khasan in August 1939. The Japanese had attacked Soviet troops dug in along the ill-defined Manchurian, Korean and Soviet borders and been bloodily repulsed.

▶Air support by the Red Army's air forces had been crucial both in Spain and in the battles with the Japanese. Here three Soviet airmen, bearers of the award of Hero of the Soviet Union, for valour in the skies over Spain and Mongolia, at an airfield in the Khalkin Gol area, immediately after the fighting, August 1939. Left to right: Yakov V. Smushkevich, Alexander I. Gusev and Sergei I. Gritsevets.

▼◀ Soviet infantry waiting to go 'over the top' and assault Japanese hill defences in the Khalkin Gol battles. Unlike the First World War, these Russians would go with massive firepower in support and first-class leadership. Logistics played its unglamorous but vital role; the Soviet 1st Front Army was supported by more than 4,200 trucks.

▶A new Russian sting – BT-7 Model 1937 Fast Tank, armed with a 45mm gun. The Japanese had concluded in their manual on how to fight the Soviets that the accumulated deficiencies of the Russian fighting man were such that he would be incapable of co-operating to conduct flanking maneouvres and encirclements. They had never met Georgi K. Zhukov and the armoured force designed, trained, and equipped by the lately murdered and revered Marshal Tukhachevsky. Zhukov rapidly turned the Japanese southern flank with his tanks and then struck the northern flank, finally crushing vicious resistance with flame-throwing tanks, and encircling the Japanese 23rd Division.

◄Soviet soldiers planting their unit colours on Remizov Height, recaptured from the Japanese, 28 August 1939, in the Khalkin Gol area of operations. This position was originally taken in the Japanese corps-sized attack across the Mongolian border but lost again in the Red Army's combined arms sledgehammer-like counter-attack.

►The ruthless and redoutable Georgi K. Zhukov, commander of the First Soviet Army Group, addressing his troops after their thorough victory in the Battle of Khalkin Gol, August 1939. Zhukov instilled absolute terror in his officers but had the common touch with the troops. His gift to Stalin of bundles of Samurai swords also showed a deft touch.

Army General (Later Marshal of the Soviet Union) Georgi K. Zhukov. Junior NCO in the First World War and winner of two St. George Crosses for valour, he joined the Red Army in 1918 and rose to command a cavalry squadron in the Civil War. After the war, his ability and driving, relentless will earned him rapid promotion. By 1939 he commanded 1st Army Group which defeated the Japanese at Khalkin Gol in Mongolia. He rose through native ability and a relentless will to command 1st Army Group which defeated the Japanese at Khalkin Gol in 1939. In February 1941 he was made Chief of the General Staff and a member of the High Command for his perceptive portrayal in a war game of the coming German invasion. His counsel to Stalin to abandon Kiev in August 1941 to avoid encirclement resulted in his dismissal and assignment to command the Reserve Front. In that command he drove the German Army out of the Yelnya salient it had formed after the Battle of Smolensk. A brilliant and ruthless commander, his decisiveness at Leningrad saved the city. The future had much in store for him.

in corps strength along the River Khalkin Gol, their initial success was crushingly reversed in midsummer. A Soviet combined arms force of three divisions and five tank brigades with strong air support and under the command of General Georgi K. Zhukov counter-attacked and drove the shattered survivors out of Mongolia. The Japanese had lost 18,000 men and were so dispirited by the application of Russian firepower and mass that they lost all appetite for further lessons. This battle marked the first appearance of the remarkable and ruthless Zhukov. His victory was decisive for the Red Army and the Soviet Union to an extent out of all proportion to the forces and immediate prizes involved. The defeat turned the Japanese to the south and west for easier prey. They were to be fully occupied when the fate of the Soviet Union hung in the balance in 1941-2.

As soon as a treaty was signed with the Japanese on 16 September 1939, Stalin felt free to implement the secret protocol of the Molotov–Ribbentrop Pact and invade eastern Poland. Three armies of the Belorussian Special Military District (MD) and three from the Kiev Special MD crossed the border into a Poland already collapsing under the weight of the earlier German attack from the west. There was little fighting in what was essentially a movement to make contact with the advancing Germans. Anxious to prevent the Baltic States from becoming German staging areas for operations against the Soviet Union, Stalin then demanded that they submit to the stationing of large numbers of troops or face an invasion. They submitted and were swiftly occupied by the Red Army in October.

Overconfident with bloodless conquest, Stalin next turned his eyes upon Finland which was also seen as a potential staging area for the Germans. He demanded the cession of the Karelian Peninsula to add depth to the defence of Leningrad. The Finns refused and Stalin contemptuously thought an artillery bombardment would bring them to heel. On 30 November 1939 the Red Army's air forces and artillery struck at the Finns. The Finns fired back – accurately. The Soviet Union now had its first major war on its hands. Incredibly, as Khrushchev related, there had been no military Intelligence preparation of the battlefield. The first Soviet assault on the Mannerheim Line of fortifications in the Karelian Peninsula was easily repulsed with great loss. Similar attacks into eastern Finland resulted in the outright destruction of several roadbound Soviet divisions woefully ill prepared for winter warfare. In all six Soviet spearheads had been repulsed. To the glee of the Germans, the awful effects of the purges and the commissar system on the basic efficiency of the Red Army had been made glaringly public. The Red Army's solution was to mass 54 divisions on the Karelian front and grind the Finns down. On 1 February the attack began, and in two weeks succeeded in unhinging the Finnish front with a profligate indifference to loss of life. By 12 March the Finns were exhausted and sued for peace.

Stalin had won his Karelian glacis for Leningrad but at enormous cost. Finnish losses of 25,000 killed and 43,000 wounded were matched by estimated Soviet losses of 200,000 killed and 400,000 wounded. Khrushchev reckoned Soviet losses to number almost one million. Amid the waste, however, something useful was gleaned. Stalin recognized the damage done to the officer corps and made a number of reforms. The grip of the commissar was loosened and the principle of unity of command as well as a strict miliary discipline were restored. A number of the more obvious incompetents were weeded out. The cruelty of the winter fighting also induced the Red Army to produce and stock vital cold weather lubricants and clothing. Tactics were severely re-examined and put on a more practical basis. From this point the Red Army would have barely one year to absorb the lessons of the Finnish War and repair some of the institutional losses of the purges.

◀A column of Soviet BA-32-6 Armoured Cars moving into the area of the Northwest Front on the Karelian Isthmus, December 1939. The BA-32-6 turret armed with a 45mm gun was originally designed for the T-30 experimental light tank. This model could have tracks fitted to the rear wheels for cross-country movement. Trapped on narrow woodland roads and by deep snow, large numbers of vehicles such as these were destroyed by the more mobile and flexible Finns.

▼Red Army troops inspecting a hard-won objective, one of the many deadly fortifications of the Mannerheim Line on the Karelian Isthmus, shortly after the war in March 1940. Note the older headgear, the pointed cap designed during the Russian Civil War and modelled after the pointed helmets of medieval Russian warriors such as Alexander Nevsky.

THE TITANS PREPARE FOR WAR
THE STRATEGIC SETTING

After his victories in the west, Hitler turned his eyes east to his ultimate goal – the destruction of the Soviet Union. Confident of the proven abilities of the Wehrmacht and contemptuous of the proven disabilities of the Red Army, he predicted the utter defeat of the Soviet Union by winter in a campaign code-named 'Barbarossa'.

Planning proceeded with thoroughness and on an awesome scale. The Army allocated 75 per cent of its field strength – 3,050,000 men in 148 divisions. Of these nineteen were panzer and fifteen panzer grenadier divisions. This strength was deceiving, however. Hitler had doubled his mobile divisions by reducing divisional tank strength from two regiments to one. The Luftwaffe devoted 2,770 aircraft or 65 per cent of its operational strength. Finland and Roumania were brought in as co-belligerents because of the necessity of staging troops from their territory. The Finnish Army contributed 500,000 men in fourteen divisions and Roumania provided another 150,000 in fourteen understrength divisions. These forces fielded 3,350 tanks, 7,184 artillery pieces, 600,000 motor vehicles and 625,000 horses.

German forces formed three large army groups. Field Marshal Gerd von Rundstedt commanded Army Group South, with an area of operations from the Black Sea to the Pripet Marshes. He was to seize Kiev and Ukraine to the River Dnieper. Field Marshal Fedor von Bock's Army Group Centre was to strike towards Smolensk and then Moscow. Field Mar-

◀Men of a Red Army ski battalion armed with Tokarev SVT-40 7.62mm automatic rifles on the Northwest Front in the Karelian Isthmus, December 1939. Few Red Army men in the war against Finland were so well equipped for winter war at this time.

shal Wilhelm von Leeb's Army Group North was to attack through the Baltics to seize Leningrad. Among the three army groups were seven field armies and four panzer groups which were panzer armies in everything but name.

Soviet forces were organized with the peacetime military district structure responsible for training, mobilization and administration. They were not converted to a wartime structure until the outbreak of war. Each frontier military district then became a front or army group. Leningrad MD became the North Front (three armies), commanded by Lieutenant-General Markian M. Popov, and was responsible for the Baltic area and operations against Finland. The Baltic Special MD became Northwest Front (three armies), commanded by Colonel-General Fyodor I. Kuznetsov, and defended the East Prussian border. The Western Special MD became West Front (four armies) commanded by Army General Dmitri G. Pavlov. The Kiev Special MD (four armies) commanded by Colonel-General Mikhail P. Kirponos, became Southwest Front. These last two fronts divided responsibity from East Prussia to the Carpathians at the Pripet Marshes. The Odessa MD (two armies), commanded by Army General Ivan V. Tyulenev, became South Front, responsible for operations from the upper River Bug to the Black Sea.

These military districts were manned by 2,680,000 men in 170 divisions, none of them at full strength. They were equipped with 1,475 modern KV-1 and T-34 tanks, 37,500 guns and mortars, and 1,540 combat aircraft of new types. They also had thousands of older and obsolete tanks and aircraft. In fact, at the time of the attack, the Red Army had 22,600 tanks and self-propelled guns of which 16,500 were in need of major or medium repairs. Despite the masses of older equipment, Soviet industry was rapidly modernizing its inventory with world-class equipment, some of it like the T-34, far superior to

anything in existence. Significant weaknesses remained. There was a great shortage of motor vehicles of all types, a problem that would not be solved until Lend Lease. As it was, non-mechanized formations would have to rely on a quarter of a million mobilized civilian vehicles and 40,000 farm tractors as artillery prime movers. Communications were poor, relying far too much on telephone because of a crippling shortage of radios.

After the fall of France war with Germany appeared certain, but not before 1942. Apparently Stalin and the General Staff concluded that the main German blow would strike at the Ukraine. They were wrong. The Germans would put their weight north of the Pripet Marshes in Army Groups Centre and North. In January 1941 a major war game was held in which Army General Georgi K. Zhukov took the German side. In his memoirs he stated that the game 'abounded in dramatic situations for the Red side' that 'proved to be in many ways similar to what really happened after 22 June 1941'. Playing the German instinctively with the right plan of campaign, he won the game. Stalin sacked the Chief of the General Staff and appointed Zhukov in his stead.

The initial Soviet war plan called for the military districts to act as a covering force in three offensively deployed echelons to allow national mobilization to proceed and then combine for a crushing offensive operation. The three echelons contained respectively, 56, 52 and 62 divisions, but these divisions were too spread out and much of the front was still uncovered. In the spring the General Staff began the movement of large forces from interior military districts to the west. A total of 800,000 reservists were called up, bringing armed forces strength to about 5,000,000 men. There was an absence of field fortifications in the border areas because of their recent incorporation into the Soviet Union. The older line of fortifications, the Stalin Line, had been effectively dismantled by Stalin's order.

Worst of all, the Red Army did not seriously consider defensive operations or the possiblity of surprise attack. The Soviet leadership assumed a delay of at least three weeks between the declaration of war and the beginning of active opera- tions and reckoned that this would give time for mobilization and forward deploy- ment of their own offensive operations.

Stalin refused to believe the mounting evidence of immediate German offensive operations, and not until the evidence became overwhelming was even tentative action taken. The night before the Ger- man attack a war alert to man defensive positions was issued, but it forbade any response to provocation or the initiation of any action without approval from Moscow.

A Study in Unpreparedness
The Western Special Military District, June 1941

When the Wehrmacht struck the Western Special Military District on 22 June 1941, it was in the midst of a major reorganization and reequipment meant to be completed in 1942. Additionally, it had been lulled into a state of unreadiness by Stalin's refusal to take seriously the German buildup and unmistakeable provocations. The details are as follows:

Strength on 22 June 1941:
Personnel: Red Army – 627,000 plus 19,519 NKVD Border Guards
Artillery: 10,087 (including mortars above 50mm)
Tanks: 2,201
Aircraft: 1,909

Manning
1. 37–71% of wartime establishment
2. Many formations were 6–7,000 men short of wartime establishment.
3. Large drafts of experienced personnel had been drawn off to build new tank and aviation units.
4. Manning levels of mechanized corps were 45–55% for tank officers and 19–36% for tank NCOs
5. There were only 70.3% crews for available aircraft.

Mechanized Corps
1. Only one (VI) of six mechanized corps had complete equipment set.
2. Half of eight tank divisions in cover armies were understrength; 3 of 4 motorized divisions had no tanks.
3. Tank fleet consisted of 83% obsolete models.
4. Only one corps (VI) had modern tanks (KV-1, T-34)
5. Five corps had only 7–30% of artillery prime movers
6. Four corps had only 8–26% of motor transport
7. In four corps 30% of motor vehicles needed major repairs
8. Eleven types of tanks in VI Corps alone.

Aviation
1. Of 855 fighters, only 253 were new types (29.6%).
2. Of 466 front bombers, only 139 were new types (29.8%)
3. There were only 85 ground attack aircraft.
4. There was no centralized air command at front level.
5. Training was incomplete – only 20% of crews could fly during daylight under instrument conditions.
6. Of 57 operational airfields west of Minsk, only 22 had fuel.
7. Large number of new fighters based at airfields within artillery range of border.

Communications
1. Only 10–20% of materials available to maintain front communications under wartime requirements.
2. Radios were available for:
a. Army and airfield:	26–27%
b. Corps and division:	7%
c. Regiment:	41%
d. Battalion:	58%
e. Company:	70%
3. Primary reliance placed on wire communications and national telephone/ telegraph system.

Operational/Planning
1. Planning for an army level offensive plan due 1 July 1941.
2. Planning for an army level defensive plan due 1 November 1941.
3. Artillery for three armies were absent at artillery courses on 22 June.
4. Little attention given to joint planning of field and fortified army forces.
5. Training plan called for corps-level proficiency to be achieved by the end of 1942.
6. Training plan called for platoon and company-level proficiency to be achieved by end of July 1941.
7. Tactical training emphasized offensive operations.
8. Staffs were largely unorganized
9. Large numbers of reservists called up but had received not training.

Source: Major V.A. Semidetko, 'The Sources of Defeat in Belorussia', *Voyenno-istoricheskiy zhurnal*, No. 4, April 1989.

BLITZKRIEG IN THE EAST
Battles of the Frontier, Smolensk and the Ukraine

The German and allied hosts, assembled from the Baltic to the Black Seas, struck at the frontier military districts at 04.00 on 22 June 1941, curiously only one day earlier than Napoleon's invasion in 1812. In the opening and crucial two weeks of the campaign the Germans had no greater ally than Stalin himself. His refusal to believe the increasing warnings of attack resulted in the Red Army's initial crippling tactical and operational unpreparedness. Then, before the enemy situation had clarified at all, he issued orders for immediate counter-attacks by all Fronts when those same headquarters were desperately seeking the most elemental information of the situation from their subordinate commands. Finally, he seems then to have lapsed into a paralyzing fit of depression that lasted until 3 July. By then most of the frontier Fronts were in a shambles.

Had the Red Army been in position and prepared for the 'Sunday Blow' of 'Barbarossa', the history of the war would have been far different. One common theme in the German accounts of those days is the bitter resistance and tenacity of Soviet troops. Given tactical and operational coherence, that tenacity would have been multiplied many times. As it was, con-fusion and deep encirclements left the Red Army soldiers little opportunity for the collective action and heroism that make a group of men into an army.

By 29 June the two panzer groups Army Groups North and Centre had pulled off a huge encirclement against West Front forces in a long pocket running west of Bialystok to Minsk. In one week, West Front, which guarded the direct road to Moscow, had been penetrated almost 300 kilometres and lost its heavy concentration of armour in the Bialystok bulge. The Minsk pocket alone yielded 300,000 prisoners, 2,500 tanks and 1,400 guns. Thirty-two of 43 divisions had been smashed. A few days later, the panzer armies had reached the River Dvina west of Vitebsk and the Dnieper near Mogilev. Army Group North had reached Riga and was crossing the upper reaches of the Dvina. The only bright spot for the Red Army was Southwest Front whose large armoured forces had exerted enough pressure to limit the advance of Army Group South to shallow penetrations to Lvov and Rovno. On 25 June the Finnish Army had attacked Northwest Front, and German Forces in northern Norway had attacked towards Murmansk. The Germans would shortly declare 89 Soviet divisions destroyed. By 3 July General Halder, Chief of the General Staff, was already crowing that the campaign against the Soviet Union had been won in fourteen days.

The Soviet High Command did not quite agree. The initial offensive strategy was quickly seen as disastrous and was replaced by an attempt to go on the defensive to allow mobilization to prepare the means for a strategic counter-offensive. Four reserve armies (37 divisions) were moved up to support West Front in the area west of Smolensk. The call to the colours had mobilized 5,300,000 men by 1 July. The Soviet Union was fielding forces far beyond the wildest German estimates which had put the total Red Army field army at 170 divisions. The western frontier military districts had had that number alone.

By 3 July the battles for the frontier had ended, and Army Groups North and Centre were on the line Dvina – Dnieper. Hitler's thoughts turned to options in the north and south rather than to Moscow. First the still potent West Front had to be dealt with. Again, the panzer groups of Generals Hoth and Guderian cut deep and met at Smolensk, trapping West Front's mass of manoeuvre to the west. By

▶One of the first Soviet counter-attacks in the opening hours of the German invasion by West Front in Belorussia, June 1941. The immediate order from Moscow to counter-attack was issued before the enemy situation had clarified enough to make sound operational decisions. The counter-attacks served to hold many Soviet units in place while the panzers encircled them.

5 August the pocket, with 300,000 men, had been liquadated. Army Group South was still meeting stubborn resistance from Southwest Front, but by 11 July had trapped two Soviet armies in a pocket between Uman and Pervomaysk and taken 100,000 prisoners. South Front, which had been facing only Roumanian armies, was now threatened by a German drive that would pin it to the Black Sea. Abandoning Odessa, it retreated to the Dnieper line.

In late July Hitler had identified the two main objectives as Leningrad and the Ukraine. Now that West Front was crippled by its latest débâcle at Smolensk and posed no immediate threat, forces could be diverted from Army Group Centre for the drive on the Ukraine, which was given even higher priority than Leningrad. Half of Army Group Centre's forces (Second Army and Guderian's 2nd Panzer Group) became the northern arm of a great pincer that would close far east of Kiev. Army Group South would provide the southern arm of the pincer. Recognizing the danger, Zhukov urged Stalin to abandon Kiev and save the armies. Stalin instead ordered Southwest and South Fronts to hold Kiev and the line of the lower Dnieper and dismissed Zhukov as Chief of Staff, assigning him command of Reserve Front behind West Front. Marshal Budenny commanding Southwest Front begged for permission to withdraw on 11 September when the catastrophe was unmistakeably imminent. He too was sacked and replaced by Marshal Timoshenko as overall commander of both Fronts, who arrived just in time to oversee the calamity. By 16 September the German pincers had closed on much of the two Fronts and within a week had taken 665,000 prisoners, the greatest capture bag in history.

The Battle for the Ukraine had one more act – the capture of (1) the Soviet Ruhr – the Donets basin; (2) the communications hub of Rostov on Don on the lower reaches of the Dnieper; (3) and the Crimean peninsula. Von Manstein's Eleventh Army attacked into the Crimea against the Soviet 51st Army while his rear on the Nogay Steppe was lightly covered by Roumanian forces. Southern Front seized the opportunity and struck at the covering force with two armies. As it was on the point of a collapse that would trap Eleventh Army against the Crimea, 1st

STATE OF MODERNIZATION AND REORGANIZATION IN MECHANIZED CORPS, WESTERN SPECIAL MILITARY DISTRICT, JUNE 1941

Tank Types	Wartime TOE	VI	XI	XIII	XIV	XVII	XX	Total by TOE	Actual
KV-1 (new)	126	114	3	–	–	–	–	756	117
T-34 (new)	420	238	28	–	–	–	–	2520	266
BT-5,7	316	416	44	15	6	24	13	1896	518
T-26	152	126	162	263	504	1	80	912	1136
G-27, 28, 37, 40	17	127	–	16	10	11	–	102	164
Total:	1031	1021	237	294	520	36	93	6188	2201

Source: Major V.A. Semidetko, 'The Sources of Defeat in Belorussia', *Voyenno-istoricheskiy zhurnal*, No. 4, April 1989.

The Voice of Old Russia

The German invasion threw Stalin into a fit of depression. For twelve days, the nation waited to hear from him; yet he continued to cower in his dacha. State and Party were without a head, it seemed. But other voices were not silent. The day of the invasion, the only national figure to rally the people was Metropolitan Sergei of Moscow and Kolomna, the head of the Russian Orthodox Church. While Soviet Power was silent, old Russia stood up to defend the people and nation. Sergei's broadcast went out over the airwaves:

'The times of Khan Baty, German knights, Carl of Sweden, Napoleon are brought back. . . Our fathers never lost their hearts even under worse conditions, because they thought of their sacred vow, and not of personal dangers and profits; that is why they faced triumph. Let us live and fight to the Glory of our ancestors and their glorious names, since we are kin to them in flesh and blood and belief. Let us remember the holy leaders of the Russian people: Aleksandr Nevsky, Dmitri Donskoi, who vouchsafed their souls for the sake of the people and Motherland. . . Let us remember the innumerable thousands of soldiers. . . May their names be gloried!'

◄Duelling with a German tank, this Soviet soldier prepares to throw an anti-tank grenade, on the approaches to Minsk, West Front, June 1941.

The First Period of War
22 June 1941 - 18 November 1942

German attacks (1941 Campaign)	Limit of German advance as of:
Finnish and Roumanian attacks	22 June 1941
Soviet attacks	30 September 1941
Soviet attacks (1942)	5 December 1941
German attacks (1942 campaign)	12 November 1942
	Soviet pockets

0   100   200
miles

Panzer Group crossed the Dnieper to the north and came down upon their rear. Once again the hunter had become the hunted. The resulting encirclement netted another 65,000 prisoners. First Panzer Army went on to seize Rostov while Eleventh Army continued its attack into the Crimea. By 15 November the entire Crimea save the fortress of Sevastopol had fallen. Most of 51st Army had been destroyed, only its headquarters and some heavy units escaping to the mainland from the Kerch peninsula.

While half of Army Group Centre was committed in the Ukraine, Zhukov, now commanding Reserve Front, took the opportunity on 30 August to strike at the German Fourth Army which had occupied a salient at Yelnya east of Smolensk. The operation drove the Germans back 12 kilometres but failed to encircle them due to a lack of tanks and aircraft. Nevertheless it was the first substantial, successful Soviet offensive operation of the war.

Hitler then allowed Army Group Centre to regroup and aim for Moscow in Operation 'Typhoon'. The drive on Moscow became so serious that Stalin was desperate for a diversion anywhere. Timoshenko had done a good job of rebuilding South Front with two new armies in early November. Seeing a gap opening between First Panzer Army at Rostov and Seventeenth Army to the north, he acted quickly and struck 1st Panzer Group north of Rostov on 17 November with his 9th and 37th Armies. Early results were disappointing, but South Front eventually massed 22 divisions against the panzer corps defending Rostov. Under extreme pressure, First Panzer Army ordered the abandonment of Rostov and fell back more than 70 kilometres to the River Mius line. Hitler countermanded the order and sacked his Army Group South commander, Field Marshal von Rundstedt who had supported his subordinate's decision to fall back. A rare personal visit to the front finally convinced Hitler to accept the withdrawal which had already occurred on 30 November. The German armies in the east had suffered their first major defeat. The news gave hope to the desperate Soviet defenders of Moscow. It also gave pause to their attackers – Guderian grimly commenting, 'This is the first ringing of the alarm bells.'

MECHANIZED CORPS AND TANK STRENGTH AT THE BEGINNING OF THE WAR

Military Districts	Assigned Corps	Tanks	
		Total	T-34s/KVs
Leningrad	1st, 9th	1,506	15
Baltic Special	3rd, 12th	1,393	109
Western Special	6th	1,021	352
	11th	237	31
	13th	294	
	14th	520	
	17th	36	
	20th	93	
Kiev Special	4th	892	414
	8th	858	171
	9th	285	
	15th	733	131
	16th	608	
	19th	280	11
	22nd	647	31
	24th	222	
Odessa	2nd	489	60
	18th	280	
Moscow	7th, 21st, 51st bn	1,134	9
Kharkov	25th	300	20
Orel	23rd	413	11
North Caucasus	26th	184	
Trans-Caucasus	28th	869	
Central Asian	27th	356	
Transbaykal	5th, and 57th, 61st TDs, 82 MD	2,602	
Far Eastern Front	30th and 59th TD, 69th MD	2,969	

Source: V.P. Krikunov, 'In Search for Truth', *Voyenno-istoricheskiy zhurnal*, No. 4, April 1989.

◀The end came for this German Ju 88 in the first days of the war, somewhere over the West Front. Notice how the swastika has been airbrushed in backwards on the vertical stabilizer. Lieutenant Mikhail P. Zhukov made a name for himself in the first week of the war by introducing the tactic of aerial ramming, downing the first Luftwaffe bomber over Lake Pskov. Actually surviving the introduction of this unorthodox technique, he went on to become an ace with nine kills and five partials. He died in combat in 1943.

▶German tanks did not have it all their own way. Here one of them dies under a shower of sparks and flame from a direct hit by a Soviet gun on the outskirts of Minsk, June 1941.

▼The Red Army extracted a price for the encirclements that looked so dramatic on the map. German Mk III tanks destroyed on the outskirts of Minsk, late June 1941.

◀A delegation of Moscow workers turns over early model T-34s to the men of a tank brigade, autumn, 1941. Despite losses to the Germans, and the move of much production capacity to the Urals, Soviet tank production jumped in 1941 to 6,590 from 2,794 in 1940. Of the 1941 production, 1,100 were T-34s and 393 were KVs. The T-34s were coming into service just in the nick of time.

▶Another nasty surprise besides the T-34, in the early days of the war, was the 'Katyusha' multiple rocket-launcher or 'Stalin's Organ' as the Germans called them. Here they are conducting a vivid night-time fire mission, West Front, July 1941.

▼Barring the road to Moscow, these Soviet gunners manning a 45mm anti-tank gun, are trying to stop German tanks somewhere west of Minsk, West Front, early July 1941.

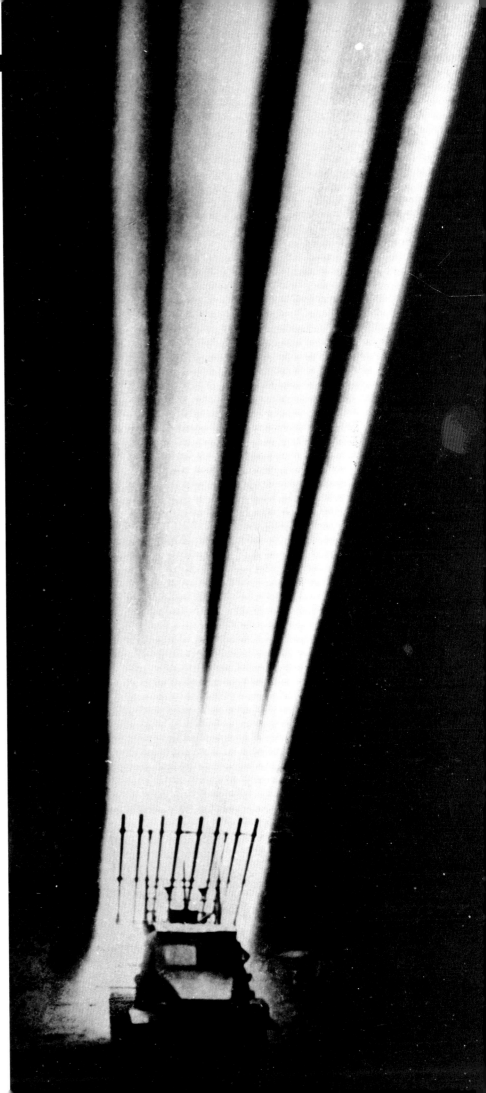

◀A local infantry counter-attack supported by 7.62mm Degtyaryov submachine-guns and 7.62mm Tokarev rifles, West Front, July 1941.

▶A Soviet MiG-3 fighter assembly line in Kuibyshev, December 1941. In the opening days of the war the Luftwaffe achieved air superiority. Thousands of Soviet aircraft, mostly obsolete, were destroyed on the ground and in the air. However new advanced types comparable to German types had been introduced, such as the MiG-3, YAK-1, and LAGG fighters and the Il-2 Stormovik ground-attack aircraft. Only the MiG-3, however, had the 370mph plus speed to match the German Me-109. The Red Army took delivery of 2,739 such modern aircraft in 1941. A total of 12,377 combat aircraft were produced in 1941, up from 8,145 in 1940.

◀A Red Army rifle regiment passes in review before leaving for the front, Moscow Military District, September 1941. The Soviet mobilization initiated on 22 June called up all reservists between the ages of 23 and 37 and brought 5,300,000 men to the colours.

▶Red Army infantry attacking on the approaches to Smolensk, July 1941. As the two panzer groups of Army Group Centre swung around the forces of West Front, the Soviet armies were fixed in place by the Germans' infantry armies.

◀'Where do they come from? These Russians seem to have nine lives!' exclaimed General Nehring, commanding 18th Panzer Division east of Borisov in early July. He would not have been comforted by the sight of mobilizing Soviet reserves as shown by these gunners armed with Degtyaryov anti-tank rifles parading before departure to the fighting with West Front, August 1941.

◄Red Army artillerymen firing a 152mm gun (Model A-19, 1931-7 make), near Smolensk, July 1941.

►Cavalrymen forcing a crossing of the River Ugra near Yelnya, east of Smolensk, as the panzers closed the great pocket to the west of the city in the last week of July 1941.

◄A Red Army soldier falls in a desperate counter-attack in the Smolensk pocket, July 1941. Once again the panzers of Colonel-General Hoth's 3rd Panzer Group and Colonel-General Guderian's 2nd Panzer Group had trapped another large Soviet force. Their panzer groups met at Smolensk in the last week of July, trapping 300,000 Red Army soldiers and 3,000 tanks.

▼A scene repeated in thousands of places in that first terrible year – German infantry trudging past burning Russian, Belorussian and Ukrainian villages set alight by their own inhabitants as part of the Soviet scorched earth policy. This village was near Smolensk, July 1941.

◀Serving the guns to the last man in the finest tradition of the artillery, these Red Army gunners of West Front, are sacrificing themselves to slow the Germans after the disaster at Smolensk, August 1941.

▶A column of T-34s moves into position for an attack, Northwest Front, August 1941. By the first week of August, 4th Panzer Group was approaching Luga, 110 kilometres south of Leningrad, and Eighteenth Army was clearing Estonia.

◀The heavy firepower of the Soviet rifle company, the Maxim machine-gun, being hauled into action by its crew on the approaches to Novgorod, Northwest Front, July 1941. By early July the panzer group of Army Group North had penetrated past the old Russian city of Pskov to equally ancient Novgorod. Novgorod and Pskov had escaped the Mongols 700 years before, but would not escape the Nazis.

◀On the road to Leningrad a German soldier rings the bell of a Russian Orthodox Church, summer 1941. By the end of June, the Northern Army Group had already pushed the Soviet Northwest Front forces back to Riga and the River Dvina.

▶Young Soviet reconnaissance troops in a night raid, Northwest Front, autumn 1941. Although German Army Group North had driven north into Estonia and were approaching Leningrad, Northwest Front had suffered no large encirclements.

▲A big and nasty surprise for the Germans – the superb T-34 tank, the best in the world at the time, Southwest Front, on the approaches to Kiev, July 1941. Here a T-34 rolls over the standard 50mm-gunned Panzer Mk-III – no contest. With its tremendous cross-country capability; thick, sloped armour; robust engine; and deadly 76.2mm gun, it definitely outclassed anything the Germans had. The only salvation for German tankers in such mismatches lay in superior training and communications.

◄Soviet naval infantry making an assault landing on an island off the Baltics held by the Germans, Northwest Front, autumn 1941. Attempting to keep the approaches to the Gulf of Finland and Leningrad and its Kronstadt naval base clear, naval infantry contested a number of the small islands off the Estonian and Finnish coasts.

▲Marshal of the Soviet Union Semyon M. Budenny among the officers of 8th Tank Division near Dnepropetrovsk, July 1941. At this time Budenny commanded Southwest Front and was holding Field Marshal von Rundstedt's Army Group South to the slowest advance of any of the German army groups. He began military service in 1903 in the Imperial Russian Army, fought the Japanese in 1904–5 and the Germans in 1914–17. As a senior NCO, he won four St. George Crosses, the highest Imperial decoration for valour, and four other medals for heroism. After the Revolution he joined the new Red Army and distinguished himself in the Civil War as a cavalry commander where he served with Stalin. That relationship helped him rise to the rank of field marshal and survive the purges. It did not help him on the battlefield where he was associated with a number of disasters such as the encirclement at Kiev.

▼Soviet mortar unit armed with 120mm mortars moving to new defence lines, Southwest Front, August 1941. By the beginning of August, the forces of Army Groups South and Centre had wrapped themselves partially around Kiev, creating a salient in which were concentrated immense Red Army forces. Budenny begged Stalin to be allowed to fall back and was relieved of his command.

▲Soviet cavalry supported by a wagon-mounted machine-gun employed in an anti-aircraft role, during the defence of Rostov on Don, South Front, September 1941. After the débâcle at Kiev, Marshal Timoshenko was able to reinforce the badly shaken South Front with two fresh armies.

▼A Red Army counter-attack near Yelnya, Reserve Front, August-September 1941. The Yelnya Operation was launched on 30 August to drive the German Fourth Army out of the salient it had established after the Battle of Smolensk. Reserve Front, commanded by Army General Zhukov, drove the Germans out of the

salient in the first successful Soviet offensive operations of the war. Four rifle divisions which distinguished themselves here were the first to receive the new Guards appellation.

▲A Red Army combined-arms counter-attack, West Front, autumn 1941. Soviet tank corps were being broken down into separate divisions, brigades and battalions at this time because of a belief that they would be more effective in direct infantry support. One such unit, 8th Tank Brigade, formed in September, had a strength of 61 tanks in three models – 7 KV-1 heavy tanks, 22 medium T-34s and 32 light tanks. This photograph shows the close infantry support delivered by just such a mix of types of tanks, KV-1s and T-34s, West Front, autumn 1941.

▶The graves of seven Germans killed in the August fighting. By the end of that month the Germans had lost 409,998 men including 87,489 killed, 302,821 wounded and 19,688 missing. Only 317,000 replacements were available, a problem that would continue to grow as replacements were never enough to cover losses. By the end of war, German dead on the Eastern Front numbered 1,810,061.

◄'Katyusha' launchers supporting a Red Army tank-infantry counter-attack, West Front, autumn 1941. By this time Guderian's 2nd Panzer Group had completed its mission in the Ukraine and was returning to Army Group Centre for the next mission – Moscow. All this time the Soviet High Command was building up reserves before Moscow to be ready for the inevitable blow.

◄Street fighting in Rostov on Don by an infantry unit under the command of Senior Lieutenant Galushko. Timoshenko had achieved a correlation of forces of seven to one that threatened to overwhelm the enemy. That threat forced the first major, precipitous German retreat of the war, by First Panzer Army to the River Mius 70 kilometres away.

◄Belorussian partisans were aready in action by September 1941. They would make life increasingly miserable for Germans behind the front-lines. Here they have killed a German machine-gunner and stripped him of his MG-32 machine-gun. The partisan is already armed with a German MP-34 submachine-gun.

THE BATTLES BEFORE MOSCOW

Having gorged himself on victory in the Ukraine, Hitler was now pleased to permit Guderian and his other generals to strike at the brain of the Soviet Union – Moscow – the target they had pleaded for when the campaigning weather was still favourable. The fine weather lingered deceptively, but was almost over when the German offensive began on 30 September. Prophetically the Germans chose a code-name signifying the colossal destructiveness of nature – 'Typhoon'; it was wrong only in detail.

Army Group Centre struck hard at the two Soviet fronts arrayed before Moscow, the six armies of Marshal Semyon K. Timoshenko's Western Front and the three armies of General Andrei I. Yeremenko's Bryansk Front. Beginning on 30 September, Guderian's 2nd Panzer Group easily broke through Yeremenko's southern flank and had encircled his entire force by 6 October. Yeremenko had sensed the imminent disaster and requested permission to withdraw, but he had been put off by the High Command until it was too late. To the north 3rd (Hoth) and 4th (Hoepner) Panzer Groups had similarly encircled Timoshenko's

Front, meeting at Vyazma on 7 October. Once again the well-trained and audacious Germans had raced around their Red Army opponents. The victory was enormous even by the heady standards of 1941. Timoshenko's six armies of 55 divisions and Yeremenko's three armies of 26 divisions were almost a total loss: 81 divisions losing 663,000 prisoners, 1,242 tanks and 5,412 guns. A few men broke out of the Bryansk pocket including a badly wounded Yeremenko and his staff. The double battle of Vyazma and Bryansk had been a perfect pincer operation. The Moscow Front had been torn open.

Fatefully, on the very day that the Vyazma pocket was closed, the autumn rains began. The fruits of victory lie in exploitation; the Russian weather and countryside would now join the Red Army in the fight, sucking and pulling at every German boot, wheel and track. The advance slowed and the Red Army was able to gather more reserves to throw in front of the Germans. Hitler also came to the aid of the hard-pressed Red Army by throwing his armoured forces off the direct and shortest route to Moscow, insisting instead that they envelop the city

from the north and south. To the weather, Hitler had now added distance to the burden of his commanders.

By 14 October the Germans had reached the historic battlefield of Borodino, 62 miles (100km) from Moscow. Two new elements were now to hinder their advance: snow and the Siberians. The tough 32nd Rifle Division from the Far East had just arrived to contest the battlefield. Reinforced by two tank brigades with the new T-34 and enormous KV-2 and with Katyusha rocket-launchers, numerous anti-aircraft and anti-tank guns, and the effective 76mm multi-purpose field gun, they were a rude shock for the Germans and a foretaste of the Red Army of the future. For five days the Siberians held a superior German force before they were overwhelmed. Once again the way to Moscow lay open, but rain and snow had turned the roads to mud and the German advance slowed to a crawl.

In Moscow, the news that the Germans were within less than 100 kilometres created panic. The government appeared to have lost its nerve and prepared to relocate to Kuybyshev. Even Stalin was

▶MiG-3s on combat patrol over the Kremlin. In the foreground below left, Ivan the Great's 16th-century bell-tower and belfry, one of Moscow's architectural gems. The Soviet Moscow counter-offensive was actually conducted with a numerically inferior air force.

ready to leave. At the railway station he paced the platform beside his loaded and waiting train. Then he made up his mind. We stay! The government unpacked and went back to work, order was restored and determined efforts to scrape up every last resource continued. Several hundred thousand men were combed out of the Moscow population to fill new formations. Everywhere the Russian talent for practical improvisation was producing, if not miracles, at least workable expedients. The new formations were no match for one with the professionalism and training of the Germans, but they would fight and their numbers grew. Supplying and moving them was facilitated by the Moscow region's excellent transportation and supply system. Reinforcements were also coming. Now assured of Japanese neutrality, Stalin quickly transferred half of the 750,000 tough, well-equipped Siberian troops he had kept in the Far East and Transbaikal military districts. Forty fresh, well-trained and well-equipped divisions were on their way to the defence of Moscow. In this moment of crisis Stalin also reinforced the morale of the population and defenders of Moscow by ordering the traditional 7 November Revolution Day Parade to be held. In his speech from Lenin's Tomb he appealed to the warrior heroes of old Russia – Alexander Nevsky, Dmitri Donskoi, Alexander Suvorov and Mikhail Kutuzov – and awakened the ancient pride of the Russians. 'The war you are waging is a war of liberation, a just war. . . . May you be inspired in this war by the heroic figures of our great ancestors.' The spark flamed in the ready tinder of long-suppressed Great Russian patriotism. By now the Russians had become aware that the Germans brought not liberation but extermination.

The early winter mud had frozen with the first November frosts. For a while the Germans had hard roads to speed their advance, but the deepening cold quickly began to cancel this advantage. Frostbite began to take a crippling toll of the poorly clad and exhausted German troops while the Russians operated confidently in a familiar environment, effectively equipped and clothed. The German advance was slowing perceptibly. By early December they had reached as far as Kalinin to the north-west and Tula to the south-east of Moscow. South of Tula the fighting raged over another ancient Russian battlefield –

◀Already wearing its winter paint scheme, a KV-1 heavy tank, damaged in the fighting outside Moscow, is being repaired in one of the city's factories, September 1941.

▶Siberians of the 32nd Rifle Division fighting to the death against a German corps-sized force on the Borodino battlefield. These were the first Siberian troops that the Germans had encountered. Like their ancestors who fought the French on this very spot on 26 August 1812, these Russians died at their posts. In the process, they gutted the SS Division Das Reich.

◀'The Siberians are coming!' At the approaches to Moscow, Siberian infantry form the sharp edge of the great counter-attack that sends the Germans reeling, December 1941. They are equipped and conditioned for the lethal winter environment. Already hardy, they are clothed in quilted uniforms and felt boots which keep out the cold and wet.Their personal camouflage is white and they are armed for the most part with submachine-guns. Men like these, who survived and fought for weeks in temperatures of −20 to −30 degrees Centrigrade, assumed almost legendary status in the minds of the German troops.

▶At the command post of the Western Front, October, 1941. The commander, General of the Army Georgi K. Zhukov; his chief of staff, Lieutenant-General Vasily D. Sokolovsky; and Nikolai A. Bulganin, a member of the Military Council – a discreet term for commissar. After the war Sokolovsky was to play a key role in the development of Soviet nuclear warfare doctrine.

Kulikovo Polye (Kulikovo Fields) where the Russians under Dmitri Donskoi first defeated the Mongols in 1380. The spires of the Kremlin were within sight of a few reconnaissance elements, but that was as far as the Germans got. Their aggressive flame was flickering out, smothering under sheer exhaustion, losses and the numbing cold. They were at the end of their tether.

On 5 December The Soviet High Command decided to launch a series of local counter-attacks to relieve the pressure on Moscow. In some places the Germans were only 10 to 20 miles from the city. But the correlation of forces had already shifted away from the Germans. The Red Army forces opposing Army Group Centre were relatively far stronger than they had been when Operation 'Typhoon' had begun. The Soviet High Command had carefully collected its reserves while the Germans had had no replacements for their considerable losses. On the West Front commanded by General Zhukov and the Southwest Front farther to the south the Red Army had gathered fifteen armies. They now had a third more rifle divisions, twice the number of artillery regiments, five times more cavalry divisions, and two and half times more tank brigades than they had had before the twin disasters at Bryansk and Vyazma. They were also closer to their sources of supply and were well served by the transportation system from Moscow.

To the surprise of the Red Army, the Germans began pulling back everywhere although the Soviet attacks had not been particularly effective in destroying German units. But the attacks had been the last straw for the physically and morally exhausted Germans who, drained of aggression, began to retire on the slightest pretext. Now the Red Army slipped the leash and fell on the retreating Germans in great strength all along the front. Well-clothed against the crushing cold that was decimating the Germans, the Soviet armies were also well armed with equipment that defeated the cold. The broad tracks of the T-34 easily negotiated the snow and woods that kept German tanks road-bound. Soviet weapons functioned with special cold-weather lubricants, thanks to the lessons of the Finnish War.

By 15 December the first phase of the Moscow counter-offensive had ended. Zhukov's West Front eliminated the

The Marshal's Ghost

Early in December the Germans captured the wounded colonel commanding the 222nd Rifle Division. Under interrogation he revealed that there were only a few divisions left in front of Moscow. The German intelligence officer was incredulous. How could that be he insisted. Soviet resistance had stiffened everywhere on the road to Moscow. The colonel nodded. In the last few weeks many new officers, most of the them middle-aged, had joined the units defending Moscow. They were the survivors of the purges and of the Gulag. 'Active service at the front is their chance of rehabilitation. And if a man has a penal camp behind him death holds no terror for him,' the colonel said. 'Besides, they want to prove that they were no traitors, but patriots worthy of Tukhachevsky.'

Reading the report of interrogation at army headquarters, a staff officer remarked, 'The late Tukhachevsky is in command before Moscow.'

▶A ski battalion makes its way along Gorki Street in Moscow with a supply unit heading for the front, November 1941. They didn't have far to go; by this time the front was effectively on the city's north-western outskirts.

▼Heavy KV-1 and medium T-34 tanks of the 9th Tank Brigade, commanded by the then Colonel Pavel A. Rotmistrov, pass the wreckage of German tanks, October 1941. The appearance of these formidable tanks with their deadly 76mm guns put the lighter and more thinly armoured German tanks at a great disadvantage. Rotmistrov's well-earned reputation as one of the best tank commanders in the Red Army earned him rapid promotion to command of an army and in 1944 the position of Deputy Commander of the Armoured and Mechanized Forces of the Red Army.

▲The Nazis in Russia showed their true feelings about religion – they were fundamentally anti-Christian. Here they have committed a unique desecration and murdered Soviet POWs from West Front before the icon screen of a Russian Orthodox Church in Vereya, Moscow Region, in reprisal for partisan actions, December 1941. By now the atrocities of the invader had little need for the amplification of Soviet propaganda. As the horror sank in, it steeled the hearts of the Russian people. Stalin reversed his persecution of the Orthodox Church and appealed for its support which was wholeheartedly forthcoming.

Early December 1941, on the Approaches to Moscow

'Yesterday we were on the defence, we retreated, but today we went over to the offensive . . . We all . . . had thought thus: first we would stop the enemy, then we would bring up forces, prepare, and finally . . . throw ourselves on the enemy. Reality turned out to be different, harsher and more exacting: . . . we did not find the time to . . . prepare . . . It became necessary, figuratively speaking, just to turn around one's left shoulder to strike the enemy under whose pressure we had still been retreating yesterday.'

Marshal of the Soviet Union Kirill S. Moskalenko

northern arm of the German envelopment of Moscow. West Front aided by Southwest Front similarly threw Guderian's forces out of their envelopment in the area of Tula. Zhukov ordered his armies to assemble mobile groups with tanks, cavalry and submachine-gunners to penetrate deep behind German lines and strike at fuel dumps and artillery. Panic began to spread as units began withdrawing under pressure. Immense quantities of equipment were abandoned to speed their withdrawal, reducing their strength even more, but the German generals knew that equipment could be replaced far easier than veteran troops.

The second phase saw the transfer of some of Zhukov's armies to the two new Kalinin and Bryansk Fronts to his north and south. The aim was nothing less than the envelopment of the reeling Army Group Centre. In less than two weeks the hunter had become the hunted. Army Group Centre was disintegrating. By the end of December the Red Army had pushed the Germans back as much as 150 kilometres despite Hitler's orders to stand fast.

Stalin's confidence grew with each of Zhukov's successes. On 5 January he announced a general offensive with five major operations along the entire front and employing nine of the ten Soviet Fronts, of which Zhukov's continuing offensives in the centre and the campaign in the Crimea were a part. Two new operations were now added – to free Leningrad from the siege of Army Group North and to recover the Donets basin held by Army Group Sputh.

The Volkhov and Northwest Fronts struck von Leeb's Army Group North on 7 January. Volkhov Front's 2nd Shock Army made a deep penetration, but the Germans recovered and isolated it. Farther south Northwest Front encircled a German corps in the Demyansk pocket. There the battle stalled as both sides sought to relieve their trapped forces in a grinding brawl. Hitler refused to allow the trapped corps to break out, but it was kept alive and fighting by a massive air supply effort. So successful was the Luftwaffe on this occasion that later Hitler would be fatally confident that the German troops later trapped at Stalingrad in 1942 would also be able to hold out. South of Moscow the second major offensive was launched by Southwest and South Fronts against

von Bock's Army Group South on 18 January and developed a large bulge (the Izyum salient) in the German lines which the Germans were eventually able to contain. In the Crimea, where Soviet amphibious landings at Feodosiya had begun on 29 December, two Soviet armies of the Crimean Front (formerly Transcaucasus Front) were ashore on the Kerch Peninsula. In the centre, the Kalinin and West Fronts were lunging for Vyazma, hoping to bag most of Army Group Centre. Large German forces were almost isolated in a long salient whose apex was at Rzhev. The base of the salient was almost severed by 1st Guards Cavalry Corps and 33rd Army which in turn were cut off and encircled by the Germans. By the end of February the Soviet offensives had all bogged down as Soviet strength exhausted itself. The fighting dragged on until the spring rains immobilized everyone.

The final dregs of the general offensive were bitter for the Red Army. Second Shock Army was eventually crushed in its pocket; the Germans relieved their trapped corps at Demyansk; and the isolated forces of West Front were eventually destroyed. On the Kalinin Front 29th Army, which had been trapped south of

Rzhev, was also destroyed. In the Crimea, General Erich von Manstein's Eleventh Army confined the Crimean Front to control of the Kerch Peninsula. Losses had been enormous; by the spring the Germans had lost well over a million men on the Eastern Front. The Red Army had lost 1,500,000 men before Moscow alone, a figure only released in 1990 by the Chief of the General Staff, Army General Mikhail A. Moiseyev. Nevertheless the Red Army had shattered the myth of German invincibility and gained an enduring self-respect and expertise that would carry them through the next three years.

SOVIET MATERIAL LOSSES IN 1941

	% Pre-War Inventory	Replaced by Industry
Small Arms:	67.0	30.0
Tanks*:	91.0	27.0
Artillery/Mortars	90.0	55.0
Combat Aircraft	90.0	55.0

Note*: The Red Army lost 20,500 out of 22,600 tanks available before the war broke out on 22 June 1941. Of these 16,500 were in need of medium or major repair.

Source: Army General M.A. Moiseyev, Chief of the General Staff, *Voyenno-istoricheskiy zhurnal*, No. 3, March 1990.

▲Firing over open sites from the meagre shelter of low snow berms in the environs of Moscow, November 1941, these 45mm anti-tank gun crews under the command of Commissar Nemirov racked up a particularly effective record of kills – 59 tanks, two aircraft and 600 infantrymen.

◄ Infantry attacking during the Moscow counter-offensive, December 1941. Note the greatcoats, felt boots and fur hats which gave them such an advantage over their German counterparts in their summer uniforms and tight, leather boots. The Russians understood their environment and were able to function in it while the Germans found themselves losing more men to frostbite than bullets.

▼The Red Army on parade in Red Square on 7 November 1941 – the Revolution Day parade. Stalin's decision to hold the parade with the enemy at the gates was a stroke of nerve and bravado that inspired the Red Army, the Muscovites, and then the whole nation. As a military event, it went off surprisingly well, given the fact that it was put on at only three days' notice and under threat of air attack.

◄The mass formation of a general military training battalion marching past Lenin's tomb under Stalin's gaze during the 7 November Revolution Day parade. From here they marched straight off to the front.

►Soviet submachine-gunners during the attack near Moscow, December 1941.

►Exhausted, freezing and hungry Germans surrendering outside Moscow during the counter-offensive, December 1941. Tough and professional veterans of victories across Europe, these men had been pushed beyond endurance by Hitler.

◄The Moscow counter-offensive begins, 5 December 1941. Nothing illustrates better the awesome effect of the Soviet steamroller than this photograph.

►A German nightmare – Cossacks with drawn sabres in the German rear during the defence of Moscow, November 1941. The II Guards Cossack Corps commanded by Major-General Lev M. Dovator, raised hell deep behind the front as they struck supply depots, convoys, headquarters, communications and artillery units. In this attack they sabred the enemy's 3rd Battalion, 430th Infantry Regiment near Volokolamsk. A gifted cavalry commander, Dovator, whose motto naturally was, 'A commander must be in front', inspired his men and earned repeated praise for his bravery. He was killed on 19 December attempting to lead a dismounted Cossack attack across the River Ruza.

▼Following the success of the Moscow counter-offensive in December, Zhukov's Western Front continues its attacks against Army Group Centre as part of Stalin's new general offensive from the Crimea to Leningrad, January 1942. Here T-34/76s, built with the aid of donations from the Khabarovsk Komsomol, are supported by Il-2 Stormovik ground-attack aircraft.

◀A reconnaissance element of Zhukov's Western Front attacks with the support of T-60 light tanks in the area of Mozhaisk about 100 km west of Moscow, January 1942. These men would pave the way for the breakthrough of 33rd Army and I Guards Cavalry Corps into the German rear that almost severed the base of the Rzhev salient into which much of Army Group Centre had been compressed. The T-60 was a new light tank produced from November 1941, based on the T-40 chassis but armed with a 20mm cannon and increased frontal armour. More than 6,000 were produced during the war and issued on a lavish scale to reconnaissance units.

▲A Soviet 45mm anti-tank gun in action in the area of Maloyaroslavets, Western Front, January 1942. Red Army attacks in this area were part of the effort to cut off the Rzhev salient.

▶Men of Captain Provorotsky's rifle company attacking in the direction of Kaluga, Western Front, February 1942. The Soviets took and held the vital road and rail junction at Sukhinichi despite strong German attempts to recover it, until the spring rains immobilized both sides.

◀Siberian ski troops armed with Shpagin submachine-guns attacking along Zhukov's Western Front, January 1942. Hitler's 'No Retreat' order made the Germans finally dig in their heels. Their resistance stiffened and the retreat became a vicious struggle of hedgehogs and strongpoints.

▶Soviet ski troops slipped deep through the porous German lines, which were little more than a string of loosely connected hedgehogs and strongpoints, to disrupt German logistics and communications units in the rear. Here a couple of men from Zhukov's Western Front prepare a railway line for detonation, somewhere in the rear of Army Group Centre.

▲The Red Army's solution to helping the infantry keep up with the tanks. Submachine-gunners and T-34 tanks of Marshal Timoshenko's Southern Front attacking in the direction of Barenkovo as part of the drive to liberate the industrial Donets region, February 1942.

◄This solution also worked to the north on the Volkhov Front commanded by Army General Kirill A. Meretskov. Here, troops armed with submachine-guns launch an assault from the cover of a T-34 on a German-held village, January 1942. On this front each side managed to encircle large formations of the other. The Germans trapped 2nd Shock Army south of Leningrad; the Red Army encircled a German corps in the Demyansk pocket. By spring, as the Germans recovered, the Soviets suffered reverses in both areas. Second Shock Army perished in its pocket as the Germans relieved their troops trapped in the Demyansk pocket. Post-war Soviet military historians ascribe the Soviet failures to the difficult terrain, weaknesses in support and inexperienced commands.

THE AGONY OF LENINGRAD:
THE BATTLE AND SIEGE, 1941-3

Field Marshal Ritter von Leeb's mission was clear and direct. Take Leningrad. For Hitler, this city had immense significance, representing everything that he hated most about Russia and Bolshevism. It was the great former imperial city of the Russian people and the birthplace of the Revolution itself, bearing the name of that devil Lenin. He planned to show it less mercy than the Romans had shown Carthage – break down its defences, wall in its millions to starve, then level and flood its site.

Now von Leeb's powerful Army Group North had driven the Red Army out of

most of the Baltics and was closing quickly on the city from the south. The Red Army had hoped to hold the Stalin Line running south-east from Lake Peipus, but Colonel-General Hoepner's 4th Panzer Group had already pierced it on 6 July. According to Hitler's plans, Hoepner would now try to swing east to seize Novgorod, cut the Leningrad-Moscow Road at Chudnovo and envelop the city from the east with the help of the Finns. The geography was not co-operative in this grand sweep. In Hoepner's path the terrain was heavily wooded and swampy, no ground for tanks – the same ground

that had saved northwest Russia from Mongol cavalry centuries before. Now the Red Army hung on to this hinge formed by Novgorod and Lake Ilmen as the Germans sought to break through.

Frustrated at Novgorod, Hoepner shifted west to better ground closer to Leningrad, and crossed the River Luga 100 kilometres south of the city at the western end of the Soviet line that reached to Lake Ilmen. The crossings came as a complete surprise to the Soviets who had no reserves in the area. Hurriedly troops, including officer cadets from Leningrad, were scraped together and thrown into the bridgeheads. They failed, and the Germans expanded their positions to strike over the short remaining distance to the city. All Hoepner needed was infantry to support his attack, but Hitler continued to insist that the Soviet hold on Novgorod be broken and the city be enveloped from the east. Hoepner received no infantry, the fighting continued around Novgorod, and time passed – enough for the Red Army to reinforce the new front south of Leningrad. The new heavy KV-1 and KV-2 tanks appeared, some manned by their factory crews from Leningrad, and by a brigade of women from Leningrad University. Behind them new fortifications

▼A skirmish line of Soviet infantry of the Volkhov Front in its attacks to relieve Leningrad, January 1942. The Red Army's recovery of Tikhvin opened the airway through which Leningrad could breathe – just barely. The siege itself had not been broken and could close to choke the city again. Desperate efforts continued to break the German grip. On 13 January Army General Kirill A. Meretskov's Volkhov Front and Lieutenant General Ivan I. Fedyuninsky's 54th Army of the Leningrad Front attacked the Germans south of Lake Ladoga. Exhausted, underfed and poorly equipped Soviet troops fought not only the

Germans but the most brutal winter in memory. The battle dragged on throughout that awful winter and then stalled. Meretskov wrote: 'I will never forget the endless forests, the bogs, the water-logged peat fields, the potholed roads. The heavy battle with the enemy went on side by side with the equally heavy battle with the forces of nature.' He was echoed by Fedyuninsky: 'The four months of constant blood-letting and, worst of all, unsuccessful fighting in the forests and marshy regions between Mga and Tikhvin remain a terrible memory.'

were springing up, the work of thousands of civilians brought from Leningrad.

On 8 August the Germans broke out of the bridgeheads against ferocious Soviet resistance, anticipating by hours a major Soviet attack on the bridgeheads themselves. By the 14th the formidable Soviet defences had been broken, but still the panzers had insufficient infantry for a clear thrust into Leningrad. Red Army forces withdrawing into Leningrad along the Baltic coast posed a risk to an unsupported German attack. A Soviet attack west of Lake Ilmen forestalled Hoepner's reinforcement. On 12 August Marshal Voroshilov, who commanded the northwest sector of the front, struck the flank of Sixteenth Army south-east of Lake Ilmen with his 34th Army and pushed the Germans back against the lake. He planned to cut south-west to Lake Peipus and cut off all the Germans facing Leningrad. Von Leeb threw General von Manstein's panzer corps at the flank of 34th Army and overran it in a slashing attack. In addition to 246 guns, the Germans captured the first of the dreaded Soviet Katyusha multiple rocket-launchers, the Stalin organs. Voroshilov had lost an army but kept the Germans from advancing on the most vulnerable road to the city. At Novgorod on 9 August the German assault made little headway against stiff resistance until the defence plans of the Soviet 48th Army were found on a dead officer. Their luck flown, the Red Army defenders of Novgorod stayed and fought to the death. The city fell on the 16th. A few days later vital Chudnovo fell. The Red Army continued to hold the line of the River Luga west of Novgorod even though it had been outflanked by the loss of Chudnovo. The Germans quickly chopped the position into pockets which yielded 21,000 prisoners, 316 tanks and 600 guns. On the 31st Voroshilov lost the rail junction at Mga just south of Lake Ladoga, which severed the last rail link with the rest of the country. So frightened was Voroshilov because of this loss that he failed to report it to Stalin for several days.

▶ Throughout the siege, German artillery shelled the city. Much of it was random, intended not for military targets but for sheer *Schrechlichkeit* (frightfulness), to slaughter and terrorize the civilian population.

▶When the war began, Leningrad was the major war production centre in the Soviet Union. Much of that production continued despite the siege, sending weapons directly to the fighting front around the city. Incredibly, the armouries of Leningrad hummed throughout the siege, sending critical weapons and components to the rest of the Red Army by air and over the ice bridge. But the cost was high. When reserves were exhausted workers marched off to the front, most never to return. Workers died at their machines from German artillery and air raids. Workers fell down and perished from hunger. From January to March the sick rate from hunger at the Kirov works was about 60 per cent. On 20 February barely 23 per cent of 10,424 workers reported for duty. By March the rolls had fallen to 6,000 of whom 2,300 had died by April.

▶One of the most moving and animating posters of the war, this one of a Russian mother and child, begging, 'Soldiers of the Red Army, save us!' No Russian man had to ask himself why he was fighting. The children of Leningrad were priority evacuees when the ice bridge finally opened.

Instead he roamed the battlelines vainly attempting to recapture the junction, courting death like an old soldier rather than face Stalin.

Despite these victories, Hoepner still had no infantry support and could make little headway as August wore on. Stalin made better use of the time, pouring reserves and equipment into the city. Troops retreating from Narva formed a pocket west of the city at Oranienbaum on the Gulf of Finland that was to hold out throughout the siege as a threat to the German northern flank. Within the city itself ten militia divisions were formed in the first three months of the war and sixteen separate artillery and machine-gun battalions. All saw combat and their losses were heavy, but they were a vital addition to the fighting manpower of the city. Ceaseless work by the population had achieved two rings of defences around the city that tied into the River Neva east of the city. The outer ring was about 40 kilometres from the city centre; the inner barely 25 kilometres.

On 8 September, finally reinforced by Eighteenth Army, Hoepner began his assault on the city. Everywhere the Germans were pressing in, overwhelming the

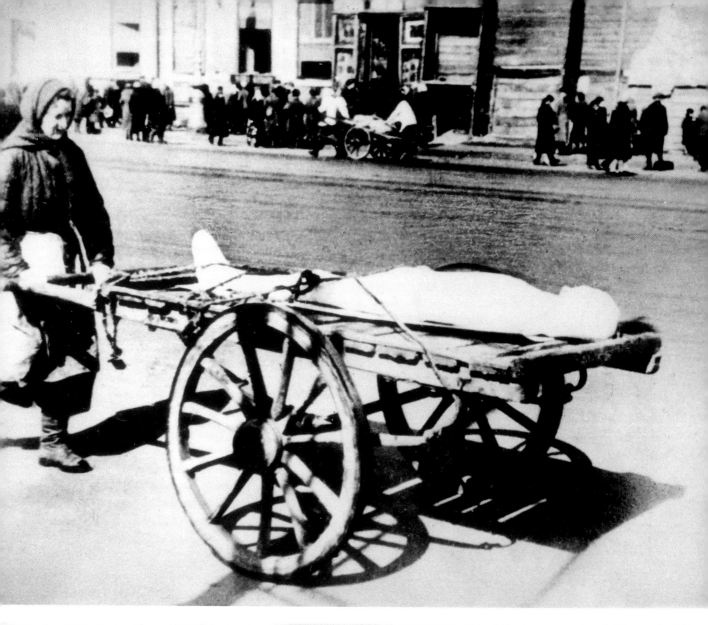

▲Death was everywhere in this great city. With the exception of Hitler's concentration camps, no such small space saw so many non-combatants perish. No city suffered such loss even in the most horrendous bombings of the war – not Hamburg, Dresden, Berlin, Tokyo, or even Hiroshima and Nagasaki. An estimated 800,000 Leningraders are buried in mass graves at the Piskaresvsky Cemetery and another 300,000 at the Serafimov Cemetery. Military deaths in the fighting range from one to two hundred thousand. The actual figures may never be known.

◄By 22 November Lake Ladoga had frozen deep enough to take truck traffic, but it was not until January with the freeing of the Tikhvin railhead that a massive resupply could be undertaken. From January until the end of April 400 hundred trucks were making a daily round-the-clock circuit delivering food, fuel and munitions to Leningrad on the way in and evacuating a half million non-combatants on the return trip. More than a thousand trucks were lost, falling through the ice or destroyed by German air raids.

Soviet defences, frustrating every measure. The battle flared around the Duderhof Hills where the tsars had reviewed and manoeuvred their guards regiments. To the east Sixteenth Army cut off the last lifeline out of the city by seizing Schlusselburg, the terminus of the lake transportation system that tied into the Russian network of canals and rivers. The city was in a state of panic and its defenders demoralized as the situation slid towards catastrophe.

Then Stalin sent a general. Army General Georgi Zhukov arrived by air from Moscow on 10 September. He handed Voroshilov Stalin's brusque note of dismissal and immediately began to restore order. Working all night, he relieved a shortage of anti-tank guns by transferring dual-purpose anti-aircraft artillery and organized six brigades of naval infantry and students to reinforce the front; he relieved the confused commander of the 42nd Army on the 14th and replaced him with a fighting general and then reinforced

the army with troops from the Karelian Isthmus. On the 17th he issued a declaration that retreat would constitute a crime against the Motherland punishable by death. His determination to act and act boldly and even harshly was a bracing slap in the face to the despairing garrison and the population. Then he took every opportunity to seize the initiative by incessant counter-attacks, raids and patrols to fatigue and bleed the enemy and frustrate his offensive plans. As the Australian commander, Vasey, had done at Tobruk, Zhukov on an even larger scale was 'besieging the besieger'.

Still the Germans attacked. By the night of the 11th the Soviet positions at Duderhof had been overwhelmed, their defenders dead. The Germans had pierced both defensive rings and entered the city's suburbs, only 10 kilometres from the city centre. On the 13th they struck 42nd Army and penetrated towards Uritsk, a key to the inner defensive ring near the Gulf of Finland. Zhukov committed his

last reserve, 10th Rifle Division, to a counter-attack the next morning, and the Germans were driven out of all their gains. On the 16th the Germans broke through to the Gulf of Finland isolating the Oranienbaum pocket. On the 17th, the Germans hit again at 42nd and 55th Armies further south in the area of Pulkovo and Kopino. Zhukov was trading sledgehammer blows with Army Group North, throwing everything he had into the fight. Massed artillery, naval gunfire and aircraft attacks fell on the Germans. Zhukov's artillerymen were firing hundreds of guns over open sights near Pulkovo. The Germans attacked again towards Uritsk, but Zhukov had prepared 8th Army in the Oranienbaum pocket for just such a manoeuvre. On the 19th a shock force of four divisions lashed out and pulled the Germans away from Uritsk. Still von Leeb's armies continued to thrust and lunge at the Soviet defences running from Uritsk to the Pulkovo Heights to Peterhof. Somehow the Red Army held the line. Zhukov and the city braced themselves for repeated shocks but found in early October that the Germans were building defences and that 4th Panzer Group was departing for Moscow. Hitler had called off the attack to let Leningrad starve under siege. Like a glittering lure, the prize of Moscow had broken his interest in Leningrad. Soon Zhukov would be recalled for the defence of Moscow, and Leningrad would settle in for the horrors of siege.

Siege was the very contingency the defenders of the city had not expected or prepared for. By the end of August this city of 3,000,000 souls had barely a month's supply of food. A massive air raid on 6 September set fire to the city's main warehouses and everything was lost except 2,500 tons of sugar which melted and filled the cellars with a salvageable rock-like candy. Since the Germans had cut the last land route to Soviet territory, the city could only be supplied by barge across Lake Ladoga. From mid-September to mid-November less than half of the 1,000 tons the city needed daily got through, but it kept the city alive. Barely alive. Starvation was creeping through the city despite the most stringent control and efficiency. People began to die. By 20 November rations had been reduced to the lowest point of the whole siege – 250 grams of bread a day for manual workers, less than one-third the normal requirement. Hitler's hideous plans for the city were ripening. The only hope was to wait for Russia's old ally, winter, to freeze Lake Ladoga hard enough to take wheeled traffic. By 17 November men were walking across the freezing lake marking out the route with coloured flags. By the 20th horse-drawn sledges were bringing a few tons of food across. By the 22nd truck convoys were crossing. Still thousands were dying of hunger. The Red Army then drove the Germans out of Tikhvin on 9 December, opening a major rail line to the east shore of Lake Ladoga. Not until January did the ice route fulfill its promise when 400 three-ton trucks crossed on a daily basis. To relieve the city further the trucks carried 500,000 civilians out of the city on their return. In the spring and summer another half million would be sent out by barge. So successful was the resupply effort that eventually rations returned to normal and even a bit higher than in the rest of the country. They were well-earned rations for Leningrad continued to be a major centre of war industry. Not only civilians but huge quantities of war materials and weapons manufactured under the most appalling conditions left by truck and barge over the lake and by air to feed the fighting in the south.

For the remainder of 1942 the siege settled into a relatively quiet front as the great battles were fought far to the south. As the drama at Stalingrad was playing itself out in December, the High Command ordered the reopening of the land

Marshal of the Soviet Union Georgi K. Zhukov

'A commander of strong will and decisiveness. He possesses a wealth of initiative and skillfully applies it to his job. He is disciplined. He is exacting and is persistent in his demands. In military respects he is well trained. He loves military matters and constantly improves himself. . .'

Officer efficiency report written by General Konstantin K. Rokossovsky, *c.* 1930 when Zhukov commanded the 2nd Cavalry Brigade

'Zhukov: Outspoken man of action whose qualities are more those of the will than of the intellect. He is highly regarded in Soviet military circles and is considered to be an especially capable officer and good organizer. He was the first to stand up for the massed use of tanks and successfully carried it off in practice.'

Captured German intelligence analysis, May 1943,

'Zhukov is my George B. McClellan. Like McClellan he always wants more men, more cannon, more guns. Also more planes. He never has enough. But Zhukov has never lost a battle.'

Joseph Stalin

'Highly illuminating to me was his description of the Russian method of attacking through mine fields . . . Marshal Zhukov gave me a matter-of-fact statement of his practice, which was, roughly, "There are two kinds of mines; one is the personnel mine and the other is the vehicular mine. When we come to a mine field our infantry attacks exactly as if it were not there. The losses we get from personnel mines we consider only equal to those we would have gotten from machine-guns and artillery if the Germans had chosen to defend that particular area with strong bodies of troops instead of with mine fields. . ."'

General Dwight D. Eisenhower, *Crusade in Europe*, 1947

'. . .sometimes his severity exceeded permissable limits. . .I shall remark that at the height of combat actions at Moscow our *front* commander sometimes, in my view, was guilty of unwarranted abruptness.'

Marshal Konstantin K. Rokossovsky, *Voyenno–istoricheskiy zhurnal*, November 1966.

◄The Soviet battleship *Oktyabrskaya Revolyutsia* (October Revolution) in the Gulf of Finland adds her heavy guns to the landward defences of Leningrad, Baltic Fleet, September 1941. The Red Banner Baltic Fleet had been driven back to its great naval base at Kronstadt in the Gulf of Finland outside Leningrad. Trapped by German and Finnish minefields, the fleet fed the land fight to the hilt. Gun crews continued to serve their guns even when the ships had been sunk and had settled up to their decks. Air attacks were incessant. *Oktyabrskaya* once beat off twenty 20 dive-bomber attacks in one day, downing five aircraft.

route south of Lake Ladoga in an offensive code-named 'Iskra'('Spark'). Leningrad Front would attack from the west and meet Volkhov Front attacking from the east. Stalin ordered Zhukov back to Leningrad to co-ordinate the fronts. The offensive was launched on 12 January 1943 and achieved complete surprise. In six days of heavy fighting Schlusselburg was captured and the spearheads of the two fronts met. The blockade of Leningrad was finally broken. The Germans still maintained their siege works to the south from which they continued to bombard the city. Bombardment, fighting for their city and famine all contributed to a sickening death toll. More than a million people had died by the time the Germans were finally driven away in January 1944.

▶ Here the new Commander of the Leningrad Front, Army General Georgi K. Zhukov, takes notes at an observation point on the city's perimeter, September 1941.

▼ Workers' militia and Black Sea Fleet sailors formed a vital part of the city's landward defences. Ten divisions of militia were formed from the city's population and saw action. The Baltic Fleet stripped non-essential personnel from its facilities and ships and provided Zhukov with six brigades of naval infantry. One of the lads fighting outside Leningrad was a young sailor named Aleksandr Yakovlev. Badly wounded in the open, five of his mates dashed out to save him. Four were killed, but the fifth dragged him to safety. His wound left him crippled, but he survived. One day he would serve Mikhail Gorbachev as the architect of *Perestroika*.

A Soviet sniper on the Leningrad Front. The siege continued throughout 1942, but the war's centre of gravity had shifted far to the south along the Volga and into the Caucasus Mountains.

A Degtyarev anti-tank gun crew changes position at the double, on the approaches to Leningrad, September 1941. Zhukov injected energy and will as a powerful antidote into the stricken city. He made the right military decisions and none too soon. The Germans attacked him immediately, but he scraped together every resource, every last man and gun, and threw them skillfully into the fight. The city held.

Soviet partisans made life hell for the Germans of Army Group North. As early as the end of 1941 partisan groups totalling 14,000 men and women had been established in the area around Leningrad. Here a partisan unit attacks in the rear of Army Group North in the autumn of 1943.

THE CAMPAIGN IN THE FAR NORTH, 1941-4

The sweep of Operation 'Barbarossa' reached not only south to the warmth of the Black Sea but brushed the frozen coast of the Kola Peninsula on the Arctic Ocean as well. Hitler's obsession with economic objectives – defending the Finnish nickel mines at Petsamo and closing the Soviet Union's only all-weather port of Murmansk – drew his attention northward. He was less concerned with objective realities. General Dietl, Commander of Mountain Corps Norway, warned him '... the landscape up there in the tundra outside Murmansk is just as it was after the Creation. There's not a tree, not a shrub, not a human settlement. No roads and no paths. Nothing but rock and scree. There are countless torrents, lakes and fast-flowing rivers with rapids and waterfalls. In the summer there's swamp – and in winter there's ice, snow, and it's 40 to 50 degrees below. Icy gales rage throughout the eight months of Arctic night. This 100 kilometres of tundra belt surrounding

Murmansk like a protective armour is one big wilderness. War has never before been waged in this tundra, since the pathless stony desert is virtually impenetrable for formations...'

Dietl suggested that the Kirov Road leading to Murmansk from Central Russia be cut in just one place farther to the south. Then Murmansk would simply wither away. Instead Hitler ordered three major, separate attacks along a 550-kilometre line running south from the Arctic, to complicate enormously the Soviet defence of the region. The Soviet 14th Army, then part of Northern Front, was charged with the defence of this vast area, its duties to cover the north coast of the Kola Peninsula, hold the Rybachiy and Sredniy Peninsulas on the Arctic, and finally to prevent penetration into the Murmansk, Kandalaksha, and Kasten'ga areas. The commander, Colonel-General V. A. Frolov, was well aware that the loss of any one of the latter three areas would collapse the entire theatre, and to prevent

that catastrophe he had five divisions in a single echelon along 550 kilometres of front! The Germans attacked with three corps, sending one against each of Frolov's three primary areas of defence.

Mountain Corps Norway with two mountain divisions attacked on 29 June and in bitter fighting had pushed 52nd Rifle Division back across the West Litsa River by 7 July. Frolov retrieved the situation with an adroit amphibious landing by NKVD border guards in the German rear. With the Soviets behind, the Germans withdrew across the river. They tried again a few days later, but again were frustrated by another well-timed Soviet amphibious landing. Reinforced in September, the Germans again forced the river. Sensing an impending German breakthrough, Frolov rushed the 168th 'Polar' Rifle Division into the fight. This 'Polar' division was little more than an untrained mob of sailors, fishermen and workers from Murmansk, mobilized, armed and sent off to fight in rapid and

▶ Soviet naval infantry make one of the several amphibious landing operations in Litsa Bay that were to support 14th Army so well, July 1941.

desperate succession. The 168th, however, was a lucky improvisation and an exception to the rule that scratch formations usually fail. It made the difference, and Dietl was forced to suspend operations by 17 July after advancing only 20 kilometres.

Several hundred kilometres to the south, XXXVI Corps began its attack on 1 July. The German corps had only one good division; its other was the poorly trained so-called SS Mountain Division Nord. They faced the strongest element of 14th Army – 42nd Rifle Corps of three divisions occupying three defensive belts. For the next forty days the Red Army exacted a heavy toll from XXXVI Corps as it withdrew to the second belt. German reinforcements finally forced a retreat to the third belt in September, but beyond that they could not go. XXXVI Corps was used up.

On the third axis, the Finns made much more rapid progress than the German corps to the north. Their two divisions faced several regiments and had driven them, despite fierce resistance, back beyond Kasten'ga by early August. The defences improved, however, when all the

Soviet units were placed under a single headquarters. Finally the arrival of 88th Rifle Division from Archangelsk stabilized the situation. The Finns made one more advance in November but were driven back to their starting-point.

By the end of 1941 the troops of 14th Army could look back with satisfaction on their performance. Nowhere had the enemy achieved a strategic breakthrough. Murmansk and Kandalaksha were still in Soviet hands and operational, and while Kasten'ga had been lost, communications with Central Russia were still intact. Enemy casualties had also been high, 21,501 Germans and at least 5,000 Finns. General Frolov had handled his army well, taking advantage of superior internal lines of communication such as the Murmansk railway to move troops laterally from one threatened sector to another. For most of the campaign he conducted economy of force operations, but when opportunities appeared, massed his troops to launch limited but effective counter-offensives. The men of 14th Army had also fought well. They adapted well to the difficult terrain and subsisted on limited food supplies. The Germans, on the other

hand, had dissipated their efforts on three axes. Communications were poor, their logistics not up to the effort, and their troops, by their own admission, had had a hard time adapting to the heavily wooded conditions found around Kandalaksha.

In 1942 the Red Army was able to launch two operational level offensives in theatre. In August 1941 a new Karelian Front was created consisting of 14th Army, responsible for operations from Murmansk to Kandalaksha, and the new 26th Army operating in the Kasten'ga area. The first offensive was kicked off by 26th Army on 24 April to force Finnish III Corps out of Kasten'ga. Three Soviet divisions and three brigades hammered at the corps' flanks and came within three

▲Troops of 14th Army in action on the Kola Peninsula, April 1942.

▼The Soviet Destroyer *Gromky* of the Northern Fleet, escorting an Allied convoy, heads for Murmansk, summer 1943. The Northern Fleet was the only one of three major Soviet fleets that had not had its bases overrun in the German advances of 1941-2 and continued to provide effective support to 14th Army of Karelian Front. Not only did it conduct effective amphibious landing operations with its naval infantry brigades, but protected Allied convoys on the last leg of their voyage to Murmansk and waged a campaign against German resupply efforts by sea from Norway to XIX Mountain Corps in the direction of Murmansk. In 1943 the Northern Fleet's strength grew to 216 ships and craft and 347 aircraft including 191 combat aircraft.

◀ In the far north the land front may have been stagnant in late 1942 and throughout 1943, but the Northern Fleet stayed active. Here a naval infantry unit makes a raid behind German lines, summer 1943.

▶ In the autumn of 1944 Hitler finally agreed to abandon the campaign in the Far North and withdraw XIX Corps (53,000 men) into Norway. Simultaneously, the Red Army had prepared a major offensive with its 14th Army (97,000 men) reinforced to six corps and supported by two naval infantry brigades. The first phase of the attack struck the Germans guarding the valuable nickel mines at Petsamo (Pechenga) on 7 October. The attack made such speed that the Soviets had outrun their logistics in two days. A German counter-attack at this critical moment fell apart as 63rd Naval Infantry Brigade struck in their rear in assault landings deep into Pechenga Bay. By 15 October Petsamo had fallen with a loss of 6,000 Germans.

kilometres of cutting off the road to Kasten'ga. Reinforced by German troops, the Finns were able to counter-attack, cut off the enveloping Soviet formations and nearly destroy them. The spring thaw then came to the aid of the Red Army and delayed a Finnish-German counter-attack until 15 May. By then 26th Army had built elaborate field fortifications. In tough fighting III Corps was finally able to restore its original lines, but by 23 May had halted operations.

In the second offensive operation, 14th Army with two divisions and two ski brigades attacked 6th Mountain Division on the Murmansk axis to drive it beyond the River Titovka. The Soviets hit both German flanks and landed a naval infantry brigade in the enemy's rear. Then nature this time intervened to help the Germans. One of the worst snowstorms on record hit the region and froze both sides in place, giving the Germans time to bring up reinforcements and restore their original positions by 12 May.

Both Soviet offensives in 1942 succeeded in their opening phases but ultimately failed. The Soviet commanders showed great aggressiveness and a sound grasp of tactics, but were unable to synchronize operations because of the low level of training and inadequate tactical communications. Stalin and the High Command decided that any strategic and operational gains in the Karelian Theatre

were not worth the effort. At approximately the same time, Hitler came to the same conclusion, and offensive operations ceased in the theatre for the remainder of 1942 and throughout 1943.

By late 1943 the Soviet strategic situation had improved greatly, and the Red Army began planning offensive operations for 1944. Stalin's goal in the north was to drive the Germans and Finns out of Soviet territory and force Finland out of the war. The latter he accomplished in a major offensive by Karelian Front, now under command of Army General K. A. Meretskov, on the Karelian Isthmus (see Chapter 13) in June. By 19 September Finland was out of the war, but the German Twentieth Mountain Army was spread out from Central Finland to the Barents Sea.

In what became known as the Petsamo-Kirkenes Operation, 14th Army, grown to six corps reinforced by two naval infantry brigades, attacked the withdrawing Germans, drove them out of Finland and pursued them into northern Norway. In the first phase of the operation the Soviets struck XIX Mountain Corps guarding the Petsamo mines on 7 October. By the 9th the advance was threatened as 14th Army lunged so far and fast that it outran its logistic support. The Germans planned a counter-attack at this critical instant but were checked by a naval infantry landing in their rear. Things went bad quickly. Petsamo fell on the 15th.

After a three-day pause to rest its exhausted troops, 14th Army began the second phase of the operation. It drove the southern wing of XIX Corps rapidly westwards while isolating 6th Mountain Division from the corps' main body. By the 22nd the Red Army was pursing the Germans on two separate axes, was 20 kilometres from Kirkenes and had an entire corps on Norwegian territory. In the third phase of the operation 14th Army sent three corps towards Kirkenes and three corps after the retreating main body of XIX Corps to the south. On 25 October Kirkenes fell. At this juncture the imminent Polar night and the rugged terrain ahead decided the Front's Military Council to go over to the defensive on 29 October.

This operation had been the most successful by far in the theatre. By 1944 the Red Army had become more expert at co-ordination at all levels, and the logistics structure had matured to the extent that it could support large-scale offensive operations. So ended the grim campaigns fought in the harshest natural environment of the entire war. While the strategic importance of the theatre had declined, the experience gained there by the Red Army paid large dividends; experienced officers such as Meretskov and his Front staff were transferred to Manchuria to conduct operations against the Japanese in conditions similar to those in Karelia.

▼The 14th Army drove the Germans across the Norwegian border on 22 October and by the 25th had taken the port of Kirkenes. The rugged terrain ahead and the coming Polar night convinced the Soviets to end the campaign at this point. In three weeks of hard fighting and hard marching under dreadful conditions, 14th Army had driven the Germans back 150 kilometres, liberated their own territory and the first corner of occupied Norway.

◄'Communists, Forward!' The classic 'Follow-me!' role of the infantry junior officer. Time and time again the Germans, who made a cult of officer leadership, were astounded at the willingness of Soviet junior officers to sacrifice themselves. This picture was taken in the first rush of success as Timoshenko's Southwestern Front lunged for Kharkov, May 1942.

▼A Soviet tank unit equipped with T-34-76s on the Southwestern Front, receiving its banner just before the Timoshenko offensive towards Kharkov on 12 May 1942. Such tank units with their new T-34s and KV-1s represented the carefully hoarded strategic reserve. Most would perish in the coming battle.

THE GERMAN HIGH TIDE
THE SUMMER OFFENSIVE OF 1942

The desperate winter battles of 1941-2 had finally exhausted themselves in the mud of the spring thaws. Both the Red Army and the Wehrmacht immediately began to plan and gather strength for the next round. The German General Staff preferred to direct one single-axis blow at Moscow, the brain and transportation hub of the Soviet war effort. Hitler disagreed; the bloody winter fighting had convinced him that Germany needed the economic resources of the southern Soviet Union bordering the Black Sea to sustain Germany for a long war. Therefore, Army Group South would bear the brunt of the campaign.

Stalin and his advisers followed the same logic as the German General Staff

and believed that the next blow would be aimed at Moscow. The Red Army accordingly concentrated its reserves for its defence. The result was a gross underestimation of the role of the southern direction as a theatre of military operations. Little planning was done to provide variants of options should a severe attack be made in that direction.

The German offensive was scheduled for early June, but the Germans planned to clear both flanks of the operation in May. Along the southern flank lay the still partly unconquered Crimea. The besieged fortress city of Sevastopol and the 44th, 47th and 51st Armies of the Crimean Front defending the Kerch Peninsula in the eastern part of the island were to be

eliminated. On 8 May General von Manstein's Eleventh Army broke the flank of the Crimean Front with an amphibious operation. Successive blows collapsed the Front which fled in disorder to the Kerch Strait. Attempts to evacuate survivors fell apart as von Manstein pressed closely on their heels; he was determined not to allow a second Dunkirk. Although 120,000 men were evacuated, the disaster cost the Red Army 170,000 prisoners, 1,133 guns and 258 tanks.

The Germans planned to clear the northern flank of the operation by destroying the Southwestern Front before Voronezh. Marshal Semyon K. Timoshenko, commanding this very targeted theatre, recommended an ambitious offensive operation employing the forces of three Fronts to recapture Kharkov. In the absence of reserves, the Soviet High Command rejected the scale of the plan but recommended that Timoshenko conduct the operation with only the Southwestern Front and the troops of Lieutenant-General Rodion Y. Malinovsky's Southern Front. Nevertheless, Stalin reinforced Timoshenko with ten rifle divisions and 26 tank brigades. Neither the Red Army nor the Wehrmacht guessed that both armies were preparing almost simultaneous offensive operations in the same sector.

On 12 May Timoshenko struck at the German Sixth Army from Volchansk and the Izyum or Barvenkovo salient with 600,000 men in five armies, and more than 1,000 tanks. Deep penetrations were made quickly in the direction of Kharkov with the Southwestern Front's 6th Army from the Izyum salient and 28th Army from Volchansk (38th Army in reserve). However, as Soviet communications lengthened, their flanks become increasingly vulnerable. Unbeknown to Timoshenko, the Germans had also planned to attack and pinch out the very Izyum salient from which he had just launched his own attack. Their attack began five days after the Soviet attack. First Panzer Army and

◄◄Soviet submachine-gunners such as these in the Kuban marshes held up Seventeenth Army's drive on Novorossisk, September 1942. Note the sensible, field-expedient flotation equipment.

◄The 'Black Death'. Soviet naval infantry of 255th Brigade of the Black Sea Fleet now subordinate to the Trans-Caucasus Front's Black

Sea Group, breaching German defences near Tuapse in the Novorossisk Defence Region, September 1942.

▲A Soviet 45mm anti-tank gun crew prepares to engage troops of First Panzer Army in the foothills of the Caucasus, Northern Group, Trans-Ccaucasus Front, August 1942.

the Seventeenth Army struck from the south, breaking through the protecting flank of the Southern Front (9th and 57th Armies). Timoshenko kept attacking toward Kharkhov until the situation was too late to retrieve. When he finally responded to this threat, pressure was relieved on German Sixth Army which quickly counter-attacked. The two German forces cut off both Soviet spearheads. Disaster had again fallen upon the Red Army. Two complete armies (6th and 57th) and parts of two others had been trapped in another classic German pincer operation. Barely 22,000 men managed to exfiltrate from the pocket. The Red Army lost 1,250 tanks, most of the total number engaged, including almost all the strategic reserve of modern T-34 and KV-1 tanks built up over the winter. A total of 2,026 guns were lost as well. By the end of May 241,000 prisoners were in German hands, and the strength of the Southwestern Front had been broken.

The gate to southern Russia and the oil-rich Trans-Caucasus was now hanging broken on its hinges. In less than a month the Crimean, Southwestern and Southern Fronts of ten armies had seen seven armies destroyed or crippled. More than 400,000 prisoners had been lost as well as more than 1,500 tanks and about 3,200 guns. Army Group South acted quickly to smash their way through. On 7 June von Manstein's Eleventh Army began the final phase of the reduction of the Crimea, the assault on the great fortress city of Sevastopol, and had secured it by 4 July. On 10 June Sixth and Fourth Panzer Armies (designated Army Group 'B' in July) attacked between Kursk and Belgorod, preparing the strategic leverage for Seventeenth and First Panzer Armies (Army Group 'A') to strike from the direction of Kharkov. Within four days Soviet reserves opposite Army Group 'B' were exhausted, and the Germans shot forward 160 kilometres to the River Don near Voronezh. The army group turned south-eastwards and thundered down the corridor of the Don and Donets heading for Stalingrad. The Soviets were so preoccupied by this drive on Voronezh that they to appreciate the deadlier thrust of Army Group 'A' which broke through the Front and raced south to seize Rostov on Don, cross the river and drive south across the Kuban in the north Caucasus. By late August it had reached the foothills of the Caucasus

Mountains. The loss of Rostov had cut the Caucasus pipeline to Moscow which forced the Soviets to transport fuel by tanker up the Caspian Sea until a new line could be laid directly to the east.

These drives had destroyed many Soviet formations, but surprisingly far fewer prisoners were taken than in 1941. The Red Army was learning to avoid the terrible German armoured pincers. Units would hold until threatened with encirclement and then retreat. Those units that had been overrun, bypassed or encircled generally slipped away to fight again. The south-easterly direction of Army Group 'A's advance also tended to drive Soviet forces north-east to be gathered in the area of Stalingrad, the objective of Army Group 'B'. By September the fighting around Stalingrad had become a campaign in its own right.

Faced with a collapse in the south, the Soviet High Command sought to prevent the Germans from reinforcing that theatre by launching major attacks from Western and Kalinin Fronts against Army Group Centre in the area Rzhev–Sychevka. Western Front broke through but was heavily counter-attacked in what became a large-scale confrontation. The successes of Western Front were exploited by Kalinin Front which pushed on to the outskirts of Rzhev. The Red Army's offensive had exhausted itself by 23 August when the defensive was resumed. Overall the operation had been a success at a time when things were still going badly in the south. Russian territory had been liberated, but more importantly Army Group Centre had not only been prevented from sending reinforcements to the south, but troops had actually been drawn away from Army Group South.

In the south-east the Germans quickly met stiffer resistance in the more easily defended mountains of the Caucasus from the newly established Soviet Trans-Caucasus Front stretching along the entire length of the great mountain chain from the Black to the Caspian Seas. The Northern Group defended the central route through the mountains, basing its defensive plan on the city of Ordzhonikidze. The Black Sea Group held the Black Sea gate into Georgia and the mountains that paralled the sea. Its forward positions were in the Kuban and the naval base of Novorossisk. The South-eastern Front was established to hold the

plains to the north-east of the mountains. Large numbers of men from the Trans-Caucasus, Georgians, Armenians and Azeris, were filling up the ranks of the formations of these mountain Fronts. Defending the approaches to their homes, their resistance was bitter and determined. Every second man in Nogorno-Karabakh, the Armenian enclave in Azerbaijan, would die in the fighting. In 1991 Eduard Shevarnadze was to recall that in this war of his childhood half the adult males in Georgia perished, many fighting on the doorstep of their own ancient homeland.

As Soviet resistance hardened, Army Group 'A's resources were being siphoned off to support the growing battle of Stalingrad. At the western end of the mountains Seventeenth Army fought with difficulty over the Kuban marshes to seize Novorossisk but was stopped short of its final objective of Tuapse by the soldiers and sailors of the Black Sea Group. In the central sector of the mountain chain First

▲ A Soviet horse-drawn machine-gun team supporting a cavalry attack in the Caucasian foothills, redeploys to a new position, Northern Group, Trans-Caucasus Front, summer 1942. Soviet cavalry swept across the flat steppes of the north Caucasus to the foothills of the mountains to savage the over-extended Germans. It was ideal country for cavalry and the Soviets made the most of it.

Panzer Army and the Northern Group had struggled from one nasty fight to another at Mozdok and Nalchik as the Germans pressed forward. By the end of October the Germans had been were held just short of Ordzhonikidze. The stalling of their attack was ominously overshadowed by the great Soviet counteroffensive at Stalingrad which would consume most of Army Group 'B' and suddenly threaten Army Group 'A' with a similar fate.

▲Soviet infantry counter-attacking in the foothills of the Caucasus, Northern Group, Trans-Caucasus Front, August 1942. Note the three most common section weapons of the Soviet infantry – the Maxim machine-gun, the M1891 bolt-action rifle and the PPsh submachine-gun.

▶A Soviet rifle regiment of the Northern Group, Trans-Caucasus Front, attacking elements of First Panzer Army in the mountainous country around Mozdok in the Caucasus Mountains, September 1942.

▲A Soviet naval infantry officer leads his men in an attack on the village of Gizel, near Ordzhonikidze, Northern Group, Trans-Caucasus Front, September 1942. So badly had the Black Sea Fleet been damaged by the loss of its bases in the Crimea that most of its personnel were released to naval infantry brigades which distinguished themselves in

mountain fighting, as far removed from amphibious operations as is possible.

▼A battery of 1910 vintage 122mm field howitzers opens fire on German positions near Ordzhonikidze, Northern Group, Trans-Caucasus Front, September 1942.

▲Soviet naval infantry scouts of 83rd Brigade stiffened the defence of Ordzhonikidze against which the last efforts of First Panzer Army finally stalled, Northern Group, Trans-Caucasus Front, September 1942.

▶A Soviet Sturmovik ground-attack aircraft production line. In their factories far from the war zone, the Soviet Union would produce 128,847 combat aircraft during the war, as against 197,760 by the USA. The year 1942 was still a year of parity in the air at best. By February 1943 Soviet production was maintaining a combat strength of almost two to one over the Germans.

▼A mountain infantry unit under the command of Lieutenant A. Yefremov, climbing a glacier to defend a mountain pass near the town of Nalchik against a final desperate attack by exhausted elements of First Panzer Army, Northern Group, Trans-Caucasus Front, October 1942. Although Nalchik fell to the Germans, they did not get far beyond it.

◀A Soviet artillery production factory in the Urals, part of the massive relocation of military production from the lands overrun earlier in the western districts of the Soviet Union.

▼◀The Merkulov tank factory brigade repairing what appears to be a damaged BT-7 medium tank, the most numerous model produced in the 1930s. The BT-7, armed with a 45mm gun, was popular with Soviet tank troops, being reliable and mobile. It had seen very effective service in the Battle of Khalkin Gol in Manchuria in 1939 and had also accompanied Soviet troops into Poland. The name of this tank under repair, 'Zoya Kosmodemyanskaya', is believed to be that of a young partisan brutally killed by the Germans near Moscow in November 1941. Her name became a symbol of sacrifice and courage. In those hard days it was common to name tanks, planes, factories, schools, etc., after fallen heroes. 'Irkutsk', painted below the name, probably indicates the town where the tank was built.

▶Fifteen 'Katyusha' rocket-launcher battalions supported 20th and 31st Armies of Zhukov's Western Front in their attack on Rzhev during the Rzhev–Sychevka Operation, August 1942. After an hour-long bombardment the attack went in during a driving rainstorm. General Konev's Kalinin Front attacked to the north with 29th and 30th Armies.

▼Collective farmers of the Moscow region at the presentation to Soviet tank troops of new KV-1 heavy tanks paid for by their donations. The inscription on the tank: 'Moscow Collective Farmers'. Donations collected by the Russian Orthodox Church were also equipping the Red Army. In 1942 Soviet industry produced a remarkable 24,668 tanks of which 13,500 were the tough T-34.

▲◀A Soviet cavalry regiment attacking through the smoke during the battles around Rzhev, August 1942. Western Front attacked with 20th and 31st armies in the line supported by two Guards cavalry corps, two tank corps and five more cavalry divisions right behind them. Each army also had a special mobile group of three tank brigades.

▲A shattered farmhouse taken by Red Army infantry in the Rzhev–Sychevka Operation, August 1942. Although the Red Army reckoned the operation completed by 23 August, severe fighting continued until the middle of September.

◀A horse-drawn anti-tank gun crew rushes into action, Rzhev–Sychevka Operation, August 1942. By 17 August Zhukov had already inflicted 20,000 casualties on the German Ninth Army.

▲Soviet tank troops of 120th Tank Brigade helping a wounded crew member from a disabled Lend-Lease US Grant medium tank. It was in such fighting on 10 September 1942 that the Soviet 33rd Army and the Germans' élite Gross Deutschland Panzer Grenadier Division collided in a huge confontation. Used to dancing over the battlefield in mobile operations, Gross Deutschland tried to slug it out toe to toe with the Russian steamroller, to its great loss.

The Second Period of War
19 November 1942 - 31 December 1943

German attacks

Soviet attacks

Front Line as of:
19 November 1942
1 April 1943
31 December 1943

German/Allied pockets

0   100   200
miles

FINLAND

Lake Ladoga

Lake Onega

SOVIET UNION

Baltic Sea

Helsinki

Leningrad

Talinn

Novgorod

Lake Ilmen

Lake Peipus

Demyansk

XXXXX
LENNINGRAD

XXXXX
VOLKHOV

XXXXX
NORTHWEST

Volga R.

Gorki

XXXXX
NORTH

Riga

Dvina R.

XXXXX
2 BALTIC

XXXXX
1 BALTIC

XXXXX
WESTERN

Moscow

Mozhaisk

Memel

Niemen R.

Vilnius

Vitebsk

Vyazma

Smolensk

Tula

XXXXX
BRYANSK

XXXXX
VORONEZH

XXXXX
CENTRE

Minsk

Bobriusk

Bryansk

Orel

Voronezh

Don R.

XXXXX
SOUTHWEST

XXXXX
DON

Bialostok

Pripyat R.

Kursk

Desna R.

Stalingrad

Warsaw

Brest

Kiev

Belgorod

Voroshilovgrad

XXXXX
STALINGRAD

Vistula R.

Lvov

Dnieper R.

Kharkov

Izyum

Donets R.

Dnepropetrovsk

XXXXX
SOUTH

South Bug R.

Donetsk

Caspian Sea

Dniester R.

Zaporozhe

Rostov

Debrecen

Kishinev

XXXXX
A

Odessa

Perekop

Sea of Azov

Kuban R.

XXXXX
SOUTH

Kuma R.

Kluj

Kerch

Mozdok

ROUMANIA

Sevastopol

Novorossiysk

Nalchik

Gronzy

Bucharest

XXXXX
TRANSCAUCASUS

Ordzhonikidze

Danube R.

Black Sea

Sofia

BULGARIA

TURKEY

STALINGRAD
17 July 1942 – February 1943

talingrad: *der Rattenkrieg* (the 'The Rats' War') as the Germans came to call it – forever conjures up images of a frozen, shattered city – snow-dusted rubble, empty brick shells, sightless blank windows. These ruins crawled with death, hundreds of thousands of deaths fed into that voracious corpse factory that sprawled twenty-five miles down the length of the River Volga. How fitting then that the city Stalin named for himself should become a corpse factory!

The Battle of Stalingrad actually began during the hot summer days of 1942 as Sixth Army and Fourth Panzer Army of Army Group 'B' (as Army Group South was redesignated in July) crossed the River Don and began their advance towards the city. The advance was to have been the last operation in the first phase of Hitler's operational plan for the summer campaign of 1942. The stakes were high; if Army Group 'B' had taken Stalingrad quickly and been able to cover the left flank of the new Army Group 'A' (consisting of Seventeenth Army and First Panzer Army) as it advanced south to capture the oilfields, the Soviet war machine would literally have run out of fuel.

The commander of Sixth Army was General Friedrich Paulus, recently ap-

pointed to his command after a diligent and obedient performance on the General Staff that had endeared him to Hitler. Ominously, Paulus had had no experience of command at senior levels, but Hitler had tired of successful commanders who always wanted to argue with him. Paulus' virtue was eager obedience. Like a Greek tragedy that pivots on character, the coming campaign would be decided by the character of the officer described years before in this fitness report:

'A typical officer of the old school. Tall, and in outward appearance painstakingly well-groomed. Modest, perhaps too modest, amiable, with extremely courteous manners and a good comrade, anxious not to offend anyone. Exceptionally talented and interested in military matters, and a meticulous desk worker, with a passion for war games and formulating plans on the map-board or sand-table. At this he displays considerable talent, considering every decision at length and with careful deliberation before giving the appropriate orders.'

Paulus had, in fact, been a valuable senior general staff officer, but his record as a junior officer had explicitly commented on his lack of decisiveness. This weakness would eventually destroy his

command because in the Battle of Stalingrad he would face a man who was synonymous with ruthless decisiveness. Stalin would choose his best general for the fight, then General and later Marshal of the Soviet Union Georgi Konstantinovich Zhukov, who in August became Deputy Supreme Commander of the Red Army. Zhukov's personnel file contained fitness reports that read far differently from Paulus'. He was described by an early superior, General Konstantin Rokossovsky, whom Zhukov was later to command:

'A commander of strong will and decisiveness. He possesses a wealth of initiative and skillfully applies it to his job. He is disciplined. he is exacting and is persistent in his demands.'

This constant in character and generalship was to alter permanently the course of the war.

The German plan that summer called for Sixth Army to drive eastwards, its flank security provided by its armoured formations. Fourth Panzer Army attacked from the south-west along its southern approaches to isolate the city. The army group mission was subsidiary to the drive to the Soviet oilfields; it was to protect the flank of that operation and overrun Stalin-

▶Hero of the Soviet Union Captain M.D. Baranov, Section Leader in the 183rd Fighter Regiment, 8th Air Army. Baranov shot down 24 German aircraft in the Battle of Stalingrad. He perished in combat on 17 January 1943.

grad whose value was seen simply as an industrial and communications centre.

The road to Stalingrad lay over the crossing of the big bend in the River Don, just 45 miles from Stalingrad, which Sixth Army approached in July. Alarmed at the threat to his namesake city, Stalin gave Marshal Timoshenko the following instructions in early July: 'I order the formation of an Army Group Stalingrad. The city itself will be defended by 62nd Army to the last man.' The order was decisive but somewhat difficult to execute on the spot. At that time, the Commander of 62nd Army, General Kolpackchi, and his staff, with drawn pistols, were trying to sort out the flood of retreating Soviet units attempting to cross the big bend at the Kalach crossings. Sixth Army could have bounced the Don at that moment and thrust straight to Stalingrad. Amazingly the Soviet rearguards reported that contact had been broken. The Germans were not coming. They had simply run out of fuel. Logistics priority had been completely diverted to Army Group 'A', in much the same way as Patton's Third Army would be halted two years later in the splintered doorway to the Reich.

THE SOVIET 62ND ARMY ORDER OF BATTLE JULY-NOVEMBER 1942	
July	**November**
33 Guards Rifle Division	13 Guards Rifle Division
147 Rifle Division	37 Guards Rifle Division
181 Rifle Division	39 Guards Rifle Division
184 Rifle Division	45 Rifle Division
192 Rifle Division	95 Rifle Division
196 Rifle Division	112 Rifle Division
	193 Rifle Division
	284 Rifle Division
	308 Rifle Division
	92 Naval Rifle Brigade

The Soviets were given eighteen days, and they made the most of it. Kolpackchi drew most of his 62nd Army into defences in a bridgehead west of the Don in the Kalach area, supported to the south by 64th Army and 1st Tank Army. On 20 July Sixth Army struck. Attacking north and south of the Kalach crossing, Paulus conducted the last great encirclement of Operation 'Barbarossa'. Nine rifle divisions and two motorized corps with 1,000 tanks and armoured vehicles and 750 guns of 62nd Army and 1st Tank Army were lost in the débâcle in the pocket closed

around Kalach on 8 August and in action further south against Fourth Panzer Army. Surviving forces of 62nd and 64th Armies fell back to a defensive ring outside Stalingrad.

On 23 August the Germans crossed the Don in several places and reached the northern suburbs of Stalingrad. The next day they attacked and ran into a prepared and resolute inner defensive ring manned by surviving elements of 62nd Army and workers' militia inspired by the order, 'Not a step back', reinforced by the ruthless will of the Commander of Stalingrad and the

▲A German column advances in the area of the big bend in the Don. Some of the troops are keeping an eye on what is probably aerial combat over the battlefield.

◄The struggle for control of the big bend in the River Don. Soviet Sturmovik ground-attack aircraft and heavy 152mm artillery contest the Germans' attempts to seize the crossings, the last barrier before Stalin's City and the Volga.

►A Soviet mortar crew and infantry engaging German troops on the east bank of the Don during the encirclement battle around Kalach, late July.

SOVIET LOSSES AT KALACH

2	Motorized Corps
9	Rifle Divisions
7	Tank Brigades
1,000	Tanks and Armoured Vehicles
750	Artilllery Pieces

Southwest Front, Colonel General Andrei I. Yeremenko and his commissar, Nikita S. Khrushchev. Will may have been just about the only Soviet advantage. Sixty-Second Army alone, even with reinforcements, had been reduced to 50,000 men and barely 100 tanks against a German assault force of 100,000 quality troops and 500 tanks.

Another German encirclement of the forward defences of Stalingrad on 30 August was prevented by the rapid withdrawal of the two armies into the city itself. At the highest levels the Soviets had determined that there would be no more encirclements and had withdrawn with an alacrity that surprised the Germans.

The depleted Soviet ranks were fleshed out with 125,000 adult male citizens of Stalingrad, of whom 75,000 were assigned to 62nd Army. Seven thousand Komsomol members between the ages of thirteen and sixteen were also incorporated into the fighting formations. Three thousand young women became nurses and telephone operators. Factory workers sent their new weapons and equipment straight from the assembly lines into action, often manned by the men who had made them. There was to be one other advantage – a new commander for 62nd Army appointed on 12 September. General Vassili I. Chuikov, fresh from service in the Far East, had had none of the bellyful of defeats that had demoralized so many of the other commanders who had served in the west since 1941. He was tough, brave and gifted. And he was the right man for the job.

The Germans started the main battle with a massive fire bombing raid which severely damaged the city. The Germans had made a great mistake. A rubble-choked city has its defensive strength redoubled because the mobility of the attacker becomes restricted and his advantage of firepower dissipated. German superiority in the air and in tanks, so effective on the flat, broad expanses of the Russian steppe, was largely negated by the vicious street-fighting, the 'Rats' War' of Stalingrad.

The Red Army turned the city into a fortress. Every room, every building, every sewer, every rubble heap, every broken wall became an individual battleground to be won and lost many times during the course of the battle. The Russian soldier showed a remarkable talent for city fight-

ing, an event for which training and experience had not prepared the Germans. Until now the Wehrmacht had been inflicting almost all the lessons in the art of war. This time the Germans would assume the role of students. The Red Army would teach them well.

Nevertheless, the Germans nearly seized the prize in the first half of September. The force of the German attack was grinding up the Soviet defence. Paulus' plan was to establish a series of breakthrough corridors to the Volga to secure the western section of the city. By 14 September the defences were on the point of collapse as Chuikov desperately ferried 13th Guards Rifle Division into

◀General of the Army Georgi K. Zhukov, Deputy Supreme Commander-in-Chief of the Soviet armed forces, on his way to the headquarters of 1st Guards Army in Stalingrad on 30 August.

▲Soviet wounded receiving first aid under fire as the fighting approachesd the outskirts of Stalingrad in September.

▼Soviet infantry counter-attack on the approaches to Stalingrad in September. Note the various weapons: SKS rifles, Shpagin submachine-guns and bipod-equipped machine-guns. Despite such desperate efforts as seen here, the Lower Saxon 71st Infantry Division penetrated Stalingrad on 13 September and stormed the high ground just outside the city's centre. Next day they smashed through to the banks of the Volga.

▲ Troops of 13th Guards Rifle Division attack a German-held building in Stalingrad. The 13th Guards, commanded by Major-General Aleksandr I. Rodimstev, a legendary field commander and Hero of the Soviet Union, had already fought and been depleted on the Don in July. Refitted in August, 13th Guards crossed from the east bank of the Volga just as the last defences of the city were burning out. They checked 71st Infantry Division and kept 295th Infantry Division from securing Mamayev Hill, the city's dominant feature. The effort practically bled the division to death for a second time, but on that day, 15 September, they saved the city.

the city from the east bank of the Volga. Commanded by Major-General Rodimstev, a renowned commander and Hero of the Soviet Union, 13th Guards checked the German advance and drove them off Mamai Hill, the dominant feature of the city. The German impetus was checked, but in two days of fighting 13th Guards had been gutted.

By 16 September the situation had worsened again as all German formations in the battle were re-subordinated to Sixth Army. A direct appeal from Khrushchev to Stalin released two crack formations from the dictator's personal reserve, a tank brigade and a brigade of naval infantry from the Northern Fleet. Again the city was saved. Although the Germans were later to reach the Volga on several occasions, their bridgeheads were isolated and unable to link up. Strong counter-attacks consistently prevented the Germans from exploiting their gains. They were unable to cut the Soviet supply lines to the river's eastern bank, which allowed the Red Army continually to bring in fresh troops and ammunition to reinforce Chuikov's 62nd Army. More than 100,000 Red Army men would cross the Volga to shore up 62nd Army's desperate fingernail grip on the city during the initial phases of the battle.

The Stalingrad meatgrinder firmly fixed the attention of both Paulus and Hitler on the operational elements of the battle. While excusable in an army commander, it was a grievous error for a man like Hitler, who styled himself a 'warlord'. The real threat, however, lay in the Soviet bridgeheads on Sixth Army's northwestern and southern flanks. These areas were defended by Roumanian, Hungarian and Italian troops of relatively poor quality. Roumanian units were continually reporting on the massive build-ups of Soviet tanks and infantry to their front, but the Germans, by now inured to the skittishness of their allies, ignored their warnings.

Zhukov poured everything he had into the bridgeheads as Chuikov and 62nd Army wore down the Germans. Twenty-five rifle and cavalry divisions and six tank and mechanized corps assembled in the bridgeheads between mid-September and mid-November. Stalin once described Zhukov as his 'George B. McClellan', the American Civil War general who never had enough men, enough equipment and

▲Soviet naval infantry of the Volga River Flotilla making an assault landing on the right bank of the Volga in September to counter-attack German penetrations to the river's edge.

▶A Soviet flame-thrower in action at Stalingrad in October. Flame-throwers were especially effective in streetfighting and were lavishly employed by both sides in the battle.

enough supplies but who could never bring himself to go for the enemy's jugular. Stalin knew that this analogy was only partially correct because, he commented, like McClellan, 'he always wants more men, more cannon, more guns. Also more aircraft. He never has enough. But Zhukov has never lost a battle.'

Like McClellan, Zhukov would not be hurried, but unlike McClellan, he knew when he was ready. On 19 November the great Stalingrad counter-offensive began. Soviet forces broke out of their bridgeheads and crushed the Germans' allied forces on Sixth Army's flanks. They raced immediately for the Kalach crossings on the River Don. The southern pincer was counter-attacked and stopped by a reserve German division which was then mistakenly withdrawn. The Soviets surged forward to Kalach and slammed the door on Sixth Army.

In one of the boldest counter-strokes of the war the Soviets had reversed roles with the Germans. Sixth Army was now the defender while the Soviets were on the attack, the initiative firmly in their hands.

For the next two months the Soviets steadily tightened the noose. Paulus was forbidden by Hitler to attempt a breakout from Stalingrad in those fleeting days before Zhukov could thoroughly rivet his encirclement in place. Completely cut off

and isolated in Stalingrad, Paulus was forced to rely on the tenuous and inadequate Luftwaffe air bridge that Reichsmarshal Goering had boasted would support Sixth Army. On its best day, the Luftwaffe's deliveries were still 150 tons short of Sixth Army's daily minimum requirements for food, fuel and ammunition. Sixth Army was doomed. It grew weaker as its defensive perimeter, centred on the Germans' remaining operational airfields, steadily shrank.

Paulus remained true to his nature to the end. In its moment of supreme crisis, Sixth Army found itself commanded by a man who found more comfort in unquestioning obedience than in discharging his moral duty to his men. Even as Field Marshal von Manstein launched his own attack to break through to Sixth Army, Paulus could not summon the moral courage at least to attempt to link up with von Manstein. As it was, von Manstein came so close to breaking the ring that a supporting attack from Sixth Army would have clinched its success. Paulus could only bring himself to inform Hitler on 22 January that his position was hopeless. Hitler's response was to repeat the order he gave to Rommel at Alamein, that Sixth Army 'defend their positions to the last'. By a strange twist of logic, he promoted Paulus to field marshal eight

days later on the grounds that no German field marshal had ever surrendered. But the lack of character that prevented Paulus from disobeying his orders to save his army could not create the courage that refuses to accept defeat. The very next day, on 2 February, he surrendered the remnant of his army.

Many German soldiers refused to surrender and made off in organized combat groups, platoons, or individually to break out of the encirclement. Only one man is known to have succeeded – a Sergeant Nieweg from a flak battery – he was killed by a random mortar round twenty-four hours after his escape. Of the 230,000 German and allied troops trapped in the Stalingrad pocket, barely 5,000 survived to return home after the war.

GERMAN LOSSES FROM ENCIRCLEMENT TO SURRENDER

German and Allied troops trapped in Stalingrad	230,000
Evacuated by air (wounded, sick, specialists)	42,000
Taken prisoner from 10 to 29 January 1943	16,800
Taken prisoner from 31 January to 3 February	91,000
Dead on the field or died of wounds	80,500
Survived captivity to return home after the war	6,000

◀The forges of Stalingrad kept pace with the guns. Although tank production at the Stalin Tractor Factory slowed in the autumn, it did not cease. T-34 tanks fresh from a frantic assembly went directly into the city fighting often without a coat of paint. Here a KV-1 Heavy tank is repaired as fighting rages outside the repair shop in October.

▶Factory workers did more than work. Here a workers' battalion commanded by V. Kibas of the Red October Factory defend their workplace reinforcing 13th Guards Rifle Division which was contesting every pile of rubble against 79th and 94th Infantry Divisions.

▼Sturmoviks! Aircraft designer Ilyushin's armoured Il-2s on a ground-attack mission near Stalingrad in November. The Sturmovik, literally 'Attacker', was a formidable and rugged aircraft.

◄More fighting below Stalingrad on the Southwest Front, the main axis of the great Soviet counter-attack. A rifle company of Major-General Ivan M. Chistyakov's 21st Army attacks under worsening weather conditions near the village of Kletskaya. For its feats here, 21st Army would be honoured with redesignation as 6th Guards Army.

▲The fighting flared north and south of Stalingrad as well. Here well-equipped and well-clothed submachine-gunners of 57th Army, commanded by Fedor I. Tolbukhin, dismount from T-34s deploying south-west of Stalingrad in October, to repulse an enemy attempt to break out of an encirclement.

▼A T-34 emblazoned with the legend 'Rodiny' ('Motherland'), that mystical Russian word that resonates with a Russian's soul, charges into battle through the snow and rubble of Stalingrad as the fighting reaches its crescendo in November.

▲ An officers' conference in the front lines.

◄ A Soviet submachine-gunner using a Stalingrad apartment as a firing position, in November. The Soviets fed countless thousands of men like this soldier across the frozen Volga to keep the defences alive. Every such man fulfilled a strategic mission – to fix Hitler's attention firmly on this one sector of the front and feed his relentless obsession with capturing Stalin's City.

Three slogans were driven home to each soldier as he crossed the Volga in those desperate months: 'Every man a fortress!' 'There's no ground left behind the Volga!' 'Fight or die!'

▶ Men of iron, granite and ice – the men who held Stalingrad – the command group of 62nd Army in December. From left to right: Major-General Nikolai I. Krylov, Chief of Staff; Lieutenant-General Vasily I. Chuikov, Commander of 62nd Army; General Konstantin Gurov, a member of the Military Council (Political Officer); Major-General Aleksandr I. Rodimstev, Commander of 13th Guards Rifle Division. Now they were no longer just defending but were part of the contracting iron vice around Sixth Army.

▲Soviet infantry closing with the Germans as the great encirclement swings its arms north and south of Stalingrad to meet deep in the rear of German Sixth Army. On 19 November four Soviet armies shattered the Roumanian-held flanks and raced for the German jugular – the bridgehead on the big bend in the River Don at Kalach.

▲In the great tradition of Russian artillery, Soviet 122mm howitzers keep up the pressure on the Germans night and day in Stalingrad, regardless of the weather. As December slips away so do the hopes of the Germans. Every pull of the lanyard drives a 122mm nail into the coffin of Sixth Army.

▼The aftermath of a tank battle; the remnant of the German tank force attempting the relief of Stalingrad in December. The Panzer Mk IIIs seen here, though usually more skilfully handled, were simply outclassed by the tough and deadly Soviet T-34s.

▲The ring tightens. A trainload of Panzer Mk IIIs, ammunition, food and other supplies captured at Kantemirovka railway station, Voronezh Front, on the Don north-west of Stalingrad in December.

▼Lieutenant-General Konstantin K. Rokossovsky, Commander Don Front, at an observation post during the reduction of the Stalingrad pocket, January 1943. While other Soviet Fronts fought off desperate German attempts to relieve Stalingrad, Rokossovsky's Don Front was squeezing the pocket's entire perimeter. On 10 January he launched the attack that would break up the pocket.

▲On 26 January the forces of Don Front finally split the Stalingrad pocket in two. Infantry of 21st Army attacking from the west took Mamayev Hill in Stalingrad as tanks of Chuikov's 62nd Army, attacking from the east, linked up in a moment of triumph. So desperate had the situation become for Sixth Army that it was begging for airdrops of food only. Two days later the wounded were no longer being fed.

▼The wreckage of Sixth Army and the hopes of German victory, February 1943.

THE SOVIET TIDE RUSHES BACK

'All the forces in Stalingrad were now being moved – towards Rostov and the Donets ... trucks, horse sleighs and guns, covered wagons, and even camels pulling sleighs – stepping sedately through the deep snow as though it were sand. Every conceivable means of transport was being used. Thousands of soldiers were marching, or rather trudging in large irregular crowds, to the west, through this cold deadly night. But they were cheerful and happy, and they kept shouting about Stalingrad and the job they had done.

Westward, westward! How many, one wondered, would reach the end of the road? But they knew that the direction was the right one. In their felt boots and padded jackets, fur caps with the earflaps hanging down, carrying submachine-guns, with watering eyes, and hoarfrost on their lips, they were going west. How much better it felt than going east!'

So wrote Alexander Werth, correspondent for the Sunday Times, as he watched the victorious Russian host emerge from the ruins of Stalingrad, graveyard of German hopes. Even before the end came for Sixth Army, the Red Army had been pounding at the receding

German front, obliterating Hungarian, Roumanian and Italian armies that the Germans had fed into their over-extended lines. The German units were being beaten back as well, but made of sterner stuff, they had not cracked. The front itself, though, was cracking from the Caucasus to Voronezh. Too few German units were holding off an enemy with the intoxicating taste of blood in his mouth.

For the Soviets, the prospects were heady after two years of defeat. German Army Group 'A' (Field Marshal von Kleist) was nervously holding fast in the Kuban and north Caucasus as Soviet forces were racing to slam their escape shut at Rostov while Trans-Caucasus and North Caucasus Fronts were pressing them from the south and east. To the north, Army Group 'B' was in even more serious straits – Bryansk, Voronezh and Southwest Fronts, co-ordinated by High Command representative Marshal Vasilevsky, had torn a 250-kilometre hole in the front from Voronezh to Voroshilovgrad by the end of the third week in January. Linking Army Groups 'A' and 'B' like a bent hinge was the newly created Army Group Don commanded by Field Marshal von Manstein. That hinge was near breaking-point as von Manstein pedalled backwards without losing contact with the flanking army groups. Marshal Zhukov was after him, trying to hammer the hinge to bits. As Stalin's star, he was co-ordinating the Soviet winter offensive's main effort by Southwest and South Fronts commanded by Army Generals Vatutin and Yeremenko.

The stress point of the hinge was on the lower Don near Rostov. Here South Front's 2nd Guards Army with Rotmistrov's III Guards Tank Corps of Stalingrad fame in the lead threw advance elements across the River Manych on 20 January at Manychskaya 30 kilometres north of Rostov. To the south the Don crossings at Rostov were clogged with the trains of First Panzer Army. Thirty kilometres to go and von Manstein's hinge

would snap. Just as III Guards Tank Corps was about to surge through the bridgehead, a panzer grenadier battalion threw itself into the breach and held it for two days. That was time enough for von Manstein to counter-attack and break the Soviet hold on the bridgehead. Rotmistrov's Guards were spent. The fighting around Stalingrad and down the Don had left the once powerful 2nd Guards Army with only 29 tanks and eleven anti-tank guns. Now the hinge would hold long enough for First Panzer Army to escape through Rostov.

Before the hinge broke again under pressure, von Manstein allowed it to slip. Field Marshal von Kleist wanted to pull the whole army group out through Rostov which would have provided the Germans an enormous reinforcement in the area of the Soviet main effort. Instead Hitler had von Kleist pull Army Group 'A' into a huge bridgehead around the Taman peninsula where they would largely sit out the rest of the fight. The Red Army had hoped to trap von Kleist, but the cautiousness of Trans-Caucasus Front Commander, Army General I. V. Tiulenev, enabled him to concentrate his 400,000 men in safety.

Barely had von Manstein been freed of the necessity to maintain a suicidal contact with Army Group 'A' in the south, when Vatutin's Southwest Front broke his northern flank at the end of January. The newly created Popov Group, commanded by Lieutenant-General Markian Popov, consisting of four tank corps and a rifle corps, shot through the 60-kilometre gap and raced south-west. After wasting much time pleading with Hitler, von Manstein was allowed to withdraw to the line of the River Mius. Just in time the units transferred from Army Group 'A' slipped through Rostov before it was abandoned on 14 February. By the 18th von Manstein's forces were safely across the river, on the same defensive line to which Timoshenko's Rostov counter-attack had driven them in November 1941. It almost didn't hold. Third Guards Mechanized Corps followed across on the Germans' heels and penetrated 25 kilometres west. Only a thaw allowed the Germans to eject them before reinforcements could expand the penetration. There was no respite; 3rd Tank Army and 5th Shock Army followed and fought their way across the Mius at several points. The situation was worsening quickly to the north as Popov Group and 1st Guards and 6th Armies were across the German lines of communication and threatening the critical junctions at Dnepropetrovsk and Zaparozhye. At one point Soviet tanks were within 50 kilometres of Army Group headquarters at Zaparozhye where Hitler had come for one of his rare visits to the front. For one brief day there were no German combat units between them and the greatest capture in military history.

At the same time as Zhukov was reaching for von Manstein's throat, Vasilevsky's Voronezh Front had driven Hitler's new II SS Panzer Corps out of Kharkov, the Soviet Union's fourth largest city, on 16 February. Army Group 'B' was reeling. By the middle of February the Soviet High Command's confidence had sky-rocketed; Voronezh Front's new objective was Poltava and the Dnieper between Kiev and Kremenchug. Southwest Front's objective was to clear the Donets basin.

Imperceptibly, however, the situation had shifted slightly in the Germans' favour. The Red Army had undertaken its offensive with less than half the necessary transport for such an operation. It was now running on momentum and was dangerously overstretched, as the exhausted condition of Rotmistrov's Guards near Rostov indicated. The Germans, on the other hand, had retreated to their supply bases and were bringing reinforcements into action. Von Manstein was drawing 100,000 men out of the Taman bridgehead, and other divisions were arriving from the West. He built a new Fourth Panzer Army around its headquarters at Dnepropetrovsk, including the reinforced II SS Panzer Corps. The Luftwaffe's 4th Air Force was also reinforced to a strength of almost 1,000 modern aircraft and reorganized to maximize efficiency.

Von Manstein attacked on 18 February when German fortunes were at their bleakest. Fourth Panzer Army attacked north-eastwards from Dnepropetrovsk

◀Kuban Cossack 'Guards' cavalry of the South Front attacking in the north Caucasus, January 1943. The fighting in the winter of 1942/3 was the heyday of the Soviet cavalry. The difficult winter conditions put a premium on the mobility and manoeuvrability of the horse, especially across the plains of the north Caucasus and eastern Ukraine. Soviet cavalry and fast tank units, often in combination, were darting across the vast, snowy spaces of the region and savaging the German lines of communication.

▶The Soviets had based their offensive on the ability to capture German supplies, but the commander of Army Group 'A', Field Marshal von Kleist, was an exacting and miserly general who ensured that the Red Army would capture little of value. Here Soviet infantry of the North Caucasus Front are fighting the German rearguard at a railway station on the approaches to Krasnodar in the Kuban, February 1943.

◀While Marshal Zhukov was hounding von Manstein back along the lower Don, Marshal Vasilevsky was breaking in to the north with Bryansk and Voronezh Fronts along the seam between Army Groups 'B' and Centre. Here an 82mm mortar supports the attack of winter-camouflaged submachine-gunners.

◀A Soviet cavalry reconnaissance unit operating deep inside German lines during the winter battles. Note the 7.62mm submachine-guns PPSH1941. Operated on a blowback principle, this weapon had no safety features other than the 20 – 25lb trigger pull. Although the weapons shown here have box magazines, a drum magazine modelled after that of the Thompson submachine-gun was normally used. The barrels were salvaged from the obsolete M1891 rifle, each rifle barrel making two submachine-gun barrels.

▶Soviet infantry of South Front supported by a 45mm anti-tank gun, fighting near the railway station during the recapture of Rostov-on-Don.

and severed the over-extended spearheads of 1st Guards and 6th Armies, trapping numerous units and throwing the rest north across the River Samara. To the south 1st Panzer Army encircled Popov Group which managed to fight its way north to Barvenkovo where it ran out of fuel, fought where it stood and died. Southwest Front had been crippled. The reorganized Luftwaffe quickly achieved air superiority and delivered the type of air support not seen since the first year of the war.

Racing against the spring thaw, von Manstein continued Fourth Panzer Army's attack now into the flank of Voronezh Front with Kharkov as the objective. The Germans crushed three rifle divisions and a tank brigade of 3rd Tank Army that were in their path; 1st Guards Army remnants struggling away from their earlier defeat were thrust aside or overrun as German armour swept north. Fourth Panzer swung west of Kharkov intending to go north around the city and encircle it, but II SS Panzer Corps attacked into the city and, after three days of savage fighting that saw the massacre of Soviet wounded in their hospital beds, had cleared it by 15 March. On the 18th II SS Panzer Corps struck north for 50 kilometres and captured Belgorod.

With the fall of Kharkov the position of Voronezh Front was untenable. Covered by the newly arrived 21st and 64th Armies, Vasilevsky pulled back 100-150 kilometres to the east across the Donets and northwards, forming what was to

become the southern face of the Kursk salient. By the 18th both armies were stuck in the mud of the spring thaw, exhausted by the titanic struggle that had gone on nonstop from the beginning of the German summer offensive in May 1942.

Millions of men had been consumed and Russia had been scorched along a great swath from the Volga to the Caucasus Mountains, but the Germans had been flung back to the very lines from which they had started.

◀Soviet infantry commanded by Captain Sedykh pursue the rapidly retreating troops of Army Group 'A' who have abandoned this heavy artillery piece, South Front, February 1943.

▶Soviet 152mm heavy howitzers camouflaged against a snowy, featureless plain, on the approaches to Novocherkassk on the River Don north of Rostov, South Front, February 1943. The Germans acknowledged the Russians to be their masters at camouflage and concealment.

▼Soviet tanks attacking on the upper Don, during the Ostrogozhsk–Rossosh offensive, 13-27 January 1943. Soviet infantry dismounting in the assault from a KV-1 heavy tank, Southwest Front, February 1943. Soviet motorized rifle troops were the élite of the infantry, but they had very few vehicles. They rode into battle aboard tanks, a practice called *tankoviy desant* or tank assault. A motorized rifle company would have a high proportion of automatic weapons: nine DP machine-guns, 27 rifles, 57 submachine-guns, and five machine pistols.

▼A Soviet tank regiment inspecting its KV-1 heavy tanks, Steppe Front, April 1943. In 1942 the Red Army was mixing KV-1s, T-34s and light tanks in the same brigades. Although the armour of the KV-1 was tough and its gun the same as the T-34's, its mobility was inferior to the T-34 with which it could not keep up. By 1943 homogeneous units of T-34s were being created and the slower KV-1s were relegated to tank regiments with infantry support missions.

▶Marshals Georgi Zhukov, Nikolai Voronov, and Kliment Voroshilov inspect a captured German Tiger (Mark VI) at an exhibition of war trophies in Moscow. The Germans' shock at encountering the tough and heavily armoured KV-1s and T-34s of the Red Army accelerated development of this first heavy German tank. With appalling ill judgement it was introduced in penny packets before its teething problems had been resolved, in wooded, unsuitable tank terrain near Leningrad in August 1942.

▼Officers of the US Military Mission in Moscow at the same exhibition of war trophies, June 1943. Although the Soviets had been warned of the Tiger tank by its premature field testing in August 1942, they were not prepared for the impact of its mass deployment by II SS Panzer Corps when it retook Kharkov in March 1943. The Tiger's 8.8cm gun was lethal to even the heavily armoured T-34.

◄Partisans such as these men of Narodny Mstitel (People's Avenger) Belorussian partisan brigades, commanded by R. Pokrovsky, had stepped up operations along the entire eastern front, to support the coming struggle at Kursk. In June the number of attacks on railroads increased to 1,092 compared to 397 in January; the number of damaged locomotives increased from 112 to 409, and damaged railroad bridges from 22 to 54.

▼Another German troop train that failed to arrive to support German operations at Kursk, derailed by the Frunze Partisan Detachment, Kursk Region, summer 1943.

THE GREATEST BATTLE IN HISTORY
KURSK – 1943

'This attack is of decisive importance. It must succeed, and it must do so rapidly and convincingly. It must secure for us the initiative for this spring and summer. The victory of Kursk must be a blazing torch to the world.' – Adolf Hitler, 2 July 1943.

The Red Army had rushed westward after its victory at Stalingrad, but by the spring thaw, its offensive capabilities were spent – both armies were stuck fast in the mud. A remnant of the advance was a huge salient in the line in the area of Kursk. As the armies gathered their strength in the months that followed, the strategic attention of both was drawn to that area, attracting the metal-shod armies like a lodestone for the great showdown of the war. The adversaries had by then reached a delicate equilibrium; the initiative of the war lay on the wet Russian earth between them. The ultimate victor in this war would be the army that held it when the battle ended.

As the German Army repaired its losses, Hitler became increasingly hungry for a great victory to sustain the morale of Germany and its allies. Increased war production, new tanks and manpower replacements would give the German Army the capability to fight one more great offensive battle. Thereafter, German strength could only decline. That battle then had to be a victory of great proportions, and Kursk was identified as the most promising opportunity. Hitler initially set the date for the attack, codenamed 'Zitadelle', in May but repeatedly postponed it until war production could supply enough of the new heavy Tiger, Panther and Ferdinand (Elefant) tanks. Arguments to go over to the defensive and bleed the Red Army to death fell on deaf ears. Like a spendthrift with money in his pocket, Hitler could not assemble a reserve without using it at the first opportunity.

The Soviet High Command had also foreseen a great showdown battle, but Stalin proved a more patient and subtle war leader. He accepted the advice of the General Staff and his major commanders in early April to ride out the first German attack and then go over to a counter-offensive that would drive the enemy out of the Motherland. It was the best of both worlds. The Red Army would have qualitative superiority in equipment and numbers, and it would have the initial advantage of the defence. Its operational capabilities had also dramatically improved; a winning team of capable and even brilliant commanders had been sifted through the first two hard years of the war. In addition, the Red Army was benefitting from unsurpassed strategic Intelligence. Churchill sent Ultra intercepts directly to Stalin. Agents in a huge underground network fed the Soviets minute details on German troop movements, industrial production and foreign policy that allowed them to calculate the German war effort with great precision.

The German plan was to pinch off the Kursk salient with a great double envelopment from the north and south. Army Group Centre (Field Marshal von Kluge) would attack south from the direction of Orel with Fourth Army and elements of Second Army. At the same time, Field Marshal von Manstein's Army Group

▶On the southern face of the Kursk salient on 5 July, the redoubtable von Manstein struck Vatutin's Voronezh Front with a sledgehammer blow that staggered it. On the first day Lieutenant-General Chistyakov's 6th Army took a mortal wound. T-34s of Lieutenant General Katukov's 1st Tank Army attempted to staunch the collapsing front and were mauled on the 7th. The Soviet High Command released 5th Guards Tank Army from reserve, but it would take three days to travel the 300 kilometres from the south. By the 9th von Manstein had torn a 35km deep hole in the front. Only the timely commitment of a heavy tank corps from neighbouring Steppe Front prevented the collapse of Voronezh Front. By 11 July the wrecked 6th and 1st Tank Armies had been compressed back into the defence. The Germans were ready to roll over them.

South would attack north from the direction of Belgorod with Fourth Panzer Army and Armeeabteilung 'Kempf'. The two forces would meet in the rear of the salient at the city of Kursk. Fifty divisions, including sixteen panzer and panzer grenadier divisions were concentrated in the area of the salient of which 39 would be used in the attack. This force numbered 900,000 men, 2,700 tanks and SP guns, 10,000 guns and mortars, and 2,000 combat aircraft. Hitler was gambling everything on the battle – these forces represented 70 per cent of panzer divisions, 30 per cent of panzer grenadier divisions, and 65 per cent of combat aircraft in the east.

The Red Army had been assembling an even mightier host, 40 per cent of its entire operational forces. The Central (Army General Rokossovsky) and Voronezh (Army General Vatutin) Fronts which occupied the northern and southern halves of the salient would total 1,336,000 men, 3,444 tanks and SP guns, 19,100 guns and mortars, and 2,172 combat aircraft. On Vatutin's southern flank was Army General Konev's Steppe Front with another 553,000 men, 7,401 guns and mortars, and 1,551 tanks and assault guns – held back for the great counter-offensive. To the north of Rokossovsky's Front were Bryansk (Army General Popov) and Western (Army General Sokolovsky) Fronts. Behind the first echelon were stacked powerful additional reserves of the High Command that included several armies, two tank armies, and one air army.

Not only were vast forces assembled, but their combat power was steadily improved. Manoeuvre forces were reinforced with artillery, anti-tank and mortar units. Rifle divisions were re-equipped with modern automatic and anti-tank weapons and combined into rifle corps to improve command and control. New artillery formations were created and armed with improved model weapons. High Command artillery reserves, consisting of breach brigades, divisions, and corps were formed to create a high fire density on the main sectors. By that summer five tank armies had been created, consisting of two tank and one mechanized corps. Each Front was allotted anti-aircraft divisions and its own air army of 700 to 800 aircraft of new types. Logistics support reached a degree of sophistication and equipment hitherto unseen as Soviet industry and Lend Lease in the form of tens of thousands of Studebaker trucks delivered huge quantities of supplies to the theatre. Within the salient itself, the Red Army was preparing for the German attack by transforming the area into one vast network of field fortifications and minefields. For the first time in the war the Soviets were able to construct three defensive belts to a depth of 60 kilometres within which they sited anti-tank weapons and strongpoints, employing direct and indirect artillery fire, mobile obstacle construction detachments, as well as tanks and assault guns. The Germans would be attacking a fortress consisting of 5,000 kilometres of trenches strewn with 400,000 mines. On the main breakthrough sector of Central Front, 112 kilometres of barbed wire were laid, 10.7 kilometres of which were electrified. Adding to the effectiveness of the defensive works was the masterful job of camouflage which hid much of it from the Germans.

Soviet Intelligence had pinpointed the timing of the German offensive to the early morning of 5 July. Zhukov acted swiftly to get in the first punch. He described the moment when 'he' began the Battle of Kursk:

'At 2.20 a.m. the order was issued to begin the counter-preparation. Everyone raced round and round, twisting and twirling, a terrible rumbling was heard and a very great battle in the Kursk area began. The sounds of the heavy artillery, the explosion of bombs and the M-31 rocket projectiles, the outbursts of the Katyushas and the constant hum of aircraft engines merged into what was like the strains of a "symphony" from Hell.'

The artillery counter-preparation of both Fronts struck barely two hours before the Germans attacked, catching the infantry in their assembly areas and savaging the German artillery. At dawn the Red Air Force struck at the German airfields, but the Luftwaffe was already in the air. The Germans attacked on schedule, but their command and control had been disrupted and they had taken heavy casualties before firing a shot.

▲A burning German Panther Mark V hit by Soviet artillery on the Central Front during the Battle of Kursk, July 1943.

▼Rokossovsky's defences were particularly tough for Ninth Army to penetrate. Its initial assault ground to a halt against the village of Ponryi defended by 307th Rifle Division massively reinforced with artillery. General of Panzer Troops Lemelsen, commander of XLVII Panzer Corps described the problem. Here it must be pointed out once again that the Russians were masters of camouflage. Neither mine fields nor anti-tank weapons could be detected anywhere before the time the first tank had moved into the minefield or the first Russian gun unexpectedly opened fire.

Fourth Army attacked Central Front's 13th, 48th and 70th Armies, the brunt being borne by the 13th. The Germans steadily ground through the mesh of stoutly defended positions at great loss. Whole units were consumed in the fighting – Captain Igishev's anti-tank battery of 13th Army died to a man but took nineteen German tanks with them. In the northern part of his Front's sector Rokossovksiy was forced to bury some of his tanks as pillboxes with orders to fire only on infantry and armoured personnel-carriers. His tank units had been hurling themselves on the heavier Tiger and Panthers and had been badly cut up. This new tactic stripped the panzers of their infantry support and held them up for four days. By the 7th, von Kluge's corps had gouged a 10-kilometre wedge into the defences in the direction of Ponryi where they were halted by the firepower of 307th Rifle Division, reinforced by 5th Artillery Division, 13th Anti-tank Brigade, and 11th and 22nd Mortar Brigades. By the 8th the Germans were still attacking, and Rokossovsky committed his entire reserve. It was then that the great counter-stroke was set in motion. Bryansk and part of the Western Fronts attacked to the north of Central Front on 12 July. Code-named 'Kutuzov', this counter-stroke in the direction of Orel took the Germans completely by surprise and made good headway. Almost immediately the pressure on Central Front was relieved as Army Group Centre drew divisions away from the Kursk salient to counter 'Kutuzov'. On the 15th Central Front also went over to the offensive.

To the south against Voronezh Front the Germans under the redoubtable von Manstein were having better luck. Two panzer corps struck the main blow at General-Lieutenant Chistykov's 6th Guards Army supported by 1st Tank Army. By the end of the day they had penetrated 20 kilometres, crushing 52nd Guards Rifle Division and brushing aside 67th Guards, whose commander was to write:

'. . . the German infantry bypassed our emplacements and infiltrated between the batteries. The tenacity of the Fascists bordered on insanity. They fought to break through our defences . . . no matter what the losses. The infantry at our first echelon was routed and the artillery regiments were smashed. The remaining infantry elements retreated to the north. All that was left at the emplacements were wrecked guns and dead soldiers.'

By the end of the 6th, Vatutin's Front had been badly hurt. The second defensive line had been pierced in the sector of 6th Guards Army; the Soviet High Command then released the hard core of its reserves, 5th Guards Tank Army commanded by Lieutenant-General Rotmistrov. But 5th Guards was 300 kilometres to the south, and it would take almost three days to reach Voronezh Front. On the 7th and 8th the situation reached crisis point for Vatutin. His 1st Tank Army had been badly mauled and 6th Guards Army was on its last legs. 1st Tank Army Commander, Lieutenant-General Katukov, watched the Germans approaching across a narrow scorched field and said, 'They are regrouping . . . advancing in a spearhead . . . I think we have had it.' By the 9th, von Manstein had achieved a 35-kilometre breakthrough in the direction of Oboyan while Abteilung 'Kempf' Army had a 10-kilometre penetration to the south towards Korocha. The Front was barely saved from collapse by the intervention of heavy corps from Steppe Front. By the 11th the situation had worsened. In desperation Vatutin ordered Katukov's battered 1st Tank Army to dig in its tanks with those of Chistyakov's equally wounded 6th Guards Army to reinforce

the defence The Germans continued to press Vatutin's defences toward Prokhorovka in the north and towards Rzhavets to the south. Voronezh Front was unravelling in Vatutin's hands. Then Rotmistrov's 5th Guards Tank Army arrived.

Rotmistrov had arrived only to be presented with a crisis even worse than he had expected. Rotmistrov:

'On the evening of 11 July, German formations reached the area immediately in front of Prokhorovka. My previous decision to mount a counter-attack could not be carried out under these circumstances. Because of the withdrawal of our formations to Prokhorovka, the two-day-long artillery preparatory fire supporting the counter-attack of Fifth Guards Tank Army had to be interrupted and new assembly areas had to be designated. Missions for our troops had to be changed and discussed again. The capture of Prokhorovka on 11 July forced me to commit two tank brigades west of Prokhorovka that evening to halt the enemy attack. The army had to be prepared for our counter-attack all over again. There were only ten hours to do this; only three were left after daybreak. Under these circumstances the troops' combat preparations had to suffer. The corps and brigade commanders had no time to reconnoitre their new assembly areas and to designate the line of their main effort.'

▲On the night of the 11th, the 5th Guards Tank Army arrived in the rear of the dying Voronezh Front. The 5th Guards consisted of XVIII and XIX Guards Tank and V Guards Mechanized Corps. They were further reinforced with II Guards Tank Corps and II Tank Corps. This host was commanded by Lieutenant-General of Tank Troops Pavel A. Rotmistrov, shown here at a forward headquarters. Rotmistrov's plan for the counter-attack became useless when the

Germans overran his planned staging areas at Prokhorovka on 11 July. He had to commit two brigades immediately to prevent a German breakthrough. Then he had ten hours left to prepare his army for the decisive action of the war.

▼By 12 July Voronezh Front was on the point of collapse from the sharp attacks of Field Marshal von Manstein's Army Group South. On

that morning II SS Panzer Corps marshalled its more than 600 tanks and SP guns for a major push towards Kursk that would have shattered the front. His attack ran into the attack of the theatre reserve, 5th Guards Tank Army, commanded by General-Lieutenant Pavel Alekseyevich Rotmistrov, at a village called Prokhorovka. The exploits of his Guardsmen on that day would earn him the epithet, 'Lion of Prokhorovka'.

▲The despair of the lost battle – a German corporal sitting on the trail of his smashed gun.

▼As night closed over Prokhorovka, the greatest armoured battle in history had fought itself out. The field was strewn with more than 300 German tanks, including 70 of the huge Tigers, eighty-eight SP guns and 300 trucks. Rotmistrov's 5th Guards Tank Army had suffered a 50 per cent loss of his 850 tanks and SP guns. Strewn among the smoking, broken steel carcasses of hundreds of armoured vehicles and thousands of corpses, were smashed remains of fighters and ground-attack aircraft that had struggled in the sky over the battlefield. The dazed Germans described the day as the *Blutmähle von Belgorod* (the bloodbath at Belgorod).

It was a general's ultimate challenge – to fight the decisive action of the war by the seat of his pants.

On the morning of the 12th, II SS Panzer Corps was preparing to attack with more than 700 tanks and SP guns towards Kursk. Unknown to them Rotmistrov was sending his 850 tanks and SP guns towards them in two great echelons. With the Soviet tankers was 5th Guards Army. The two iron hosts collided near Prokhorovka in the greatest single armoured engagement in history. At the same time Vatutin threw his tired armies into the attack all along the line. By the end of the day both sides were exhausted and the great tank battle had essentially been a draw. But the Germans had shot their bolt; their tank reserve had been spent.

Next day, the 13th, Hitler abruptly cancelled 'Zitadelle'. Two new crises had seized his attention. The Allies had landed in Italy on the 10th, and he desperately needed reserves to contain them. The Soviet counter-offensive 'Kutuzov' had sucked the life out of Army Group Centre's attack and was threatening the army group's entire deployment. On the 15th Hitler forbade any further offensive operations by Army Group South; that order was unnecessary because Army Group

Centre, already reeling from 'Kutuzov', was now being hit by Central Front's own energetic offensive. Soviet armies were attacking now throughout the theatre. The eastern front was now moving westwards and would only stop when the Red Army's tide broke over Berlin.

Losses on both sides at Kursk were enormous. Zhukov claimed that the Germans lost 1,500 tanks, 3,000 guns and 1,500 aircraft. Soviet losses are harder to gauge. Army Group South claimed to have taken 32,000 prisoners, inflicted 85,000 other losses and destroyed about 2,000 tanks and an equal number of guns on Voronezh Front. After the tank battle at Prokhorovka, Soviet operational tanks may have fallen as low as 1,500 from the almost 4,000 when the battle began. But control of the battlefield is one of the great dividends of modern warfare. The Red Army was able to recover and repair large numbers of its tanks while depriving the Germans of that same opportunity. Two weeks later the number of Soviet operational tanks had climbed to 2,750.

The Tank Battle at Prokhorovka

'The tanks were moving across the steppe in small packs, under cover of patches of woodland and hedges. The bursts of gunfire merged into one continuous mighty roar. The Soviet tanks thrust into the German advanced formations at full speed and penetrated the tank screen. The T-34s were knocking out Tigers at extremely close range, since their powerful guns and massive armour no longer gave tham an advantage in close combat. The tanks of both sides were in closest possible contact. There was neither time nor room to disengage from the enemy and reform in battle order, or operate in formation. The shells fired at extremely close range pierced not only the side armour but the frontal armour of the fighting vehicles. At such range there was no protection in armour, and the length of the gun barrels was no longer decisive. Frequently, when a tank was hit, its ammunition and fuel blew up, and torn-off turrets were flung through the air over dozens of yards. At the same time over the battlefield furious aerial combats developed. Soviet as well as German airmen tried to help their ground forces to win the battle. The bombers, ground support aircraft, and fighters seemed to be permanently suspended in the sky over Prokhorovka. One aerial combat followed another. Soon the whole sky was shrouded by the thick smoke of the burning wrecks. On the black, scorched earth the gutted tanks burnt like torches. It was difficult to establish which side was attacking and which defending. The 2nd Battalion, 181st Tank Brigade, of 18th Tank Corps, attacking on the left bank of the Psel, encountered a group of Tigers which opened fire on the Soviet armoured fighting vehicles from a stationary position. The powerful long-range guns of the Tigers are exceedingly dangerous, and the Soviet tanks had to try to close with them as quickly as possible to eliminate this advantage of the enemy. Captain P.A. Skripkin, the battalion commander, ordered: 'Forward, follow me!' The first shell of the commander's tank pierced the side of a Tiger. Instantly another Tiger opened fire on Skripkin's T-34. A shell crashed through its side and a second wounded the battalion commander. The driver and wireless operator pulled their commander from the tank and took him to the cover of a shell crater. As a Tiger was making straight for them, Aleksander Nikolayev, the driver, leapt back into his damaged and already smouldering tank, started the engine and raced up to meet the enemy tank. Like a flaming ball of fire the T-34 raced over the ground. The Tiger halted. But it was too late. The blazing tank rammed the German Panzer at full speed. The detonation made the ground shake.'

General-Lieutenant Pavel A. Rotmistrov

▲After Kursk the German Army for the first time felt the fury of the new Soviet air offensive. Here a German transport column is savaged by Il-2 Shturmoviks on the approaches to Belgorod. During the attacks on Orel and Kharkov, three Soviet air armies, 16th, 2nd and 5th, supported the ground operations of Central, Voronezh and Steppe Fronts, employing 1,450 aircraft against 900 German.

▼A T-34 is followed into action amid German artillery fire by a Soviet recovery vehicle, a turretless T-34. The Soviets produced no custom-built recovery vehicles during the war, but did modify some T-34s for recovery work, usually those that had sustained too much damage to be repaired as combat vehicles.

THE SOVIET SUMMER OFFENSIVE – 1943
ACROSS THE DNIEPER

Kursk – the great battle – had been won. As its last echoes faded, new offensives rippled across the front. Unlike Hannibal after Cannae, the Red Army knew in its bones that the fruits of victory are gathered in the pursuit. The army was imbued rather with the Russian spirit of Aleksandr Suvorov, the legendary general of Catherine the Great, '. . . one must plan quickly and carry on without delay, so as to give the enemy no time to collect himself . . . it is the moment which gives victory. Master it . . .' Running on the heels of Kursk, the Red Army leapt into a summer campaign that would drive the Germans across the Dnieper.

The Soviet High Command feared that the Germans could conduct an orderly retreat behind a fortified River Dnieper Line which would allow them to continue to feed off the considerable resources of right bank Ukraine. The river offered them just such an opportunity. The Dnieper is the second greatest Russian river of these East Slavic lands and like all of

them, its right bank was much higher than the left. In places it was 300 feet above the river and offered excellent observation and fields of fire to the flat left bank. Southwards from Kiev the river was covered by Field Marshal von Manstein's Army Group South. It was his force that would have to be smashed if the Dnieper was to be snatched from the Germans. As in the winter campaign after Stalingrad, Army Group South would be the primary objective of this first Soviet summer offensive.

The first blow was struck by Voronezh (Army General Vatutin) and Steppe (Marshal Konev) Fronts at the left flank of Army Group South, Fourth Panzer and Eighth Armies, with the objectives of seizing Kharkov and driving on to the Dnieper. Reinforced with armies held in reserve during the Battle of Kursk, they were powerful offensive formations. On 3 August, 6th Guards Army (Voronezh Front) pulverized the German 167th Infantry Division with its artillery and then rolled over the survivors with 200 tanks and waves of infantry. A diversionary

attack wrecked 332nd Infantry Division as well. The next day two Soviet tank corps were racing through the gaps, brushing aside German counter-attacks. On 5 August Belgorod was liberated as was Orel by Central Front farther north. Stalin celebrated the twin victories with 120 gun salutes in Moscow and awarded the honorifics of the cities' names to the first divisions to enter them.

Voronezh Front pushed Fourth Panzer Army west and away from Kharkov while Steppe Front pushed down on the city and Eighth Army from the north. At the same time, Southwest Front's 57th Army attacked west across the River Donets. Vatutin's thrust was held up for a while by the stout German defence at Akhtyrka to the west of Kharkov. Between Akhtyrka

▼Supported by a 1910 model Maxim machine-gun, Soviet infantry attacking a German armoured personnel-carrier, on the approaches to Orel, Central Front, 4 August 1943.

▲On the night of 3 August units of the 5th, 129th and 380th Rifle Divisions and 17th Guards Tank Brigade of 36th Rifle Corps, 11th Guards Army, initiated the main attack of the Central Front towards Orel. The 2nd Battalion, 190th Rifle Regiment, 5th Rifle Division, was the first to break into Orel, earning 'Orel' as one of the division's honorifics.

▶Soviet tank-infantry assault by Central Front which captured Orel on 5 August 1943. Here the Soviets are using some of the 3,782 British and Canadian-supplied Valentine tanks.

▼Requiem for the fallen liberators of Orel. People of Orel and men of 17th Guards Tank Brigade, commanded by Colonel Boris Shulgin, honour the men of the brigade who fell in the battle, Central Front, 6 August 1943.

and Kharkov the Germans had lost contact with one another. The way to Poltava in the German rear was open. But Stalin wanted Kharkov. Vatutin threw Rotmistrov's 5th Guards Tank Army east against the defences of Kharkov. In a great grinding battle amid fields of giant yellow sunflowers, the Lion of Prokhorovka was fought to a standstill by several SS and panzer divisions. Soviet spearheads probed deeper and deeper into the shrinking pendant-shaped German positions around Kharkov. Finally the Commander, Army Group South (Field Marshal von Manstein) concluded he would rather lose a city than an army and ordered his bleeding Eighth Army out of Kharkov on 22 August. Stalin now had Kharkov. Four times in the last 22 months, the city had changed hands. There would not be a fifth.

While Army Group South was preoccupied on its northern flank with the defence of Kharkov, the Red Army struck its southern flank. The main blow fell on the reconstituted Sixth Army – since Stalingrad bad luck was to cling to any army so numbered. Army General Tolbukhin, commanding Southern Front, exploited the element of surprise by deceiving the Germans as to the reinforcement

of his Front. The Germans were looking for the arrival of reinforcing formations which normally signalled a Soviet offensive. This time Tolbukhin fleshed out his existing units instead, a clue the Germans missed. On 18 August Southern Front's 5th Shock Army tore a gap in Sixth Army with a crushing barrage on a narrow front and then poured mechanized forces through. A German counter-attack nearly closed the gap but the exploiting IV Guards Mechanized Corps turned around and 'counter-attacked' the German counter-attack from the west. By 23 August Sixth Army could no longer cope with the situation. II Guards Mechanized Corps reached the coast at Taganrog, isolating the German XXIX Corps. A ruse by the Germans allowed their corps to break out and von Manstein ordered Sixth and First Panzer Armies to withdraw to the River Kalmius.

As the Kharkov operation played itself out, the Soviet High Command prepared another strike just to the north against German Army Group Centre. On 26 and 28 August Central (Rokossovsky) and Western (Colonel-General V. D. Sokolovsky) Fronts successively attacked the flanks of Army Group Centre (Field Marshal von Kluge) with Central Front

conducting the main effort. Rokossovsky pried apart the hinge between Army Groups Centre and South, provoking a slow withdrawal of von Kluge's armies to the River Desna. By this time the Soviet High Command had decided to concentrate its strength against the left flank of Army Group South rather than continue a separate operation into Belorussia.

Voronezh Front was rapidly reinforced and attacked the right flank of Army Group South's Fourth Panzer Army on 4 September while Rokossovsky's Central Front continued to hammer its left flank. Fourth Panzer Army alone was straining under the attacks of six tank and mechanized corps and up to nineteen rifle divisions; by 14 September the Soviets had broken it up into three segments. The road to Kiev was now open.

On the same day Army Group South's southern flank had withdrawn to the River Kalmius. Before Sixth and First Panzer Armies could establish themselves in their new line, Army General Malinovskiy's Southwest Front was upon them. On 6 September I Guards Mechanized Corps and nine rifle divisions broke through almost on the boundary of the two German armies. Next day XXIII Tank Corps followed through the gap. The two mobile

corps then dashed west and within two days had penetrated 160 kilometres and were within 30 miles of the Dnieper. Extracting permission from Hitler, von Manstein abandoned the Kalmius line and ordered his southern armies to assume a mobile defensive role as they withdrew towards the Dnieper. Freed of static defence missions, the German armies made good time and re-established contact, trapping the two Soviet corps. With their supply line severed, the corps had no choice but to fight their way out of encirclement, taking heavy losses.

The Soviet High Command was now free to develop two main thrusts at the recoiling Germans army groups. The secondary would be towards Smolensk against the northern flank of Army Group Centre; the primary would be towards the Dnieper on the northern flank of Army Group South. Hitler's determination to control operations from his HQ in East Prussia had delayed decisions until they had become crises. Now these crises were joining in a single great rupturing catastrophe of the entire front. Hitler had deprived his armies of the ability to manoeuvre, in effect nailing their feet to the ground. The Red Army was all too eager to pound these immobilized targets. Now when Hilter had agreed finally but still grudgingly to allow his reeling armies to retreat across the Dnieper, he had waited too long for it to be an orderly retreat. Now it would be a race for the Dnieper. Who would cross first – pursued or pursuer?

The firm Soviet grip on the initiative was paying dividends to the north. Against Army Group Centre's northern flank, Kalinin (Marshal Yeremenko) and Western (Colonel-General Sokolovsky) Fronts drove north and south of Smolensk against Third Panzer and Fourth Armies. Von Kluge had had to strip his Fourth Army to send to von Manstein, and against this force Western Front struck in the direction of Smolensk on 14 September. By 2 October Sokolovsky's Front had liberated Smolensk and Roslavl and commenced the liberation of Belorussia. Against Army Group Centre's southern flank, Central Front collapsed the flank of Second Army as it drove on the Desna, passing on both sides of Chernigov by the middle of September.

Against Army Group South, the Red Army was racing neck and neck for the

◄ Soviet Il-2 Shturmoviks being assembled at an aviation factory in Kuibyshev (now Samara) in the summer of 1943. Throughout the war 41,129 Shturmoviks, mostly the Il-2 model were produced.

◄▼ A column of German Mk III and IV tanks destroyed by Soviet ground-attack aircraft ranging ahead of Soviet ground forces on the road to Kharkov, early August 1943. Shturmoviks extended the reach of the Red Army during artillery preparations as they ranged just beyond the strike of the guns into the depth of the German defences.

▼ Soviet T-34 tanks and infantry attacking through German artillery fire in the attack on Kharkov, August 1943.

Dnieper. The Germans had five main crossing points. The Soviets aimed for the wide stretches of the river between the crossing points. The crossing had become the great unifying goal of the Red Army, animating its spirit and quickening its pace and ingenuity. Stalin was to shower 2,000 Hero of the Soviet Union medals upon those who crossed first. Four of them were awarded to Guardsmen I. D. Semenov, V. N. Ivanov, N. Y. Petukhov and V. A. Sysolyatin. In the company of partisans which had scouted an unprotected spot, they were the first to slip across the river early on 22 September. Shortly before, Colonel-General Vatutin had been informed by the Chapayev partisan group that the Germans had a mere picket line north of their Kanev bridgehead in the

bend of the river below Pereyaslav at Burkin. He immediately ordered 51st Guards Tank Brigade of Rybalko's 3rd Guards Tank Army to cross any way they could. The four Guardsmen were the first; The rest crossed on barrels, rafts, planks and anything that would float. In two days the bridgehead was four kilometres deep and six kilometres wide. Repeated German counter-attacks could not dislodge it; it was the old story – once the Russians had seized a bridgehead, these masters of stubborn defence were almost impossible to dislodge. At this time the High Command launched the largest Soviet airborne operation of the war to support the bridgehead. It was a disaster. There had been no time to plan the operation, and the transport aircrews were

not well trained. As a result three brigades of 7,000 men were dropped haphazardly around the bridgehead only to be overrun by German forces.

The same day that Vatutin's Guardsmen had slipped across the river, Rokossovksiy's Central Front secured a bridgehead near Chernobyl in northern Ukraine. The Germans had not expected a crossing in the marshy area of the confluence of the Rivers Dnieper and Pripyet, but the partisans had prepared the way with a hidden corduroy log road through the marsh. By the end of the month the bridgehead was fifteen miles long. At the same time, Steppe Front took three bridgeheads between Kremenchug and Dnepropetrovsk. The Red Army then paused for a week as it brought its strength up to the river line. At this time, Voronezh, Steppe, Southwest and South Fronts opposing Army Groups South and 'A' (Sixth and Seventeenth Armies) were renamed 1st, 2nd, 3rd and 4th Ukrainian Fronts.

Although the airdrop at the Burkin bridgehead had failed, Vatutin's 1st Ukrainian Front would strike the jackpot at another crossing just north of Kiev itself two days later. There on 26 September General Moskalenko's 38th Army threw themselves across on whatever would float. Several of the first regiments were shot up, but finally a platoon of 22 men commanded by Sergeant Nefedov of 842nd Rifle Regiment got a toehold and held on near the village of Lyutezh. By the 30th most of 240th Rifle Division was

across. But if the Red Army was to make a strategic crossing at Lyutezh, Moskalenko needed armour. The nearest tank unit was V Guards Tank Corps, but the Desna stood between it and the hard-pressed 240th to the west on the Dnieper. Ordered to find a way to Lyutezh, V Guards Commander, Lieutenant-General Kravchenko, went to work. Local peasants helped him find a shallow crossing over the Desna. His men feverishly sealed their tanks with tallow, pitch, putty and oiled canvas, and installed vertical pipes over the exhausts. With a dash he crossed his 90 tanks underwater up to the hatches. At the Dnieper he found two barges abandoned by the Germans and ferried 60 tanks into the bridgehead by 6 October. The bridgehead was now safe. Vatutin now switched Rybalko's 3rd Guards Tank Corps from the Burkin area to Lyutezh in secrecy.

On 9 October Tolbukhin's 4th Ukrainian Front resumed its attacks with overwhelming superiority on Sixth Army on the Nogay Steppe just north of the Crimea. The key to the German defence of the Dnieper here was the city of Melitopol 150 kilometres to the east; they held it for fourteen bitter days of fighting before giving way. Then Tolbukhin released two reserve armies which sealed off the Perekop isthmus thus severing the Crimea from the German front and drove on to the Dnieper. Von Manstein intended to use a large armoured force transferred from the west to eliminate the Soviet

bridgeheads over the upper Dnieper and then riposte south to re-establish contact with Seventeenth Army trapped in the Crimea. Marshal Konev beat him to the punch by pouring strong forces through his 2nd Ukrainian Front bridgeheads to the west bank of the Dnieper and striking south towards the key communications junction of Krivoi Rog opposite First Panzer Army. Von Manstein's panzer reserve barely managed to blunt this drive. At the same time, 3rd Ukrainian Front attacked out of its bridgehead and drove First Panzer Army out of Dnepropetrovsk.

Shortly afterwards Vatutin's 1st Ukrainian Front expanded its bridgehead north of Kiev and erupted into west bank Ukraine on 3 November. In the morning 2,000 guns and 500 Katyushas of 38th Army smothered the three defending German divisions. Fifth Guards Tank Corps led the attack with shouts of 'Ura!' Moskalenko had ripped a 10-kilometre hole in the German front. In two days' fighting Fourth Panzer Army's front was broken, and its corps were retreating out of contact with each other. Rybalko's 3rd Guards Tank Army attacked south-west of Kiev, while Moskalenko's 38th Army fought through Kiev itself on 5 November, wiping out the German 88th Infantry Division. Rybalko drove west and seized the vital communications and rail hub at Fastov. By the middle of December Army Group South had lost the entire Dnieper line except for a 50-kilometre stretch between Kiev and Cherkassy.

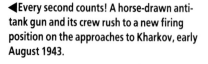

◀Every second counts! A horse-drawn anti-tank gun and its crew rush to a new firing position on the approaches to Kharkov, early August 1943.

►One of the natural warriors summoned to leadership during the crisis of the war, Lieutenant-General (later Marshal of Tank Troops) Mikhail Ye. Katukov, Commander 1st (Guards in 1944) Tank Army, engages in one of the great privileges of command – presenting medals to his men – after the battles from Belgorod to Kharkov, August 1943.

►German prisoners taken in battles near Kharkov, August 1943.

As the four Ukrainian Fronts pushed Army Group South across the Dnieper from Kiev south almost to the sea, the new Belorussian Front was pummelling Army Group Centre north of Kiev. Created from Bryansk and Central Fronts, the new Front was commanded by the redoubtable Rokossovsky. While threatening the German bridgehead at Gomel from north and south, he launched his main attack on 15 October farther south on a 20-kilometre front near Loyev which established a large bridgehead. Successive attacks followed until the Germans resistance collapsed on 10 November. By the 14th Rokossovsky's spearheads had reached Retchitsa on the way to the Dnieper. On the 22nd Belorussian Front began another major attack further north against Ninth Army south of Propoysk, driving it back across the Dnieper. Rokossovsky's southern attack the

next day broke contact between Ninth and Second Armies. By retreating westwards the two armies were able to re-establish contact and launch a counter-attack in late December that pushed Belorussian Front's advanced formations back 20 kilometres. By then the front had stabilized.

Farther north on the boundary between Army Groups North and Centre, the Red Army had still another crisis in store for the Germans. On 6 October a strong attack against 3rd Panzer (Army Group Centre) shattered the defending Luftwaffe field division. Surprised by the ease of the victory, Marshal Yeremenko, commanding Kalinin Front, nevertheless was quick to seize the opportunity. He loaded a guards infantry division on tanks and trucks and struck behind the army group's front to seize the fortified town of Nevel. Very heavy partisan activity disrupted the

movement of German reserves. Ominously, the Soviets expanded the operation, moving the former headquarters of Bryansk Front, now 2nd Baltic Front, to take over part of Kalinin Front which itself became 1st Baltic Front. Yeremenko exploited the inability of the two German army groups to co-operate by widening his breach and driving south-west towards Vitebsk where the Germans managed to hang on until the end of the year despite repeated Soviet attacks.

In September 1943 the Red Army was not only advancing on the River Dnieper. There was other unfinished business. On the 9th, Colonel-General Petrov's North Caucasus Front attacked the German Seventeenth Army in its strong Gotenkopf position on the Taman peninsula. Strong attacks by his 18th Army were supported by a daring amphibious operation that

117

▼The race to the Dnieper was on! Hitler waited too long to give von Manstein permission to retreat across the great defensive barrier of the river. Its high bluffs on the west bank looked down on the flat, treeless east bank; it was a defender's dream. Given time and effort, the Germans could have made a dangerous rampart of it. Here horse-drawn Soviet artillery passes a failed German Mark IV tank rearguard. The Ukrainian goat seems unfazed by the whole thing.

seized the port of Novorossisk just behind the German lines. By 14 September the Gotenkopf Line was broken. Petrov's assaults had soaked up German reserves; then he committed his reserves of several Guards divisions. The Germans tried to re-establish a defence to the rear but were outflanked by more Soviet amphibious landings. Combined with Petrov's continuing attacks, the German positions collapsed. The survivors of Seventeenth Army, unable to evacuate to the Crimea, were overrun in the ports across from the Kerch peninsula by 9 October. On 1 November 1943 Colonel-General Petrov, newly promoted for clearing the Taman

peninsula, threw an amphibious assault across the beaches of the Kerch peninsula, 30,000 men carried by 150 ships and craft of the Azov Flotilla. A violent storm hit the flotilla in mid passage, but the order to turn back was too late to stop the landing of the initial forces. They hung on long enough for Petrov to push more forces through as the weather finally abated. By the end of the year he had his entire Front in the Crimea and was pushing the Germans out of the Kerch peninsula.

After its westward lunge that had carried it by successive blows from Kursk to right bank Ukraine and deep into Belorussia, the Red Army paused to built

up its strength while the Germans wasted themselves in counter-attacks that repeatedly bogged down in attrition battles. The successive Soviet blows that had rained down on the Germans since Kursk were proof that operational and strategic initiative had passed irrevocably to the Red Army. Everywhere the Germans were reduced to warding off ever more skilfull and numerous blows. Even more ruinous for the Germans, the Red Army was growing in strength, numbers and quality of equipment as German strength passed its peak. Nike, the goddess of victory, had lighted on the Red Army's shoulder where she would stay to the end.

▲Cross, cross, cross! – was the order. Don't wait for engineers and bridging, but cross any way you can. And they did – on fishing boats overlooked by the Germans or hidden by the partisans, on logs, jerry-built rafts, barrels, on whatever would float. Bridgeheads sprang up everywhere as Red Army infantry armed with what they could carry dug in on the west bank.

▼A few days later to the north of Kiev, troops of 38th Army commanded by General Moskalenko made repeated efforts to cross the Dnieper. Battalions of three regiments were wiped out in turn until a platoon of 22 men commanded by Sergeant Neferov of 842nd Rifle Regiment made it across and dug in.

▲Soviet gunners serving their 45mm anti-tank gun despite a near miss, Western Front, September 1943.

▼Soviet submachine-gunners attacking a village on the approaches to Smolensk, September 1943.

◄Representative of Supreme Command Headquarters, Marshal of the Soviet Union Semyon Timoshenko, Commander of the North Caucasus Front, Colonel-General Ivan Petrov, and Commander of 18th Army, Colonel-General Konstantin Lesselidze, with a group of staff officers discussing the plan of a forced crossing of the Kerch straits, September 1943.

▲On 1 November 1943 Colonel-General Petrov, newly promoted for clearing the Taman peninsula, threw an amphibious assault across the beaches of the Kerch Peninsula, 30,000 men carried by 150 ships and craft of the Azov Flotilla. Here a 57mm anti-tank gun crew fights off a German tank attack on the Kerch bridgehead.

▼By 14 September the Gotenkopf Line had been broken. Here Soviet infantry attack behind T-34 tanks towards the city of Taman.

◀Artillerymen of 51st Army, Southern Front, pulling their guns by raft across the shallows of the Sivash (Putrid Sea), 1 November 1943. It seemed a point of pride and challenge to the Soviets never to be daunted by natural obstacles.

▶On 3 November 1943 General Moskalenko's 38th Army led by V Guards Tank Corps burst out of the First Ukrainian Front's strong bridgehead at Lyutezh. Here his men are seen marching through the largely ruined city on 6 November.

▶The Germans had intended to loot east bank Ukraine thoroughly and leave nothing but ashes in a scorched earth campaign as they retreated across the Dnieper. They intended to take all grain, livestock and civilians of military age with them, but the Red Army were pressing them so hard that they got away with only a fraction of their loot. They were more efficient in the destruction of the industrial and economic infrastructure. Here they have destroyed a railway line by ripping up its ties with a huge metal 'plough'.

▲As the Germans' forced allies faded away, Soviet allies recruited from refugees of conquered nations began to form combat units under Soviet command. Here Colonel Lubvik Svoboda addresses the men of 1st Separate Czechoslovak Infantry Brigade, 1st Ukrainian Front, November 1943. A professional soldier, Svoboda first saw military service in Austro-Hungarian uniform in 1915, defected in 1916 to the Russians and joined the famed Czech Legion, joined the new Czechoslovak Army in 1920, escaped to Poland in 1938 after the German takeover of his country, escaped again to the Soviet Union in 1939 after the fall of Poland, and helped organize the first Czech units in the Soviet Union. After the war he was to become Defence Minister and finally president.

▲▶After June 1941 Stalin realized only too well that his decision to murder the Polish officer corps at Katyn was a major error. As a sop to his Western Allies, he had allowed surviving Poles who were able to do so to leave through Iran; many of them were formed into a Polish Corps that fought in the West. Many of those who remained were recruited into another Polish Army that would fight alongside the Red Army all the way to Berlin. Here 1st 'Tadeusz

Kosciuszko' Division is assembled at the Solotsky Barracks outside Ryazan, August 1943.

▶During the autumn of 1943 the Russian Orthodox Church presented the Red Army with a brigade of new tanks. They are emblazoned with the inscription 'Dmitri Donskoi', the name of the Grand Prince of Moscow who in 1380 was the first Russian to defeat the Mongols at the Battle of Kulikovo Fields. These tanks are the new Model T-34/85 armed with the 85mm high-velocity gun. The new German Tiger and Panther tanks that appeared in large numbers at Kursk were considerably upgunned and outranged the T-34/76 and were much more difficult for the 76mm gun to destroy. Soviet industry's response was a crash programme to develop a new 85mm gun. The new larger turret required by the new gun was a radical improvement that allowed a three-man turret configuration and a 360-degree vision cupola for the commander. By 1944 they formed the bulk of Soviet tank production.

◄From faraway France another contingent of allies served with the Red Army. These were the pilots of the French Air Force Régiment Normandie-Niemen. In the centre is the commander of one of the Normandie Squadrons, Captain Marcel Lefebre, who was awarded the medal Hero of the Soviet Union, a rare distinction for a foreigner.

▼As summer gave way to winter, the pace of operations did not slacken. The Red Army saw in the New Year of 1944 with fierce fighting along the front. Here Soviet infantry attack supported by a 50mm mortar, West Front, late December 1943.

THE SOVIET WINTER AND SPRING CAMPAIGNS – 1944
OFFENSIVES IN THE NORTH AND SOUTH

As 1943 drew to a close the Germans expected the Red Army to pause after the long summer offensive that had carried it over the Dnieper in continuous fighting since the Battle of Kursk. Instead of resting, the Soviets would continue the tempo of the offensive against long-suffering Army Group South and now against Army Group North.

Marshal Zhukov coordinated both 1st and 2nd Ukrainian Fronts in this new fighting and staggered their blows. On Christmas Day Vatutin's 1st Ukrainian Front began the offensive with strong

▼On Christmas Day 1943 Army-General Vatutin's strong 1st Ukrainian Front began the winter offensive aimed at Army Group South. Here T-34 tanks and submachine-gunners of 3rd Guards Tank Army go on the attack in the region around Berdichev.

attacks south-west of Kiev with 1st Tank Army in the lead. Fourth Panzer Army started to break apart under its blows. Von Manstein counter-attacked and temporarily contained the attack. To the east Vatutin had a bigger surprise. On 26 January he broke open the front along the boundaries of two German armies and, with the help of Konev's 2nd Ukrainian Front attacking from the east, encircled two German corps numbering 56,000 men in the Korsun pocket. The two fronts began squeezing the pocket and also established an outer defensive ring to prevent relief as had been done at Stalingrad. At this point control of the operation was passed to Konev. The Germans made desperate attempts to relieve the pocket but were stopped by the outer defensive ring; a breakout was then ordered. On 16 February, abandoning most of their equipment that would be a hindrance in the mud and snow, the Germans in the

pocket attacked west under the protection of a blizzard. In most places they were stopped in the murderous Soviet gauntlet, but the largest body fought their way through Soviet lines in what degenerated into mad flight. Unit cohesion broke down and hundreds drowned while trying to cross the final water barrier. The Soviets took 18,000 prisoners. The survivors had abandoned even their personal weapons to escape, but what was worse, their nerve had broken. After Stalingrad and now Korsun, the fear of encirclement spread like plague in the German Army, devouring its morale.

To the south-east along the front, Marshal Vasilevsky co-ordinated the offensives of Malinovskiy's 3rd Ukrainian and Tolbukhin's 4th Ukrainian Fronts against Army Group A's Sixth Army which was forming a great east-pointing salient. On 10 January, Malinovskiy attacked the north face of the salient fol-

▶At the beginning of the offensive the Red Army had achieved a superiority in artillery of 70 per cent over the Germans. Given that Hitler would not let his forces retreat, they made particularly good targets for Soviet artillery.

The Third Period of War
1 January 1944 - 9 May 1945

German attacks

Soviet attacks

German pockets

Front Line as of:
1 January 1944
1 May 1944
1 January 1945
9 May 1945
Unopposed March

0   100   200
miles

NORWAY

SWEDEN

DENMARK

Baltic Sea

FINLAND

Helsinki

Talinn

Lake Piepus

Riga

COURLAND

Memel
Niemen R.

Danzig

Königsberg

Vilnius

Lake Ladoga

Lake Onega

SOVIET UNION

Leningrad

Novgorod
Lake Ilmen

Demyansk

XXXX
KARELIAN

XXXX
LENNINGRAD

XXXX
VOLKHOV

XXXX
2 BALTIC

XXXX
NORTH

Dvina R.

XXXX
1 BALTIC

XXXX
3 BELORUSSIAN

Vitebsk

Volga R.

Moscow

Mozhaisk

Vyazma

Smolensk

Tula

XXXX
2 BELORUSSIAN

Minsk

Don R.

Stettin

Berlin

Poznan

Torgau
Elbe R.

GERMANY

Oder R.

Breslau

Prague

Cracow

Lvov

Warsaw

Vistula R.

Bialostok

Brest

XXXX
CENTRE

Pripyat R.

Bobriusk

XXXX
1 BELORUSSIAN

Desna R.

Bryansk

Orel

Kursk

XXXX
1 UKRAINIAN

Kiev

Korsun

XXXX
SOUTH

S. Bug R.

XXXX
2 UKRAINIAN

Belgorod

Kharkov

Donets R.

Dnepropetrovsk

Donetsk

XXXX
3 UKRAINIAN

Zaporozhe

Rostov

Dnieper R.

Vienna

Budapest

Debrecen

Kluj

Dniester R.

Kishinev

XXXX
A

Odessa

Perekop

Sea of Azov

Kuban R.

Kerch

Novorossiysk

XXXX
4 UKRAINIAN

Sevastopol

Belgrade

Bucharest

Danube R.

Black Sea

Adriatic Sea

ITALY

ALBANIA

GREECE

Sofia

TURKEY

the Germans attempted to pull back to a shorter fortified line, the 'Rollbahn', but found Red Army units had already breached it in several places. At Novgorod Volkhov Front had struck Sixteenth Army and surrounded a considerable German force. To the south of Lake Ilmen 2nd Baltic Front was adding more pressure to Sixteenth Army.

By the 23rd, Eighteenth Army was caving in. Its men were exhausted by the mud and rain of this unusually mild winter and by constant action. The two Russian Front commanders, on the other hand, were rotating their units so as to have always fresh troops in action. By this time the two German armies had lost contact with each other. Hitler replaced the army group commander on 1 February with his favourite, Field Marshal Model who managed to extricate it in a fighting retreat through forest and swamps to a solid line running from Narva on the coast south along Lake Peipus and Lake Pskov. Leningrad Front strained to snap the German hold on Narva but could not dislodge III SS Panzer Corps. By the end of March the front had stabilized.

To the south the four Ukrainian Fronts were ready to resume the offensive at the beginning of March. The Red Army had concentrated all six of its tank armies in this sector. First Ukrainian Front, the strongest, was now directly commanded by Marshal Zhukov who had just replaced a mortally wounded Vatutin. The Front's mission was to drive straight westwards to the Carpathian Mountains supported by strong drives of 2nd and 3rd Ukrainian Fronts. Fourth Ukrainian Front was to concentrate on retaking the Crimea.

Zhukov attacked on 4 March into the gap between First and Fourth Panzer Armies with 3rd Guards Tank Army in the lead. In two days Zhukov had torn open a 150-kilometre breach; however, von Manstein managed to stabilize the front and bring his two panzer armies in line running from Ternopol to Proscurov. At Ternopol Zhukov attempted to break through for his dash to the Carpathians, but Fourth Panzer Army hung on in what Zhukov described as the fiercest fighting since Kursk. On 21 March Zhukov attacked again with three tank armies and disintegrated the German front. First and 4th Tank Armies sped south, 1st turning west to drive the Germans out of Ternopol and 4th to Chortkhov, cutting First

lowed by Tolbukhin's attack on the south-east face directed at the Nikopol bridge-head over the Dnieper. Malinovskiy's 8th Guards Army under Chuikov (formerly 62nd Army) drove deep into the salient, nearly severing it. The German corps in the tip of the salient barely escaped south around the Soviet spearheads, and by the end of February had re-established a front to the west along the River Ingulets and then east to the lower Don.

Around Leningrad, Army Group North braced itself for its own ordeal. For the first time since the counter-attack before Moscow in 1941-2, the Soviet High Command had prepared a major operation against this army group comparable with those to the south. Against two large German armies, Eighteenth and Sixteenth, the Russians had Leningrad (Colonel-General L. A. Govorov), Volkhov (Colonel-General K. A. Meretskov)

and 2nd Baltic Fronts. The first two Fronts ranged themselves against Eighteen Army which was still bombarding Leningrad with its murderous heavy siege guns. Unknown to the Germans, the Red Army had amassed a great advantage: 3:1 in divisions, 3:1 in artillery and 6:1 in tanks, self-propelled guns and aircraft. At the same time the offensives against Army Group South drew off Army Group North's reserve divisions.

The Soviets attacked Eighteenth Army on 14 January at both ends of its front, the Oranienbaum pocket along the coast west of Leningrad and the sector from Mga south-east to the River Volkhov. Within four days the Germans were in trouble. The 2nd Shock Army attacking from Oranienbaum and 42nd Army attacking from Leningrad destroyed several German divisions along the coast and continued to push south. East of Leningrad

◀The air shook with the screech of the Katyushas that opened Leningrad Front's offensive against Army Group North on 14 January 1944. Leningrad and Volkhov Fronts concentrated their attack on the German Eighteenth Army besieging Leningrad. Unknown to the Germans they had achieved a superiority of 3:1 in divisions and artillery, and 6:1 in tanks and aircraft.

▼Third Guards Tank Army entering Berdichev. The city fell at the end of the first week in January 1944, barely two weeks after the offensive had begun. First Ukrainian Front had driven the Germans back more than 100 kilometres in less than two weeks of intense fighting.

▲On 26 January 1st and 2nd Ukrainian Fronts encircled two German corps of more than six divisions in the Korsun-Shevchenkovskiy pocket. On 16 February the desperate Germans attempted a breakout, having abandoned their wounded and all but tracked vehicles in order to transit the snow and mud.

▼By the end of January the Red Army had already inflicted 40,000 casualties on Eighteenth Army, crippling its combat strength. The machine-gun crew going into action in the foreground has the DPM1928 machine-gun, January 1944.

Panzer Army off from its base of supply and trapping it against the River Dniester. Zhukov fully expected the Germans to try to break out to the south and concentrated his forces in that direction. Instead von Manstein ordered First Panzer Army to attack north-west across the rear of 1st and 4th Tank Armies to escape. The mud prevented Zhukov from bringing forward much artillery, and many of his forward tank units were badly depleted from the continuous fighting. Still he threw everything he could at the retreating Germans, but it was not enough. They finally broke through to the west on 10 April.

As Zhukov and von Manstein grappled on the flank, Konev's 2nd Ukrainian Front and Malinovskiy's 3rd Ukrainian Front attacked the German Eighth and Sixth Armies also on 4 March. By the 9th Konev had destroyed the left flank of Eighth Army and was pressing west. By the 7th Malinovskiy had split Sixth Army apart and was manoeuvring 40 kilometres deep into its rear. Malinovskiy then chose to dissipate his strength going for two objectives at once, allowing Sixth Army to escape and establish temporarily a solid line behind the River Bug by 20 March. They were able to hold for it barely eight days before being forced to retreat towards Odessa closely pursued by Chuikov's 8th Guards Army and 46th Army. On 2 April a sleet storm struck the area as the Germans were trying to form a bridgehead over the Dniester that included Odessa. As the storm raged throughout the next day, Malinovskiy's tanks and cavalry attacked under its cover to sever the German bridgehead and surround Odessa. The rest of Sixth Army fled across the Dniester in scenes of complete panic and confusion.

By the beginning of April the Soviet spring offensive had largely ended, but the German armies had been badly beaten and literally kicked westwards. Repeated retreats and escapes had resulted in the abandonment of huge amounts of equipment and supplies, and many divisions had been reduced to *Kampfgruppen* (battle groups). In the gap between Army Groups South and 'A', Soviet tank columns had penetrated to the Carpathians.

As the fighting moved west the Crimea had become hopelessly isolated, yet Hitler had reinforced his Seventeenth Army to a strength of seven divisions plus seven Roumanian divisions. On 8 April Malin-

ovskiy's 4th Ukrainian Front attacked with two armies across the Perekop isthmus and the Sivash bridgehead line. The Germans held the isthmus, but the Roumanians gave way at the bridgehead. Second Guards and 51st Armies pushed into the interior of the Crimea, meeting the Independent Coastal Army (formerly North Caucasus Front) attacking west from the Kerch peninsula. The Germans retreated into the fortress of Sevastopol. By 7 May the Red Army was breaking into the city; only then did Hitler order an evacuation. Again too little too late became another German disaster. In this last week barely 38,000 Germans were rescued from an original Seventeenth Army strength of almost 100,000 men.

▶German prisoners taken in the Korsun-Shevchenkovskiy pocket. Of the 56,000 Germans trapped there, the Soviets captured 18,000. Barely 30,000 made it back to German lines, most without even their personal weapons; the panic was so great that even the renowned German unit cohesion disintegrated.

▼▶A T-34 tank of 4th Guards Mechanized Corps, of General Chuikov's 8th Guards Army in a night attack during the Nikopol-Krivoi Rog offensive.

▼152mm heavy guns of the Red Army in action with 1st Ukrainian Front.

▲The winter of 1944 was abnormally mild and rainy for Russia and Ukraine. Instead of hard, frozen ground suitable for movement, both sides struggled with deep, sticky mud. Even here the Russians were more practical in dealing with the situation. They confiscated the large numbers of peasant sledges to carry the heavy weapons of mortar and machine-gun crews so that the men could conserve their strength. Wide tracks on Soviet tanks and self-propelled guns made for easier going through the mud. American Lend-Lease trucks were also far more robust and able to deal with muddy conditions than German vehicles.

▼By the end of the second phase of the Soviet winter offensive which began on 4 March, 1st Ukrainian Front had driven the Germans back 200 kilometres in less than one month. Here 11th Guards Tank Corps commanded by General Getman are crossing the River Prut at Chernovtsy in western Ukraine which they liberated on 29 March 1944.

►Russian ingenuity born of surviving in a harsh climate simply would not be defeated by the muddy conditions of the winter of 1944. Here the troops are laying corduroy roads for their tanks to transverse.

►SU-152 152mm self-propelled guns of 3rd Ukrainian Front closing on the Roumanian border in early April. The SU-152 prototype was rushed to completion in just one month and went into production immediately so that the first regiment of twelve vehicles, formed in May 1943, was committed to combat at Kursk. It was the only Soviet vehicle that could slug it out toe to toe with the new German Tigers, Panthers and Elefants, earning the name 'Zvierboy' (Animal Hunter).

◀On 26 March 1944 3rd Ukrainian Front in its pursuit of Sixth Army reached the first of the Soviet Union's pre-war borders. Here Soviet border guards erect a frontier marker on the Soviet-Roumanian border.

▼As Sixth Army retreated toward the Roumanian border, Hitler demanded that it hold a bridgehead east of the River Dniester to include the city of Odessa. Under the cover of a sleet storm on 3 April, 8th Guards Army launched its tanks and cavalry in a slashing attack that cut the bridgehead in two and isolated Odessa.

▲Winter mud turned to spring mud as these infantrymen of 46th Army, 3rd Ukrainian Front, slog through water on the approaches to Odessa.

▶The ground quickly dried sufficiently to carry the rapid assault of tanks and infantry of 6th Army, 3rd Ukrainian Front. The mix of T-34 models is apparent in the T-34/76s in the foreground and the newer T-34/85s in the background, and depended entirely on available replacements at the time. By now light tanks had been relegated to mechanized artillery and reconnaissance roles. The slower KVs were assigned as infantry support.

▶Infantry of 3rd Ukrainian Front fighting on the outskirts of Odessa, 9 April 1944. The city which had been isolated a few days before, fell the next day after suffering German occupation since 16 October 1941.

◄Soviet MiG-3 fighters over Sevastopol. In its attack on the Crimea 4th Ukraine Front was supported by both 4th and 8th Air Armies.

◄Commander of the 6th Guards Pursuit Regiment, Hero of the Soviet Union Colonel M. V. Avdeyev, confers with British and American aircrew of an American bomber which performed shuttle flights over Germany to land in the newly liberated Crimea.

▲The evacuation that ended in disaster. A last-minute refusal by Hitler to complete the evacuation of the Crimea which was being successfully carried out, sealed the fate of much of the garrison. Of the 64,700 men hemmed-in in the Sevastopol pocket in the first week of May, 26,700 were left behind. Such was the fate of the Lower Saxons of 111th Infantry Division trapped against the shore and overrun.

▼The crew of a Soviet 76mm anti-tank gun manhandle their piece forward, Leningrad Front, January 1944.

▲ Shturmovik ground-attack aircraft flying over Leningrad to attack the besieging German Eighteenth Army during the winter offensive that liberated the city, January 1944.

▼ Winter-clothed Soviet submachine-gunners, at least three of whom on the lead tank are armed with German submachine-guns, are moved up to the front for the attack, Leningrad Front, January 1944.

▲Another example of the fertile Russian imagination and determination to dominate their harsh environment are the aero-sleighs employed by Volkhov Front in its fighting near Lake Ilmen, January 1944.

▼Lend-Lease Sherman M4 tanks of 59th Army being rafted across the River Volkhov near Novgorod, Volkhov Front, January 1944.

◄The Red Army attacked on 22 June, three years to the day from the German attack on the Soviet Union in Operation 'Barbarossa'. The Soviet attacks succeeded on every front as Army Group Centre began to crumble almost immediately. By the fourth day of the offensive, the Germans had committed their last reserves without stopping or even delaying the Red Army anywhere.

▼Artillery of 2nd Belorussian Front, part of the 24,400 guns and mortars massed to deal Army Group Centre an immediate and crushing blow, together with 4,000 tanks and 5,300 aircraft and 2,500,000 men. The Soviet deception plan enabled these enormous forces to assemble without German notice. So quiet did the front appear that Hitler permitted the transfer of the panzer corps which deployed 88 per cent of the tanks and 23 per cent of the assault guns of the army group.

SHATTERING THE EASTERN FRONT – 1944

Despite its severe beating at the hands of the Red Army in the last year, the Wehrmacht still held a coherent Eastern Front from Estonia on the Baltic to the Roumanian border on the Black Sea. Beginning in June the Red Army would deliver a succession of blows that would shatter that front and put Russian troops into East Prussia and on the outskirts of Warsaw.

The Soviet High Command's operational-strategic goal was still the destruction of an entire German army group. Only a disaster of such magnitude would be able to collapse the German position and do irretrievable damage to the enemy. For the past two years Army Group South (now Army Groups North Ukraine and South Ukraine) had been the object of such attention, but under Field Marshal von Manstein had saved itself time and time again. Now both army groups, however, had been driven west in the winter and spring offensives of 1944, leaving Field Marshal Busch's Army Group

Centre occupying a dangerous salient in Belorussia. Here was the target the Soviet High Command had been looking for.

To distract the Germans from the build-up opposite Army Group Centre, the Soviet High Command decided to settle accounts with Finland first. Finland had become a co-belligerent of Germany's in 1941 to recapture its territory lost to the Soviet Union in the Russo-Finnish War of 1940. It rapidly achieved that objective and then assumed a largely passive military posture that did little more than contribute to the Siege of Leningrad. In the late spring of 1944 the Red Army concentrated 450,000 men, 10,000 guns and mortars, 800 tanks and 1,547 aircraft of the Leningrad and Karelian Fronts for a knockout blow against Finland. The Finns were then outnumbered 2:1 in manpower, 4:1 in artillery and 6:1 in aircraft. On 9 June Leningrad Front attacked across the Karelian Isthmus and Karelian Front attacked to the northeast of Lake Ladoga in eastern Karelia. Achieving a tremendous concentration of firepower, Colonel-General Govorov's Leningrad Front broke through the Finnish defences the next day, described as the 'Black Day' of the Finnish Army. By the 14th they had reached the second Finnish line of defence, and again fire power had breached it by the next day on a 13-kilometre stretch. On the 16th The Finns retreated to their third and final line of defence running Vyborg–Vuoksi and abandoned eastern Karelia. On the 21st the Soviets finally captured Vyborg and were gnawing their way towards good tank country. By early July the last of the final defence line was lost. At this point, the Soviet High Command began shifting forces to more decisive theatres, and the front stabilized. The Finns were saved, but their 60,000 casualties in the fighting were too much. In September they made a separate peace with the Soviet Union.

As the Finns were being ground down, the Soviet High Command was conducting a massive concentration for a crushing strike against Army Group Centre. The objectives of the operation were to liberate Belorussia and advance to the River Vistula and the border of East Prussia. For this operation, Stalin put together his winning team. Marshal Zhukov would be co-ordinating 1st Baltic (Army General I. K. Bagramyan) and 3rd Belorussian (Colonel-General I. D. Chernyakovskiy) Fronts (former West Front) while Marshal Vasilevskiy would co-ordinate 1st (Marshal K. K. Rokossovsky) and 2nd Belorussian (Army General V. Zakharov) Fronts, all of which were being massively reinforced. On the front Vitebsk–Bobruysk there were 1.2 million men; a total of 2.5 million men including reserves was readied for the operation against Army Group Centre's 700,000 men. The disparity in equipment was even greater. The Red Army massed 4,000 tanks, 24,400 guns and mortars, and 5,300 aircraft, achieving superiorities of 10:1 at the breakthrough points. Incredibly, German Intelligence misread the situation and predicted an offensive against Army Group North Ukraine thus triggering the transfer of LVI Panzer Corps which included 15 per cent of the army group's divisions, 88 per cent of its tanks, 23 per cent of its assault guns, 50 per cent of its tank destroyers and 33 per cent of its heavy artillery.

The Red Army attacked on 22 June, the third anniversary of the German attack on the Soviet Union. The Soviets paid special attention to the German artillery which was close to the front and out in the open since it had had little to fear from the air in the past. This time the Soviets had overwhelming air superiority which shifted quickly to air supremacy.

Chernyakovksiy's 3rd Belorussian Front swung its sledgehammer of four armies at German VI Corps, with the point of impact on its 299th Infantry Division. The division was swept away. Into the gap rushed a tank corps and a mechanized-cavalry group racing for Vitebsk to the south and ignoring their

flanks. Within two days of such attacks all along the front, three of four German armies were in serious trouble. Third Panzer Army had lost five divisions encircled around Vitebsk by 1st Baltic and 3rd Belorussian Fronts; Fourth Army was ready to snap from the two hard, deep blows inflicted by 2nd and 3rd Belorussian Fronts; Ninth Army's northern boundary with Fourth Army was split off by 1st Belorussian Front. Everywhere the Germans were reeling from attacks that showed a sophistication and dash that had once been an exclusive German accomplishment. The result was a catastrophe advancing at a geometric rate.

By the 26th, the situation for the Germans was beyond repair. Ninth Army lost two corps and 70,000 men in a pocket around Bobruysk. By the 28th Third Panzer Army had lost two of its three corps. Fourth Army managed to retreat across the River Beresina to the east of Minsk, but Soviet spearheads of a great encirclement were already west of Minsk. On 3 July Minsk fell, sealing the fate of Fourth Army. The next day the remnant of Ninth Army were trapped. Since 22 June the Red Army had destroyed 25 German divisions, killed or captured 350-400,000 irreplaceable veterans and 31 of 47 general officers, exceeding by far their tally at Stalingrad. Out of this enormous Cannae, barely 800 German soldiers made their way back to German lines on the Vistula two months later.

At this point the Germans expected the Soviets to pause, since they had already reached the limit of similar lunges in the past, about 200 kilometres, but the Red Army just kept coming. First Baltic Front attacked north towards Dvinsk; 3rd Belorussian Front via Vilnius to the River Niemen; 1st Belorussian Front west to Brest-Litovsk; 2nd Belorussian Front remained to deal with German pockets and countless stragglers. Hitler quickly transferred his personal fire brigade, Field Marshal Model, to command the dying army group. Model's specialty was dealing with Hitler's self-imposed crises. A master of ruthlessness and improvisation, Model was determined to hold on to the rail centre at Baranovichi as the southern anchor of his army group. Zhukov was not about to let the offensive be reined in. He called General Batov of 65th Army and commanded, 'Don't give them any respite, keep fighting,and take that rail centre Baranovichi!' On the 8th both Baranovichi and Vilnius, the two endposts of the new line the Germans were trying to hold, fell. No help could come from Army Group North which was engaged in savage fighting with 2nd and 3rd Baltic Fronts. The remnant of Army Group Centre finally came to a halt by 18 July on a line Ukmerge-Kaunus-Grodno-Bialystok simply because the Red Army had outrun its supplies after a 300-kilometre advance.

To the north in the Baltics, the seam between Army Groups North and Centre was splitting on the 18th as Bagramyan's 1st Baltic Front drove in a sharp wedge, consisting of 51st and 2nd Guards Armies transferred from their victory in the Crimea. By the end of the month they had cut the last rail line linking Army Groups

▲ As a diversion to the concentration of forces against Army Group Centre, the Red Army launched an offensive against the Finnish Army. In this photograph can be seen regiments of M-31 rocket-launchers deployed in depth. KV-1 heavy tanks are in the foreground.

Centre and North at Jelgava near the Gulf of Riga. Army Group North's two armies were now isolated in a pocket Riga–Lake Pskov–Narva. Second and 3rd Baltic Fronts began slicing off large parts of that pocket on 10 August with massive strikes against Eighteenth Army around Lake Pskov. A counter-attack from the remnant of Third Panzer Army on the boundary between the two army groups reopened a corridor allowing reinforcements to stabilize Eighteenth Army's front. By the end of the month the two Soviet Fronts had gone over to the defensive as the Soviet theatre offensive ran out of steam.

When Army Group North drifted to a halt on 18 July, Army Group North Ukraine from Stanislav north had been violently propelled west by an onslaught of Marshal Konev's 1st Ukrainian Front. Konev had struck on 14 July and broken through in the Rava-russkaya and Lvov sectors. Five days later it had encircled a German corps of six divisions east of Lvov, triggering the army group's retreat. Although First Panzer Army continued to hold Lvov, the remainder of Army Group North Ukraine was stumbling

▼'Black Day' for the Finnish Army. Soviet infantry fighting in the city of Vyborg.

▲Soviet troops of Leningrad Front's 21st Army celebrating the capture of Vyborg.

backwards under a rain of blows delivered by Konev's armies. First Panzer Army's resistance at Lvov caused Marshal Konev to switch his main axis northwards towards Sandomierz on the River Vistula in Poland. By the 28th Lvov was lost too, and First Panzer Army fell back to the Carpathian Mountains. The remainder of Army Group North Ukraine as well as Army Group Centre's surviving elements were being pressed back into Poland except for Third Panzer Army which was now preparing to defend East Prussia against 3rd Belorussian Front. In two days of furious fighting, Chernyakovskiy's armies nearly broke into East Prussia. On 17 August a single Soviet platoon actually fought its way across the border before being wiped out. Not only had the Wehrmacht just been driven out of the borders of the Soviet Union but the Red Army had planted its boot, however briefly, in German soil. It was but the merest foretaste of next year's deluge.

The Red Army was not finished with Army Group North and renewed the offensive on 14 September with the intention of taking Riga. Stiffened German resistance in that direction caused the Soviets to switch their main effort to Memel which in turn weakened the defences of Riga which fell on 13 October. The fighting flickered over the East Prussian border more powerfully than before. Bagramyan's 1st Baltic Front fought its way over the River Niemen and Chernyakovskiy's 3rd Belorussian Front smashed 40 kilometres deep into German territory toward Gumbinnen, site of the first clash between defending Germans and attacking Russians in 1914.

The Soviet armies continued their pursuit of the Germans deep into Poland in the last days of July. Second Belorussian Front reached the Narew down to Roznan. First Belorussian Front, spearheaded by 2nd Tank Army and followed by 8th Guards and 69th Armies, reached the Vistula opposite Warsaw and threw themselves across the river to take bridgeheads at Magnuszew and Pulawy on 27 July. The Red Army made the most of its skill in expanding even the smallest handhold in a bridgehead at Magnuszew where a single company of 79th Rifle Division held on until there were only six men left before being reinforced. On 1st Belorussian Front's left flank, 1st Ukrainian Front's 1st Guards Tank Army had seized

a bridgehead over the Vistula at Sandomierz by the end of July and expanded a salient in the direction of Krakow. Along this line the front finally stabilized. The Red Army had again outrun its supplies and had begun to feel the debility of its own heavy manpower losses after dramatic

victories and advances of 220-450 kilometres in less than six weeks. Those losses could be made good for one last offensive, but the Germans, who had lost more than a million men and had 30 divisions destroyed since June, were now broken beyond all hope.

▲While Leningrad Front attacked across the Karelian Isthmus, Volkhov Front attacked across the River Svir into eastern Karelia forcing its evacuation by the Finns. Here Soviet infantry and T-34/76 tanks ford the Svir near the city of Lodeinoye Polye.

▼The end of a German air ace. The Soviet attack on Army Group Centre quickly achieved

air superiority then air supremacy. The Luftwaffe 6th Air Force supporting Army Group Centre was the weakest on the Eastern Front. Its 775 aircraft included 405 bombers and reconnaissance aircraft and only 275 fighters and ground-attack aircraft. A fuel shortage ensured that barely 40 aircraft could oppose 5,300 Soviet aircraft.

▲ Soviet T-34/76 tanks and infantry attacking in the direction of Minsk.

▼ SU 152 SP artillery – Forward to Minsk! Fortune turned from the Germans at every opportunity. As Fourth Army retreated on Minsk, its retreating columns were stopped by a single Soviet aircraft which destroyed ten metres of the vital bridge over the River Berezina. The next day, 30 June, Soviet tanks and SP artillery took the bridge under fire. They sounded the death knell of the German Fourth Army which was to lose 130,000 of its original 165,000 men.

◀The German Ninth Army was the first to be mortally wounded. By 26 June 1st Belorussian Front was north and south-west of the city of Bobruysk into which thousands of panic-stricken and leaderless German troops had collected. Rokossovsky encircled and crushed the pocket as he headed for Minsk. Here a Soviet soldier strides past one of the countless Germans to die in the battle for Belorussia.

▶'In executing the breakthroughs, the Russians showed an elegance in their tactical conceptions, economy of force, and control that did not fall short of the Germans' own performance in the early war years. They used tightly concentrated infantry and artillery to breach the front on, by their previous standards, narrow sectors. The tanks stayed out of sight until an opening was ready, then went straight through without bothering about their flanks.' Earl F. Ziemke, *Stalingrad to Berlin: The German Defeat in the East.*

◀Soviet machine-gunners supporting an infantry attack during the closing of the Minsk pocket.

▶On 14 July, as the remnant of Army Group Centre retreated in disarray, Marshal Konev's 1st Ukrainian Front attacked Army Group Northern Ukraine to the south. Here Soviet T-34/76 tanks, infantry, 76mm artillery and 57mm anti-tank guns make a crossing of the western River Bug at the jump.

◀Tanks of 35 Guards Tank Brigade, 3rd Guards Mechanized Corps, 5th Guards Tank Army, 3rd Belorussian Front, crossing the River Vilia on the way to Vilnius in Lithuania.

▲◄On 17 July 1944 57,600 German prisoners taken in the destruction of Army Group Centre were paraded through the streets of Moscow with nineteen of their generals at their head. The ferocity of the fighting was shown in the final Soviet count of only 85,000 prisoners and more than 200,000 German.

▲Cemetery of German soldiers in Lithuania after its liberation. The Germans lost more than a million men in the fighting from June until the end of September that saw them driven out of all Soviet territory except for the Courland pocket on the Baltic coast.

◄Destroyed German tanks and transport caught in the Bobruysk pocket in which Ninth Army lost two corps and 70,000 men.

▲Soviet infantry attacking past burning German Panther tanks on the road to Vilnius.

▼Street fighting in Vilnius which the Germans tried to hold as one of the northern end posts of a new defence line. It quickly fell on 8 July.

▶Soviet troops of 16th 'Lithuanian' Rifle Division fighting on home ground.

▼Advanced elements of 5th Guards Tank Army of Army General Chernyakovskiy's 3rd

Belorussian Front crossing the River Niemen east of Kaunus in Lithuania. By 21 July 5th

Guards had several bridgeheads over the Niemen.

◀Soviet infantry attacking into the enemy's homeland atop SU-85 assault guns, September-October 1944. Third Belorussian Front attacked from the east into East Prussia in the direction of Gumbinnen, the site of the first Russian victory over the Germans in the opening days of 1914.

◀Fighting on the East Prussian border. Infantry attempting to negotiate a barbed wire obstacle, September-October 1944.

◀German prisoners captured in the fighting around Riga, early October 1944.

▶A 45mm anti-tank gun crew in action during the battle for Riga in Latvia. Riga was liberated on 13 October 1944 after stubborn resistance. Nine days later the remnant of Army Group North were sealed off in the Courland pocket.

▶Soviet tanks and infantry attacking in the direction of Riga. The 1st, 2nd and 3rd Baltic Fronts thrust towards the Gulf of Riga on 14 September and later to Memel to cut off Army Group North.

▼Reconnaissance unit of 1st Ukrainian Front. These *razvedchiki* (scouts) are dressed in the two-piece camouflage combination over normal field dress. Their exploits became legendary.

▶▼A command group observes a tank-infantry assault on the Lvov main axis of 1st Ukrainian Front's attack on Army Group Northern Ukraine, July 1944.

▲ A platoon commanded by Junior Lieutenant Yuzhakov dismounts from tanks to make the final assault on an objective. The 322nd Rifle Division, 60th Army, distinguished itself in opening a wide breach north of Lvov, known as the Koltov Corridor, through which Konev's tanks and mechanized forces flooded.

▼ Cavalry of 1st Ukrainian Front in action towards Lvov, July 1944. By this stage in the war the Soviets were sending cavalry-mechanized Groups through the gaps in German defences in the exploitation role which they performed admirably. Groups consisted of either a tank or mechanized corps and a cavalry corps. It was just such a mixed unit that sealed off the eight German divisions in the pocket at Brody which yielded 17,000 prisoners and 30,000 dead.

▶ Polish soldiers fighting in the streets of Lublin. First Belorussian Front reached the Vistula on 27 July. Chuikov's 8th Guards Army and 69th Army immediately established bridgeheads south of Warsaw at Magnuszew and Pulawy that would be springboards for latter offensives. At the Magnuszew bridgehead 79th Rifle Division got one company across initially, 50 men commanded by Lieutenant V. T. Burba. Holding on all day under constant counter-attack, they were reduced to six men holding a sliver of river bank until reinforced that evening. In the last counter-attack Lieutenant Burba threw himself with a bundle of grenades under a tank, halting the Germans and saving the bridgehead.

▲Polish soldiers of 1st Polish Army, attached to 1st Belorussian Front, and commanded by Lieutenant-General Berling, fighting on their own soil at last.

▼Soldiers of 1st Polish Army of four divisions, attached to 1st Belorussian Front, commanded by Lieutenant-General Berling, are fighting on their own soil at last – in the direction of Warsaw.

▲Crossing the Vistula. First Belorussian Front would reach the Vistula on 27 July. Chuikov's 8th Guards Army and 69th Army immediately established bridgeheads south of Warsaw at Magnuszew and Pulawy that would be springboards for later offensives. At the Magnuszew bridgehead, the 79th Rifle Division got one company across initially, 50 men commanded by Lieutenant V.T. Burba. Holding on all day under constant counter-attack, they would be reduced to six men holding a sliver of river bank until reinforced that evening. In the last counter-attack, Lieutenant Burba threw himself with a bundle of grenades under a tank, halting the Germans and saving the bridgehead.

▶In an East Prussian border village, the Red Army has already left its mark in a dramatic historical gesture. Painted in antique Cyrillic letters on the Prussian wall are the words of the Medieval Russian hero, Prince and Saint Aleksandr Nevsky, the victor over Swedish invaders on the River Neva and Teutonic Knights in the Battle on the Ice: 'Whosoever shall come to us with the sword shall perish with the sword. Upon this stood and stands the land of Russia.'

Naval infantry of the Red Banner Baltic Fleet make an amphibious assault to clear a German garrison from one of the Moonzund Islands in the Gulf of Finland, September 1944. A joint operation by the fleet and Leningrad Front overcame determined German resistance on the four islands; the first three islands had fallen by 4 October; the fourth required one and half months, falling on 24 November. Capture of the islands gave the Baltic Fleet complete control of the Gulf of Finland and allowed it to support further Soviet ground forces' operations along the Baltic coast.

◀A KV-1 heavy tank supports an infantry attack in East Prussia, September 1944.

◀Soviet tanks and infantry supported by ground-attack aircraft attacking an East Prussian village, 18 October 1944. Senior Sergeant Belov was the first soldier to plant the Red Flag on German soil.

◀Russian infantry attacking across an East Prussian meadow in October 1944, much as their ancestors had done in August 1914. The ending would be different this time.

THE BALKAN CAMPAIGN – 1944

The Red Army's three great summer blows had broken Army Groups North Ukraine, Centre and North, and driven them in headlong flight into central Poland and East Prussia. The entire Eastern Front had been shoved west hundreds of kilometres – except in the far south where Army Group South Ukraine held a line from the Black Sea along the Dniester north to the Carpathian Mountains. On that front the Red Army had bided its time, waiting for the victories in the north to free reserves to strengthen the inevitable attack. The Soviet High Command expected victories at least equal to those already earned that summer. No one expected that their lunge would carry them to Belgrade and Budapest.

The rout of Army Group North Ukraine had pulled Marshal Konev's 1st Ukrainian Front in two directions. The main thrust had been toward Sandomierz and into a salient over the Vistula south of Warsaw. The second had followed the retreat of First Panzer Army south-west

into the Carpathian Mountains and away from the main effort by Konev's and Zhukov's Fronts in Poland. To accommodate this necessary divergence, the Soviet High Command created 4th Ukrainian Front on 30 July under General Ivan Petrov and transferred Konev's 1st Guards and 18th Armies to it as well as 8th Air Army. While 4th Ukrainian Front continued attacking south-west into the foothills of the Carpathians, a far stronger Soviet force was being readied to the south.

Against Army Group South's two German and two Roumanian armies in Roumania were poised Army Generals Malinovskiy's and Tolbukhin's 2nd Ukrainian and 3rd Ukrainian Fronts reinforced to a strength of 929,000 men in 90 divisions and six tank and mechanized corps. The two Fronts, co-ordinated by Marshal Timoshenko as High Command representative, had achieved a superiority of somewhat less than 2:1 in troops, 2:1 in artillery and aircraft, and 3:1 in tanks and SP guns. The German situation was

dangerously fragile. The Soviet winter and spring campaigns had driven the Germans back on to the territory of their increasingly demoralized Roumanian ally. To shore up the Roumanians the army group had alternated German and Roumanian armies along the front.

On 20 August the main attack by Malinovskiy's Front north-west of Iasi kicked off while Tolbukhin began a secondary but still strong effort south of Tiraspol. The artillery preparation for the offensive was unprecedented in its boldness. Colonel-General of Artillery Mitrofan Nedelin (after the war to become the first commander of the Strategic Rocket Forces), 3rd Ukrainian Front's artillery commander, recommended that non-breakthrough sectors be stripped of their artillery to reinforce the main efforts. After much hesitation, Marshal Timoshenko agreed and 73 per cent of the entire Front artillery was allocated to a breakthrough sector 18 kilometres wide, masked by careful use of deception. Under the shock of the artillery prepar-

▶A guards M-13 rocket-launcher brigade fires a salvo by night as 1st Ukrainian Front drives First Panzer Army south-west into the Carpathian Mountains in eastern Czechoslovakia.

ation, several Roumanian divisions fell apart, even before the Soviet infantry attacked.

By late afternoon both Fronts had ripped gaping holes in the German front. Malinovskiy's 6th Tank Army was in the midst of an operational breakthrough against Roumanian Fourth and German Eighth Armies. At the same time Tolbukhin had found a 30-kilometre gap between the German Sixth and Roumanian Third Armies. Caught between the plunging spearheads of the two Fronts was the mass of the ill-fated Sixth Army. As usual, Hitler waited too long to give Sixth Army permission to retreat. When it came, the situation was so far gone that the army staff in the rear was the first element to flee, Soviet tanks being about to overrun the headquarters. By the 26th Tolbukhin's Front closed the bag on Sixth Army. Eighteen German divisions and five corps headquarters were trapped in two large pockets. There would be no escape. Except for its headquarters and service troops, Sixth Army had been crushed as thoroughly as its earlier incarnation at Stalingrad.

With that, the southern half of the German front was gone; the Roumanians had already switched sides and were harassing German service units frantically attempting to escape. Tolbukhin's front rumbled southward toward Bulgaria. Hitler ordered a defensive line to be thrown across the Carpathians and southern Transylvanian Alps. On 30 August Bucharest fell to 2nd Ukrainian Front. Another wing of the front seized the mountain passes which the Germans could not defend in time, their disorganized forces being in full retreat. Army Group South was now threatened from the north where Petrov's 4th Ukrainian Front on 9 September had begun an attempt to break into eastern Czechoslovakia through the Dukla Pass toward Uzhgorod.

The Germans had made good their retreat to the River Muresul by 15 September as Malinovskiy's Front slowed due to over-extended logistics and accumulated mechanical wear on his equipment. Both sides now reinforced their forces. The Soviet High Command wanted to attack from Oradea towards Debrecen in eastern Hungary to link up with 4th Ukrainian Front's attack from Uzhgorod and trap large German and Hungarian forces in the resulting pocket. On 6

October Petrov's Front finally took the Dukla Pass, and Malinovskiy began his attack and drove a cavalry-mechanized group beyond Debrecen. On 10 October the Germans counter-attacked with a panzer division on each wing and snapped off the Soviet spearhead, trapping three corps. Sixth Guards Tank Army violently attacked across the flat Hungarian plain to free the surrounded corps, provoking one of the most free-wheeling, roller-coaster tank battles of the war. By the 12th Soviet strength had prevailed as the Soviet corps broke loose from the German grip. Again the Germans retreated with the Red Army in pursuit. But again the Germans turned and struck back and again encircled three Soviet corps at Nyiregyhaza on 23 October, in much greater strength than at Debrecen. This time their grip was too tight. The trapped corps abandoned their heavy equipment and weapons and escaped on foot six days later.

As Malinovskiy attacked west into Hungary, Tolbukhin's 3rd Ukrainian Front

crossed the Bulgarian border on 8 September. On the same day, the Bulgarian Government declared war on Germany, its ally until a few days before. Bulgaria's defection opened a new front of more than 600 kilometres against the German Southeastern Theatre Command (Army Groups 'F' and 'E') in occupation of Greece and Yugoslavia. The Germans were already evacuating Greece when Tolbukhin's armies began attacking into Serbia. Southeast Theatre Command had a personnel strength of 900,000, a misleading figure. Sixteen of its 31 divisions had been either Bulgarians or foreign collaborators. The fifteen German divisions were mostly second-class troops in what until then had been a partisan-ridden backwater of the war.

On 22 September Tolbukhin crossed the Danube west of Turnu Severin and pushed west to encircle Belgrade from the north while his 57th Army encircled it from the south and Yugoslav partisans from the west. They fought their way into

◄The infantry will always do what trucks cannot and mules will not do. Here men of Petrov's 4th Ukrainian Front haul artillery ammunition over the Carpathian Mountains in pursuit of First Panzer Army, August 1944.

▲The infantry may have to haul ammunition for the gunners, but nobody touches the guns but the gunners. Here a 76mm anti-tank gun crew manhandles their piece through the mountains, 4th Ukrainian Front, September 1944.

▼By early September 4th Ukrainian Front was hammering at the Dukla Pass in eastern Czechoslovakia as 2nd Ukrainian Front was attacking from the south-east through Roumania. The Soviet High Command hoped that they would meet in eastern Hungary to cut off most of Army Group South and First Panzer Army.

◀Cossack guardsmen of 4th Ukrainian Front tend their wounds and sharpen their sabres during a lull in the fighting in the Carpathians, September 1944.

▲Soviet 152mm heavy artillery in a camouflaged battery on the pre-war Soviet-Czechoslovak border.

▼On 20 August Army General Malinovskiy's 2nd Ukrainian Front attacked north of Iasi in the main effort against Army Group South Ukraine in Moldavia. Army General Tolbukhin's 3rd Ukrainian Front at the same time struck a secondary but strong blow south of Tiraspol. Here Soviet infantry dismount for the final assault on a German position in Roumania.

the city on the 14th and overwhelmed the garrison, of whom fewer than 12,000 managed to break out. Southeastern Army Command was in a shambles. Then Tolbukhin turned his armies north into Hungary and left pursuit of the Germans in Yugoslavia to the partisans. The Soviet High Command clearly understood that a front in Yugoslavia led nowhere but into the mountains. The fighting in Hungary led across the Hungarian plains into the Reich itself.

In Hungary Malinovskiy continued to push west against Army Group South (formerly Army Group South Ukraine). By 29 October he had crossed the line of the River Tisza, the last major natural obstacle before Budapest. Malinovskiy was eager to take the city on the jump, to lay a Revolution Day present before Stalin. The 46th Army, reinforced by a mechanized corps, attacked north and on 3 November broke into the outer defences of the city on the eastern bank of the Danube. The garrison of Budapest was too strong and 46th Army not strong enough and short of ammunition to boot. The Soviets withdrew in a few days. The Soviet High Command then directed Malinovskiy to push all his armies except 46th westwards to the north of Budapest. As these armies wheeled across the Danube, 46th seized the southern half of Csepel Island in the Danube across from Budapest.

As Army Group South concentrated against Malinovskiy's thrust north-east of Budapest, Tolbukhin broke out of two bridgeheads across the Danube in south-eastern Hungary on 22 November and headed north. The Hungarian troops in front of him melted away. By 8 December Tolbukhin's 4th Guards and 57th Armies were lunging for the gap between Lake Balaton and Lake Velencze south-west of the city. Malinovskiy's 6th Guards Tank and 7th Guards Armies were also attacking but were deflected north-east of Budapest. Hitler was now desperate to save the Hungarian capital and provided Army Group South with two panzer divisions and three 60-tank Tiger battalions. The Germans decided to deal with the more serious threat Tolbukhin represented, but the ground was too wet and muddy for tanks. They waited. Incredibly, the army group commander was ordered to split his panzer forces and send the armoured infantry and staffs to deal with

Malinovskiy's threat while the panzer units stayed behind to face Tolbukhin and wait for the ground to dry. The author of this order to destroy the combined arms effectiveness of these units was none other than Colonel-General Guderian, father of the *Blitzkrieg*. By the 20th both Soviet Fronts were on the move again. The Germans tanks counter-attacked near Lake Velencze while the Soviet infantry moved past them in the safety of woods and swamps to overrun fuel and ammunition points in the German rear. The German counter-attack was a fiasco.

As Hitler dithered as to whether to defend or evacuate Budapest, Tolbukhin's 4th Guards Army made the decision for him. Two days before Christmas 4th Guards cut the main road and railway leading west out of Budapest. By Christmas Eve it was no longer possible to withdraw troops from Budapest as 4th Guards flowed west of the city. The day after Christmas 4th Guards took Esztergom and closed the ring on Budapest, trapping more than 100,000 German troops in the city. Thus began the siege that would last three terrible months and rival only Stalingrad in its ferocity.

◄Anti-tank gun supporting infantry of 34th Rifle Corps, 46th Army, 3rd Ukrainian Front. These were the men who played a key part in trapping all eighteen divisions of Sixth Army in two large pockets on 26 August.

▼◄Forces of 3rd Ukrainian Front's 46th Army crossing the Dniester Strait in the drive that split German Sixth Army from Roumanian Third Army on the Black Sea flank of Army Group South Ukraine.

▲A Russian veteran of the Brusilov Offensive of 1916 in tsarist dress uniform displaying three St. George Crosses, greets Soviet soldiers in Kishinev, capital of recaptured Soviet Moldavia, formerly Roumanian Bessarabia annexed to the Soviet Union in 1940. The Brusilov Offensive was the only instance in the First World War in which an enemy front had been completely broken and routed.

▼Tolbukhin's 3rd Ukrainian Front passed south through Roumania and crossed into Bulgaria on 8 September 1944; the Bulgarians declared war on their recent German ally the same day. By 22 September he was attacking into Yugoslavia against the German Southeast Army Command (Army Groups 'E' and 'F') which was frantically trying to evacuate Greece. Here T-34/85s roll down a Serbian road in eastern Yugoslavia.

▲Burning German assault guns (Sturmgeschutz III) destroyed by 4th Ukrainian Front on the road to Belgrade.

▼Soviet T-34/76s and T-34/85s attacking with infantry and supported by 76mm anti-tank guns. Tolbukhin's 3rd Ukrainian Front encircled Belgrade from the north and south while Tito's partisans attacked from the west. They all fought their way into the city on 14 October and overwhelmed the garrison by the next day. Fewer than 12,000 Germans escaped.

▶▲In Hungary 46th Army, now under 2nd Ukrainian Front, attacked and penetrated into the fortified German bridgehead protecting the eastern suburbs of Budapest on 3 November. Malinovskiy had hoped to lay the city at the feet of Stalin as a Revolution Day (7 November) present, but the Germans were too strong, and 46th Army too weak and too low on ammunition. Three days later 46th Army was withdrawn from the bridgehead.

▶Soviet machine-gunners in action on the outskirts of Budapest, late December 1944.

▲Tanks and infantry of 1st Belorussian Front attacking in the direction of Warsaw, 14-17 January 1945. Zhukov's reconnaissance in force of 14 January had so unnerved the Germans that they hastily withdrew thinking it was the main attack. He unleashed his armies immediately and overran each German echelon before it could get into action.

▼Infantry attacking on the outskirts of Warsaw, 1st Belorussian Front, 16-17 January 1945. The Polish Army and the Soviet 47th and 61st Armies entered the rubble heap of Warsaw on 17 January after its systematic and barbarous destruction by the Germans.

SMASHING IN THE DOOR TO THE REICH
THE FALL OF WARSAW, BUDAPEST, VIENNA AND PRAGUE

There was no doubt in the mind of the Red Army that 1945 would be the Year of Victory. The Wehrmacht had suffered ever-heavier blows in 1944 and had been finally kicked out of the Russia. The Red Army had pursued the Germans through the Balkans, into Poland and even into the Reich itself in East Prussia. The capitals of eastern Europe and the Reich itself were within its grasp. The Germans had precious little space to trade for time.

By the beginning of the year the Red Army's strength in the field was 6,700,000 equipped with 107,300 artillery pieces and mortars, 2,677 rocket-launchers, 12,100 tanks and self-propelled artillery pieces, and more than 14,700 combat aircraft. Its strength was augmented by 347,000 men of the Polish, Roumanian and Bulgarian Armies. The Poles of 1st and 2nd Polish Armies, attached to 1st Belorussian Front, would give a particularly fine account of themselves. The Germans were still dan-gerous, and the Soviets reckoned their field army in the east numbered 3,700,000.

The Soviet High Command planned to end the war in a 45-day campaign (Vistula–Oder Offensive Operation) by striking straight to Berlin and the River Elbe with the Marshal Georgi K. Zhukov's 1st Belorussian and and Marshal Ivan S. Konev's 1st Ukrainian Fronts in the Vistula–Oder Operation. The German Army Group 'A' opposing them had been badly weakened. Army Group Centre, now hemmed into East Prussia by 2nd and 3rd Belorussian Fronts, was stronger but could not affect the campaign because of its unfavourable position. Nevertheless a powerful simultaneous attack on Army Group Centre (East Prussia Offensive Operation) was also planned. This double offensive was set for 20 January, but Stalin moved it forward to the 12th at Churchill's behest in order to take pressure off the Western Allies still slugging it out in the Ardennes.

The Vistula–Oder Operation began on an icy and foggy morning which deprived the Soviets of air support. First Ukrainian Front had an effective substitute in artillery, massing 420 guns to each kilometre of front. The Front's five armies and two tank armies shattered four corps belonging to Fourth Panzer and Ninth Armies on the first day. Of seven panzer and panzer grenadier divisions, Fourth Panzer Army lost five; the two infantry corps of Ninth Army lost half their strength. By the 13th 1st Ukrainian Front had torn open a 60-kilometre wide path into the German province of Silesia.

Zhukov's 1st Belorussian Front, the theatre main effort, began its attack on 14 January. The Germans mistook his strong reconniassance in force for the main attack and withdrew quickly. Zhukov immediately lept upon them with his full force. The German front shattered as the Soviets began driving one echelon on to the next. On the 15th Zhukov unleashed

▶The commander of 69th Army, Colonel-General Kolpakchi and the Commander of Polish 1st Army, Lieutenant-General Popawski.

his armour, 1st and 2nd Guards Tank Armies which rolled over the weakened German reserves. The German front was gone. By the 17th 1st Ukrainian 1st Belorussian Fronts had swept the Germans from the line of the River Vistula. On that day Polish 1st Army and Soviet 47th and 61st Armies of 1st Belorussian Front liberated the rubble heap of Warsaw. The rage of the Poles at the sight of their ruined capital would only be quenched in the fires of Berlin.

The Soviet High Command then ordered both Fronts to drive directly to the line of the River Oder. The German front was a shambles; Army Groups 'A' and Centre lost contact with each other as the two Soviet Fronts plunged forward in pursuit. Zhukov's Front swept around Poznan while Konev's closed on Breslau, capital of Silesia, in eastern Germany. On 22 January Konev's Front closed on a 200-kilometre stretch of the Oder. By the 31st Zhukov's front had overrun much of West Prussia and also closed on a long stretch of the river to the north and seized bridgeheads at Kuestrin and Frankfurt. In less than three weeks the two Fronts had covered 500 kilometres and had clawed their way into several German provinces. Then, barely 60 kilometres from Berlin,

they stopped. Soviet supplies had run low, and Hitler had cobbled together the new Army Group Vistula in Pomerania which seemed to threaten Zhukov's extended flank. Stalin decided to let Berlin wait. Always anxious about his flanks, he set Konev to clean out the rest of Silesia and sent Zhukov north with Rokossovsky's 2nd Belorussian Front to overrun the rest of West Prussia and eastern Pomerania.

The day after the Vistula–Oder Operation began, a similar blow fell on Army Group Centre. Colonel-General Chernyakovskiy's 3rd Belorussian Front struck at Third Panzer Army in eastern East Prussia; and the next day 2nd Belorussian Front, commanded by Marshal Konstantin K. Rokossovsky, struck north-east from Poznan into Second Army. Army Group Centre's front withstood the attacks and seemed likely to hold. With his famous sense of intuition, Hitler then ordered the transfer of the élite Panzerkorps Grossdeutschland to Army Group 'A' on 14 January. The situation worsened quickly for the Germans. Second Belorussian Front drove a wedge north-westwards until it reached the Baltic coast at Elbing on 23 January. Tanks of 5th Guards Tank Army rode into the unsuspecting town, guns blazing. By next day the Red Army

had a firm grip on the coast, severing East Prussia from the rest of Germany and with it Third Panzer and Fourth Armies. The German Second Army had been pushed west into Eastern Pomerania to be absorbed by the new Army Group Vistula. Third Belorussian Front, now joined by Baltic Front, at the same time was squeezing the Germans trapped in East Prussia back towards Königsberg and the Samland Peninsula. In early February Rokossovsky shifted his attack west into eastern Pomerania aiming at the port cities of Gdynia and Danzig but failed to achieved a breakthrough, breaking off the attack on the 19th. To the east next day the Germans launched a spoiling attack out of the Samland Peninsula, throwing Baltic Front back. The Red Army offensive was spent. Thanks to its poor performance, Baltic Front was abolished and folded into 3rd Belorussian Front which was given a month to prepare to resume the offensive.

As fighting died down in East Prussia, 1st and 2nd Belorussian Fronts attacked into West Prussia and eastern Pomerania at the beginning of March. On 1 March Rokossovskiy's 3rd Guards Tank Corps reached the coast near Koeslin. On 4 March Zhukov's 1st Guards Tank Army isolated Kolberg on the Baltic coast,

▲A Soviet battery of 76.2mm guns on the firing line in the area of Krakow, 1st Ukrainian Front, 19 January 1945. Within a week of the beginning of the Vistula-Oder Campaign on 12 January, Marshal Konev's front had taken the medieval Polish city from Seventeenth Army.

▲T-34/85s on the move west of the Vistula. When Stalin called a halt to the Vistula–Oder Operation on 3 February, the Germans had lost 35 divisions and 147,000 prisoners, and the Red Army had overrun the industrial areas of Silesia and West Prussia to the line of the River Oder.

▶Troops of 1st Ukrainian Front march through the medieval splendour of Krakow, 19 January 1945. In order to preserve the unique beauty of the city, the Red Army attacked without artillery support.

▶Anti-tank gunners of 1st Belorussian Front shelter behind a knocked-out German tank as they help reduce the German garrison of Poznan. In January Zhukov's rush from the Vistula to the Oder swept around Poznan. Hitler ordered it to be held as a fortress, and its garrison of two divisions did not succumb until 23 February.

joining up with 2nd Belorussian Front. Eastern Pomerania, the ports of Gdynia and Danzig, and 2nd Army were isolated. Third Panzer Army barely managed to escape west over the Oder. The two Fronts then collapsed the pocket on the Bay of Danzig, capturing Gdynia on 28 March and Danzig on the 30th, and driving the survivors of Second Army into the Vistula delta. After 13 March 3rd Belorussian Front resumed its attack on East Prussia; by 29 March the survivors of Fourth Army, reduced to 60,000 able-bodied men and 70,000 wounded, had retreated across the Frisches Haff to the Frische Nehrung (long cape).

While Zhukov and Rokossovsky were charging towards the Baltic, Konev turned 1st Ukrainian Front to drive Army Group Centre out of Lower Silesia. Bypassing Breslau, which the Germans had turned into a fortress, 1st Ukrainian Front cleared Lower Silesia to the River Neisse and took bridgeheads by 24 February. From 15 to 31 March Konev turned his attention to Upper Silesia, inflicting 54,000 casulties on First Panzer and Seventeenth Armies. To the south of Konev, 4th Ukrainian Front was fighting across the Carpathians into Czecho-slovakia and protecting 1st Ukrainian Front's southern flank as well as 2nd Ukrainian Front's northern flank in Hungary.

To the south in Hungary, General Rodion I. Malinovksiy's 2nd Ukrainian Front and Colonel-General F. I. Tolbukhin's 3rd Ukrainian Front tightened the siege of Budapest. As at Stalingrad, Hitler refused the garrison permission to break out. Instead he ordered Army Group South to attack and relieve the city. On 18 January IV SS Panzer Corps drove 60 kilometres into 3rd Ukrainian Front's flank, posing such a serious threat that the Red Army was forced to conduct its last full-scale defensive operation of the war. Tolbukhin held, gathered his armour and counter-attacked successfully on the 27th. With relief having failed, the Budapest garrison was doomed. On 11 February the surviving 30,000-man garrison attempted a breakout; fewer than 700 succeeded. The city was declared secured on the 13th.

Obsessed with recovering Hungarian oil refineries that were by now only twisted metal, Hitler attempted yet another offensive in Hungary north of Lake Balaton in

◀West Prussia experiences the tramping boots of the Red Army. Zhukov's infantry armies have just cleared a German pocket out of the town of Schneidemuehl, mid February 1945.

◀A German artillery column destroyed in column on the approaches to the German city of Brieg (now Bzhet), south of Breslau on the River Oder in Lower Silesia.

▶A memorial plate of the visit to Kutuzov's monument by the men of 1st Ukrainian Front. The inscription reads, 'To Field Marshal Mikhail Golenishchev-Kutuzov, the great patriot of the Russian land, on the day of the 132nd anniversary of his death, April 28, 1945. Soviet Soldiers who entered Bunzlau on February 12,1945.'

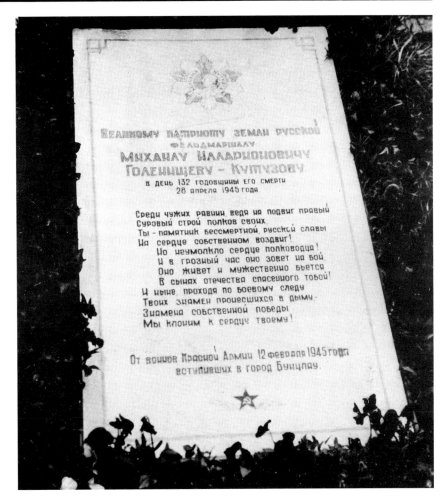

◀First Ukrainian Front, 12 February 1945. Russian soldiers pay their respects at the monument of a national hero – Field Marshal Mikhail Kutuzov (1745-1813), the Commander-in-Chief of the Russian Army that defeated Napoleon and drove him out of Russia. Kutuzov

died during the subsequent Silesian Campaign and was buried on this hill near Bunzlau, Silesia (now Boleslawiec, Poland) on 8 May. He was reburied in St. Petersburg, his heart in a silver vessel, on 25 June 1813.

▼152mm howitzers of 1st Ukrainian Front shelling the German defenders of Breslau in Silesia, encircled by 3rd and 4th Guards Tank Armies, 11 February 1945.

early March. This time he committed his last armoured reserve, Sixth SS Panzer Army, which would have immeasurably strengthened the defence of Berlin. The Soviet High Command observed these preparations, strengthened 2nd and 3rd Ukrainian Fronts and waited for Hitler to dissipate his strength once again. The German attack initially made serious inroads on Tolbukhin's Front, but he was able to counter-attack and hang on. With the Germans committed against Tolbukhin's Front, Malinovskiy to the north launched a counter-offensive (Vienna Offensive Operation) on 16 March, and caught the Germans in a swinging door. Their positions crumbled and by the 25th his breakthrough was complete. German morale was disintegrating; even the SS

appeared to be losing their nerve as the Red Army began its pursuit to Vienna. By the end of the month 2nd and 3rd Ukrainian Fronts were converging on Vienna from the north and south. Vienna was not to be another Budapest or Stalingrad. The starch had gone out of the Germans which even the infamous Otto Skorzeny's execution squads could not restore. The city was declared secure on 13 April. The Red Army had taken 134,000 prisoners and destroyed 32 divisions since the beginning of the Vienna Operation.

The Red Army's final act in the war, following the fall of Berlin, was the Prague Operation. In a great pincer 1st, 2nd and 4th (Army General Yeremenko) Ukrainian Fronts converged to encircle the

remnant of Army Groups Centre and Austria (formerly Army Group South) in western Czechoslovakia. In a short five days (6-11 May 1945) the remnant of the Wehrmacht was gathered up, yielding 860,000 prisoners.

It had indeed been the Year of Victory for the Red Army. All the great capitals of eastern Europe and their lands had been wrested from the Germans – Warsaw, Budapest, Vienna and Prague. More importantly the German Army's back had finally been broken and its outlying ancient eastern provinces occupied. This feat had cost the Red Army more than one million dead, but the toll had brought the war's end within sight. After Vienna and before the postscript of Prague, there remained one last great battle – Berlin.

◀Soviet infantry fighting in the streets of Breslau. Bypassed by 1st Ukrainian Front while it overran Lower and Upper Silesia and then joined in the capture of Berlin, Breslau was a hopeless German outpost in a Red sea. In the end the city held out longer than Berlin, surrendering on 6 May 1945.

▼German soldiers taken prisoner in battles on the outskirts of Sommerfeld (now Lubsko) in Silesia, February 1945.

▶Fourth Ukrainian Front, commanded by Army General Yeremenko, fought through the Carpathian Mountains into Czechoslovakia, maintaining contact between Konev's 1st Ukrainian Front to the north and Malinovskiy's 2nd Ukrainian Front to the south. Here 122mm guns of 4th Ukrainian Front support operations in the Carpathians, February 1945.

▶After the initial East Prussia Offensive had exhausted itself on 19 February, 2nd Belorussian Front was redirected to resume offensive operations farther west to overrun West Prussia and eastern Pomerania. On an icy West Prussian road submachine-gunners on a T-34/85 wend their way through the wreckage of yet another German forlorn hope – a Jagdpanzer IV, normally assigned to the anti-tank battalion of a panzer division on the left and a Mk IV on the right.

▼A 76.2mm gun crew commanded by Junior Sergeant T. Ponomarenko fires at German warships in the Bay of Stettin, early March 1945. On 1 March 3rd Guards Tank Corps, 2nd Belorussian Front reached the Baltic coast near Koeslin. On 4 March 1st Guards Tank Army reached the coast 20 kilometres to the west near Kolberg. Progaganda Minister Goebbels had just completed a film entitled *Kolberg* which dealt with the siege and epic defence of Koeslin during the Napoleonic Wars. The film had not been even fully premiered when the garrison, which had held out until 18 March, slipped away by destroyer after covering the evacuation of 80,000 civilians.

◄Danzig was taken by 2nd Belorussian Front two days after Gdynia on 30 March 1945. In a bizarre tableau that only war can produce, a Soviet SU-122 sits between an overturned van and a crashed locomotive. It must have been some fight.

◄With the fall of Danzig on 30 March 1945, the remnant of Second Army fled into the delta marshes of the Vistula. Some of the prisoners are seen here marching east.

►The opening bombardment by 2nd Belorussian Front on the Vistula in the East Prussian Offensive Operation, 13 January 1945. These 1931/37 Model A-19 122mm guns are giving their attention to Second Army, Army Group Centre, defending the southern approaches to East Prussia.

►Infantry of 48th Army, 3rd Belorussian Front, attacking an East Prussian town, February 1945. By 20 February the German Fourth Army had been pressed into a 50 by 22 kilometre beachhead around Heilegenbeil. The Soviet Front commander, Colonel-General Chernyakovskiy, was killed in the fighting and replaced by 2nd Belorussian Front Commander, Colonel-General Vasilevsky.

◄The East Prussian Campaign began on 13 January with the attack of 2nd and 3rd Belorussian Fronts commanded by Marshal Vasilevskiy and Army General Chernyakovskiy. The Soviet High Command concentrated in these two fronts 1,670,000 men, 25,426 guns and mortars, 3,859 tanks, and 3,097 combat aircraft. Here a Soviet military policeman regulates military traffic into 'Vostochnaya Prussiya' – East Prussia, 3rd Belorussian Front, January 1945.

▲Soviet transport drives past another overrun German defensive point and a Jagdpanzer IV that died trying to hold off the Red Army's steamroller somewhere in East Prussia, March 1945.

▼A column of heavy JSU-152mm self-propelled guns drives through the sandy pinewoods on the outskirts of Königsberg to fire upon the fortifications of the city, 3rd Belorussian Front, March 1945.

▲Il-2 ground-attack aircraft, nicknamed 'Black Death' by the Germans, on their way to deliver another strike on Königsberg, 6 April 1945, the day the final assault on the city began. On 9 April, after massive artillery and airstrikes by 1,500 aircraft, 11th Guards Army fought its way in and forced the surrender of the garrison.

▼T-34/85s and infantry on the march towards Königsberg, 3rd Belorussian Front, April 1945.

◀Infantry of 3rd Belorussian Front race beside the sea canal in Königsberg during the fighting that finally reduced the city between 6 and 9 April 1945.

◀The end! German equipment abandoned on the coast of the Frisches Haff near Königsberg as 3rd Belorussian Front constricted Army Group North into smaller and smaller pockets with their backs to the sea, spring 1945.

▼Gun cupola of Königsberg's fortifications, smashed by Soviet artillery. Fortifications in East Prussia had been built between the wars as a defence against Poland and had been stripped to equip fortifications facing the British and Americans on the Western Front.

▲German prisoners taken in Königsberg by 3rd Belorussian Front, spring 1945. The mighty Wehrmacht had burned itself out. Many of the prisoners were now over-aged Volkssturm or under-aged Hitler Jugend as can be seen in this photograph.

▶'Für Uns' – You died 'For Us' is the message of grief from a First World War monument in the ruins of Königsberg, April 1945.

◀Another collection of Jagdpanzers Mk IV that failed to stop 3rd Belorussian Front's attack down a Königsberg street, April 1945.

◀The debris of German might – abandoned equipment in the last pocket to surrender in East Prussia, Samland, May 1945.

◀The carcass of that dreadnought of tanks, the King Tiger, litters a beach on the Frisches Haff with other abandoned equipment, April 1945.

▶Lieutenant A. Samorokov's submachine-gunners of 104th Rifle Division, 9th Guards Army, 3rd Ukrainian Front, attacking a Hungarian village on the outskirts of Budapest, January 1945.

◀Soviet troops of the Samland Group (formerly Baltic Front) attached to 3rd Belorussian Front and commanded by Army General I. Kh. Bagramyan, attack to reduce the last German pocket in East Prussia – on the Samland peninsula, north of Königsberg, 13-25 April 1945. The entire front, consisting of five armies, crushed the 65,000 German defenders of Abteilung Samland, formerly Third Panzer Army, in twelve days. This concluded the East Prussian Offensive Operation begun on 13 January.

▶Hitler once again frittered away his increasingly scarce reserves by sending Sixth SS Panzer Army into another attack against Tobulkhin's 3rd Ukrainian Front at the end of March. Once Tobulkhin had held them, Malinovksiy's neighbouring 2nd Ukrainian Front launched a major counter-offensive which unhinged the entire German position in Hungary. Here the 'Katyushas' of 2nd Ukrainian Front support the counter-offensive.

◄A Soviet anti-aircraft gun and crew positioned in a Budapest square to fend off relief operations of the Luftwaffe, 2nd Ukrainian Front, February 1945.

►The savagery of the fighting in Budapest turned the city into another Stalingrad. As at Stalingrad, Hitler refused to allow the garrison to break out. Here infantry of 2nd Ukrainian Front move under cover of trolley-buses during the last day, 13 February 1945.

►Hitler had not entirely forgotten the doomed German garrison of Budapest. The Luftwaffe was able to drop a canister containing hundreds of Iron Crosses into the city. It missed its drop zone and fell into Soviet hands, providing a nice addition to the Red Army's souvenirs.

◄Volleys of BM-13 Katyusha rockets from 3rd Ukrainian Front saturate German and Hungarian strongpoints in Budapest, February 1945.

►Infantry and tanks of 2nd Ukrainian Front during the last day of the street fighting in the terrible battle for Budapest, 13 February 1945. The surviving 30,000 men of the garrison attempted a breakout on the 11th – barely 700 reached to German lines. The city was secured two days later.

◀Riflemen and submachine-gunners of Lieutenant V. Serov's platoon fighing in a Hungarian village in 2nd Ukrainian Front's March counter-offensive.

▶Motorized infantry and tankers of 6th Tank Army, 3rd Ukrainian Front, attacking towards Szekesfehervar north of Lake Balaton in the counter-offensive that would drive the Germans out of Hungary, 20 March 1945.

◄The victors in the siege of Budapest:- Marshal of the Soviet Union Rodion Malinovsky, 2nd Ukrainian Front Commander; Major-General K. A. Zykov, Chief of the Political Department; Lieutenant-General Alexander Tevchenkov, member of the Front Military Council. Hungary, April 1945.

►Red Army gunners with a 122mm howitzer supporting the advance into Vienna, 2nd Ukrainian Front, 8 April 1945.

◄On 30 March 1945 6th Guards Tank Army of 3rd Ukrainian Front, crossed the Austrian border and headed past Wiener Neustadt towards Vienna. Here a Soviet military policeman salutes the Red Banner passing the Austrian border on an SU-76 self-propelled 76mm gun. Notice the underditching log on the side of the vehicle.

►Infantrymen of 2nd Ukrainian Front attacking down a Viennese street supported by a US Lend-Lease M3A1 Scout Car. A total of 3,340 M3A1s were used by the Red Army as scout vehicles, command cars and radio vehicles.

◄Infantry of 2nd Ukrainian Front marching over the Swastika and through a burning Austrian village in the direction of Vienna.

◀Submachine-gunners of 2nd Ukrainian Front have broken through to the Danube Canal in the battle for Vienna, April 1945.

◀▲ The Soviet forces attacking Vienna were heavily equipped with US Lend-Lease M4A2 Sherman tanks as seen here equipped with the improved L/55 76mm gun, 2nd Ukrainian Front, April 1945.

◀An infantry unit of 9th Guards Mechanized Corps, 2nd Ukrainian Front, in the fighting for Vienna, April 1945.

▶Soviet infantry advance down a battered Viennese street. Note the neglible amount of equipment other than their individual weapons carried by these soldiers.

▲Red Army infantry attacking the approaches to the Imperial Bridge over the River Danube during the fighting for Vienna, April 1945.

▼The Red Army was not manned entirely by Russians – it drew its troops from all nationalities. Here a Mongol Buryat or Kalmuk soldier from as far away as Lake Baykal or the Caspian Sea attacks armed with a PPsh 1941 submachine-gun, Vienna, April 1945.

▶The Soviet Navy's Danube Flotilla played an important part in the seizure of Vienna. Here naval infantry armed with PPsh 1941 submachine-guns assault across a Danube bridge.

▼Submachine-gunners and T-34/85 tanks of 2nd Ukrainian Front speed through the Austrian town of St. Poelten 30 kilometres west of Vienna to overrun eastern Austria.

◀With the fall of Berlin, Marshal Konev could turn his 1st Ukrainian Front on some unfinished business – the reduction of Breslau, the Silesian fortress city he had had to bypass in February. A T-34/76 supporting the attack into Breslau, 1st Ukrainian Front, 6 May 1945.

▶Soviet gunners take post during the reduction of Breslau, 1st Ukrainian Front, 6 May 1945.

▼Gunners armed with the 14.5mm Simonov self-loading anti-tank gun attempting to suppress strongpoints in Breslau, 1st Ukrainian Front, 6 May 1945.

▼A scene played out in dozens of east German towns and cities in East Prussia, West Prussia, Pommerania, Saxony, Brandenberg, and Silesia – Soviet infantry of 1st Ukrainian Front street fighting in Breslau.

▲Decorated for valour in the reduction of Breslau. From right to left: Heroes of the Soviet Union Senior Sergeant I. Gavrish, Sergeant-Major N. Logoinov and Senior Sergeant I. Kuznetzov, 1st Ukrainian Front, May 1945.

▼A 1st Ukrainian Front unit commanded by Major A. Zhiba drag machine-guns and a 76.2mm gun into position for an attack behind a smoke-screen during the Prague Operation, May 1945.

▶In what must have seemed almost like a holiday after the fighting around Berlin, tanks of 1st Ukrainian Front speed into the approaches of Prague as German resistance collapses, May 1945.

▶Receiving the thanks of the city and the title of Honoured Citizens of Prague are (centre) Marshal of the Soviet Union and Commander, 1st Ukrainian Front, Ivan Konev; (third from right) Army General (Later Marshal of the Soviet Union) and Commander, 4th Ukrainian Front, Alexander Yeremenko; and (fourth from right) General Rybalko, Commander, 3rd Guards Tank Army.

▶Parade of Czech 1st Army Corps which fought as part of 1st Ukrainian Front and was commanded by General Ludvic Svoboda (later President of Czechoslovakia), Prague May 1945.

◀The end of the Thousand Year Reich – one of the 480,000 German prisoners taken in the Berlin Operation. The instrument of surrender would deliver into the Red Army's hands a further 1,250,000 Germans fighting from Yugoslavia to East Prussia.

▶In the Kuestrin bridgehead on the west bank of the River Oder, at the command post of 8th Guards Army, 1st Belorussian Front, hours before the final offensive, 16 April 1945. This army that had shielded Stalingrad so well would form the tip of the spear Zhukov was aiming at Berlin. First Belorussian Front was the mightiest of the three Fronts in the Berlin Operation with 77 divisions, 3,155 tanks, 14,628 guns and mortars, and 1,531 rocket-launchers. Left to right: Colonel-General Vasily Chuikov, 8th Guards' scrappy little Commander; General-Lieutenant Konstantin Telegin, member of 1st Belorussian Front's Military Council; General-Lieutenant of Artillery Vasily Kzakov, Commander of the Front Artillery.

THE FALL OF THE REICH
THE LAST BATTLE – BERLIN

Since late January Zhukov's 1st Belorussian Front had marked time on the River Oder. Berlin had beckoned, a bare 60 kilometres away, a distance essentially empty of defences. But Stalin flinched from the risk. Instead, he ordered the systematic reduction of German territories east of the Oder – East Prussia, Pomerania and Silesia. By the end of March he was ready, especially since the Western Allies were advancing rapidly eastwards and, as he believed, might have their own designs on Berlin.

There followed a rapid, even hasty, redeployment of forces under Zhukov's direction. First Belorussian Front narrowed its front, turning over the line from the Baltic Sea to Schwedt to Rokossovsky's 2nd Belorussian Front which had been giving its full attention to the reduction of resistance in the Danzig area; turning that mission over to a single army, Rokossovskiy's Front made a rapid about turn and closed on the lower Oder. Konev's 1st Ukrainian Front shifted its

striking forces from the left and centre to its right on the River Neisse, on the left flank of 1st Belorussian Front. These three Fronts combined for this one great effort 2,500,000 men, 6,250 tanks, 7,500 aircraft, 41,600 guns and mortars, and 95,383 motor vehicles. First and Second Belorussian Fronts alone had 110 rifle divisions, eleven tank and mechanized corps, and eleven artillery divisions. The opposing German Ninth and Third Panzer Armies had barely 25 divisions. The ratio of tanks was 5.5:1 (4,106 to 754); the ratio of artillery was overwhelming; Ninth Army had barely 344 pieces while Third Panzer Army had almost none – anti-aircraft artillery from the defences of Berlin was pressed into service as replacement. The German units were increasingly hollow having suffered irreplaceable personnel and equipment losses. Hitler further compounded these weaknesses by transferring half of Army Group Vistula's armoured strength to defend Prague and Vienna. Nevertheless, the Germans had

made good use of the two months' breathing-space Stalin had granted them to build up the forward defences of Berlin in a continuous system to the River Oder and scrape up every available man and piece of equipment. Every town, village and farmstead had been turned into strongpoint. He had also shut down all the Army's schools and training centres and committed their irreplaceable cadre to combat. What could have been almost a *coup de main* for the Russians in January would be a bloodbath in April.

Zhukov was made responsible for co-ordinating the entire plan and turned over much responsibility for 1st Belorussian Front to his deputy, Army General V. D. Sokolovskiy, in early April. That Front would make the main attack out of its bridgehead over the Oder at Kuestrin bridgehead with five armies. They would then veer north to form the great northern pincer of the encirclement of Berlin. Second Belorussian Front would cover the advance of Sokolovskiy's Front and

force Third Panzer Army against the Baltic coast. First Ukrainian Front would form the southern pincer of the encirclement but would also drive to meet the Americans approaching the River Elbe to the west. Stalin purposely left the Front boundaries in the final approaches to Berlin unmarked. He had ·cleverly manipulated both Zhukov and Konev, holding the great prize of Berlin before each, to entice them into the utmost effort.

Before dawn on 16 April the guns of First Belorussian and First Ukrainian Fronts began the operation with a massive bombardment of First World War proportions, followed by the tanks and infantry. On the first day 1st Belorussian Front alone expended 1,236,000 shells (2,450 railway wagons of ammunition or 100,000 tons of metal), in addition to 6,550 air sorties. Konev, who had the easier going, made immediate progress and pressed northwards. Zhukov, who remained with First Belorussian Front, had a much tougher nut to crack. He had packed Chuikov's 8th Guards Army (of Stalingrad fame) followed by Katukov's 1st Guards Tank Army into the spearhead that would break out of the bridgehead. Their advance sliced through the first layers of the defences but was then blocked by the Seelow Heights to which the Germans clung desperately and to which Hitler had committed a good part of the garrison of Berlin. Stalin was worried that Zhukov was not moving fast enough and decided to engage his other pincer by ordering Konev to turn his 3rd and 4th Tank Armies north for Berlin. This spurred Zhukov to action and he burst through the Seelow Heights early on the 18th.

It took two more days of hard fighting for 1st Belorussian Front to reach the outskirts of Berlin, each kilometre being contested by the Germans, but the going was easier than had been the fight for the Seelow Heights. Hitler had gambled too much of his strength on that position and lost. Zhukov now won the race with Konev when the artillery of 79th Rifle Corps, 3rd Shock Army, opened fire on the outskirts of Berlin at 1350 on 20 April, appropriately on Hitler's birthday. The next day 2nd Guards Tank Army, 3rd Shock Army and 47th Army hammered their way into the city. To the south, 1st Ukrainian Front was clawing its way north with its two tank armies in the lead, overruning the German Army's major ammunition dump on 20

▲A tank regiment of T-34/85 tanks and SU-100 assault guns advancing to the front, 1st Tank Army, 1st Belorussian Front, April 1945. Zhukov initially committed 1st Tank Army to a supporting role behind 8th Guards Army in the attack on the Seelow Heights, but resistance was so strong that he committed the tank army on the second day and burst through on the third. In the attack on Berlin 1st and 2nd Belorussian Fronts had a ratio of 5.5:1 over the Germans in tanks such as these tough T-34s and assault gun variants.

▲Veteran transport – these camels drew wagons from Stalingrad to Berlin. Despite the use of almost 100,000 motor vehicles, old-fashioned methods still were necessary.

◀As if the overwhelming Soviet advantage in tanks were not bad enough for the Germans, here a Soviet 76.2mm anti-tank gun fires point-blank at the few surviving German tanks left in front of Berlin. On 1st Belorussian Front's main attack sector there were 270 guns (76.2mm or higher) for each kilometre of front.

▲Infantry riding atop SU-76 self-propelled 76.2mm guns through a burning German city, 1st Belorussian Front, April 1945.

◄A burning Tiger II tank on the approaches to Berlin in the area of 1st Belorussian Front, April 1945. Hitler had taken personal command of the defence of Berlin and promptly sent half the tank strength of Army Group Vistula off on a wild-goose chase to protect Prague and Vienna. He then committed the core of the Berlin garrison to the defence of the Seelow Heights which barred the way of 1st Belorussian Front.

◄Hitler had packed too much of his available forces into the defence of the Seelow Heights. When that position fell, the drive to Berlin quickened, but the Red Army had to storm every farmstead and village between the Oder and Berlin, all of which had been configured for all-round defence. The Germans were no longer the élite forces of 1941-3, but they fought with a terrible desperation.

▼A IS-2 (Joseph Stalin) heavy tank with infantry of Colonel-General Rybalko's 3rd Tank Army, 1st Ukrainian Front, approaching Berlin from the south-east.

▼Engineers of 2nd Belorussian Front bridging the Oder during the river crossing of 20 April 1945. The Front crossed under cover of a smoke-screen along a 16-kilometre stretch from Schwedt to Stettin.

April. Second Belorussian Front had begun the attack four days after the other Fronts because of the need to redeploy from the Danzig area in short order, but quickly seized a 10-mile-long bridgehead over the Oder north of Stettin. South-east of Berlin the eastern encirclement was completed at Bohnsdorf which also isolated Ninth Army from the city's defence.

The garrison of Berlin now numbered barely 200,000 men consisting of LVI Panzer Corps, Volkssturm, SS and Hitler Youth formations. In any case the defences of the city which under rational control would have been formidable were still being determined by a madman in his bunker, manoeuvring forces which either did not exist or were fighting for their lives. The Germans within Berlin would fight bitterly but without effective or intelligent control except on the tactical level. On 25 April the encirclement of Berlin to the west was completed when 2nd Guards Tank Army of 1st Belorussian Front met 4th Guards Tank Army of 1st Ukrainian Front west of Berlin between Nauen and Potsdam. That same day Konev's 5th Guards Army met US First Army forces at Torgau on the Elbe, and 2nd Belorussian Front broke out of its

bridgehead and headed west. By 27 April Third Panzer Army had largely collapsed as an organized fighting force. Second Belorussian Front was pursuing the surviving 100,000 men as they fled westwards to the safety of Anglo-American captivity. The Germans were to have one final albeit small success as the war crashed down around them. XXX Corps, made up of the three youth divisions (Clausewitz, Scharnhorst and Theodor Kroener) of officer cadets, made the last attack of the German Army in the old style. They attacked 1st Ukrainian Front on 29 April in an effort to relieve Berlin and penetrated 30 kilometres to the south-west of Potsdam, but they had shot their bolt. Over-extended and unsupported, they were quickly withdrawn to join the great retreat westwards.

The situation within Berlin itself was telescoping rapidly to a conclusion. Eight Soviet armies had begun attacking through the city's S-Bahn defensive ring on the 26th and within two days had compressed the defenders into a pocket 9.5 miles long and 1 to 3 miles wide. Crushed between 1st Belorussian and 1st Ukrainian Fronts, the defenders were putting up a deadly, last-ditch struggle that would cost the Red Army 800 tanks.

But Berlin was no Stalingrad. Germany had been sucked dry – there were no reinforcements to be fed into the battle to keep hope alive. Still, the Germans, that odd mix of SS and amateur Volkssturm and Hitler Youth fought until they died. The Soviet assaults converged on the city's centre that held its great public buildings including the city hall and the Reichstag. On 29 April 266th 'Artemovsk' Rifle Division, 5th Shock Army fought its way to the city hall. Checked in the street by intense anti-tank fire, they blew open the sides of the building with dynamite and cleared it floor by floor. At the same time 150th 'Idritsk' and 171st Rifle Divisions, 79th Rifle Corps, 3rd Shock Army were fighting their way closer to the charred ruins of the Reichstag. Finally, on 30 April, elements of both divisions made a final assault at 14.25 which broke into the building and secured the lower floors in hand-to-hand combat. As the Red Army and the SS hacked and stabbed at each other, the author of this war, Adolf Hitler, blew his brains out deep in his bunker. The fight for the upper floors went on into the night until Sergeant M. A. Yegorov and Junior Sergeant M. V. Kantaria reached the Reichstag cupola

and unfurled the Soviet flag at 21.58. A few minutes later 3rd Shock Army Commander V. I. Kuznetzov called Zhukov to announce, 'Our Red Banner in on the Reichstag!'

The surviving German military authority in Berlin, LVI Panzer Corps Commander, General Weidling, ordered all resistance to cease at 11.30 on 2 May. In the Battle for Berlin, the Red Army had taken 480,000 prisoners, 134,000 from the garrison of Berlin, and itself had suffered more than 300,000 casualties. When the final surrender came on 9 May a further 1,250,000 troops fighting from Yugoslavia to East Prussia would march into captivity. The war against the Germans had ended.

▶The heroes of Stalingrad, the men of 8th Guards Army, fighting in Berlin under a poster addressed to them: 'Stalingraders, forward! Victory is near!'

▼The Soviets had unquestioned air superiority in the Berlin Operation. The once proud Luftwaffe had been devoured in the skies over Germany and the Eastern Front. Now it was reduced to furtive and desperate flights. The rest was wreckage or useless for lack of fuel, pilots and parts. Irreparable twin-engined

bombers abandoned on an airfield in the environs of Berlin, late April 1945.

▶House-to-house fighting in Berlin, the realm of the flame-thrower and the submachine-gunner. Here the flame-thrower team includes a submachine-gunner in body armour.

▶▼A column of German prisoners being marched to the rear as Soviet T-34/85 tanks speed to the fighting in Berlin. From the faces of the middle-aged POWs can be seen the decline in the quality of the Wehrmacht.

SOVIET OPERATIONAL NORMS (12 January – 8 May 1945)

Forces on Front Breakthrough

Sectors	%of Total
Combined arms large strategic formations:	75.0
Tank and mechanized large strategic formations:	90.0
Artillery and main air forces:	75–90.0

Operational Densities on Breakthrough Sectors Per Kilometre

(Vistula-Oder Offensive Operation)

Tanks and SP Artillery:	80–115
Artillery and Mortars:	230–250
Engineer Companies:	13–17

Force Ratios on the Warsaw-Berlin Axis

Personnel:	4:1
Tanks:	5.5:1
Artillery:	6:1
Aircraft:	8:1

◀One of the last to die. Red Army infantry charge past a fallen German in the last few days of fighting in early May 1945.

◀Remember Warsaw! Revenge for six years of horror – infantry of Polish 1st Army attached to 1st Belorussian Front took part in the capture of Berlin.

▶Sited in the archway of Heinrich Himmler's house, this 76.2mm anti-tank gun fires point-blank at the Reichstag, 29 April 1945. The 79th Rifle Corps of 3rd Shock Army had fought its way to the area around the Reichstag, the symbolic centre of Berlin. The building, still a charred husk from its burning in 1933, had a large and determined SS garrison.

Note: In the Vistule-Oder Offensive Operation, advance rates reached 1.2–2.5 km/hr or up to 20 km per day.

Source: Colonel V.N. Shevchenko, 'Military Art of Soviet Forces in Operations in Europe in 1945', *Voyennaya mysl*, No. 4, April 1990.

SOVIET CONCENTRATION OF FORCES (Vistula-Oder Offensive Operation – 1945)

1st Belorussian and 1st Ukrainian Fronts

4 Tank Armies
5 Separate Tank Corps
1 Separate Mechanized Corps
(Total: 16 Tank and Mechanized Corps)
6 Separate Tank Brigades
23 Separate Tank Regiments
2 Separate SP Artillery Brigades
41 Separate SP Artillery Regiments
32 Separate SP Artillery Battalions

Tanks and SP Artillery numbered over 7,000. Of that 68% were in tank armies and separate corps and were intended for exploiting success. The remaining 32% were in separate brigades and regiments as part of combined arms armies and were employed for infantry close support. Tank armies' rates of advance were 20–40 km daily average and from 50–60 km to 100 km per day for the maximum rate. Forward detachments played a vital role in maintaining these rates. For that reason they were usually replaced every 50–60 km.

Source: Colonel V.N. Shevchenko, 'Military Art of Soviet Forces in Operations in Europe in 1945', *Voyennaya mysl*, No. 4, April 1990.

SOVIET LOSSES IN THE FINAL PERIOD OF WAR (12 January – 8 May 1945)

Personnel (dead):	1,000,000
Tanks and SP Arty: -	12,500
Artillery and Mortars:	11,550
Aircraft:	11,800

Source: Colonel V.N. Shevchenko, 'Military Art of Soviet Forces in Operations in Europe in 1945', *Voyennaya mysl*, No. 4 April 1990. Other sources list 1,085,000 dead.

▲A T-34/85 attacks quickly down a Berlin street, early May 1945. In the reduction of the German pocket in central Berlin, the Red Army lost 800 tanks.

▼The mighty Russian war cry, 'Ura!' indicates the surrender of Berlin on 2 May 1945, around the Victory Column that marked the German victory in the Franco-Prussian War in 1871.

▶In the enemy's fallen capital, these Red Army officers can now be tourists. Here one of them is photographing the bronze plate on the Chancellery, May 1945.

▼In the shadow of a faded victory, citizens of Berlin clear the the wreckage of war from their streets. The Victory Column commemorating the Prussian victory over France in 1871 is in the background. So heavy had been the manpower drain of the war on Berlin that of its remaining population at the time of the battle, barely 500,000 of the 2,500,000 citizens were males. Despite the horrors of the battle, the citizens of Berlin suffered a far kinder fate than that planned by Hitler for the Muskovites.

▲Men and women of the Red Army – trying to capture that indestructible bond of shared deeds and memories in a photograph, Berlin, May 1945.

◄Marshal of the Soviet Union Georgi K. Zhukov, Deputy Commander-in-Chief of the Armed Forces of the USSR, signing the instrument of Germany's unconditional surrender in Karlhorst, Berlin, at the German Army's military engineering school, at midnight on 8 May 1945. This was a repeat performance of the surrender the day before to the Western Allies in Rheims, France. Stalin insisted on another ceremony, a justifiable demand in light of the achievements and sacrifices of the Red Army. This day – 9 May – would become the official Soviet Victory Day.

◄On behalf of the German High Command, Field Marshal Wilhelm Keitel, Chief of the General Staff, signs the instrument of unconditional surrender. Nothing could have shown more clearly the depths to which the once proud German Army had sunk than its utter defeat being ratified by a man such as Keitel. Distinguished only in his slavish devotion to Hitler, Keitel was held in comtempt by his peers who called him 'Lakeitel' a play on the German word for lackey. This heir to von Moltke, von Schlieffen and von Hindenburg was hanged for war crimes in Nuremberg Prison on 16 October 1946.

◄After the victory the Supreme Commanders of the Allied Forces, posed for this picture in Berlin, June 1945. From left to right: Field Marshal Bernard Montgomery, General Dwight Eisenhower, Marshal of the Soviet Union Georgi K. Zhukov, General Jean de Lattre de Tassigny. Both Montgomery and Eisenhower were award the highest Soviet military order, the Order of Victory.

▶General Dwight D. Eisenhower, Commander-in-Chief of Allied Forces in Western Europe, awards Army General (later Marshal of the Soviet Union) Vasili Sokolovskiy, Deputy Commander of 1st Belorussian Front, an American military order on behalf of the President of the United States, Germany, June 1945. Marshal Zhukov had left much of the actual operation of his 1st Belorussian Front to Sokolovskiy, because he was co-ordinating the operations of all three Fronts in the Berlin Operation. Sokolovskiy later became one of the most respected military theorists in the Soviet Armed Forces. His book, *Soviet Military Strategy* (1961), became the foundation for Soviet nuclear war-fighting strategy.

▼Victory Day – 9 May 1945! Moscow salutes its heroes and the end of the war that had lasted 1,418 terrible days for the Soviet Union. The instruments of surrender were signed in Berlin on 9 May 1945.

◄▲ The first trainload of demobilized Red Army men and women departs Berlin, proudly festooned with laurels and proclaiming 'We are from Berlin!'

◄◄ Taking her time out. At last there was hope for a normal life.

◄A fortunate child whose father has come home. In countless families, the father's chair at the head of the table would be for ever empty. The Soviet Armed Forces suffered 8,668,400 dead and another 20,000,000 wounded and sick in this most terrible of all wars.

▲They returned home by the millions, here luckily to an intact home and living parents. Too many of them found only ruins and graves.

▼Commander of the vast Soviet Victory Parade on Red Square, Marshal of the Soviet Union Konstantin K. Rokossovsky, Moscow, 24 June 1945.

◀The idol of the Russian people and the Red Army, Marshal of the Soviet Union Georgi K. Zhukov, rides a splendid white stallion, as he reviews the Victory Parade. It was to Zhukov that the cheers and shouts of 'Saviour' were directed as he rode through the streets of Moscow. They placed him in the pantheon of Russian heroes next to Alexander Nevskiy and Alexander Suvorov which earned him the undying emnity of the man watching from atop Lenin's Tomb – Stalin.

▼The BM-13 Multiple Rocket-Launcher – the legendary 'Katyusha' rumbling by in a well-earned place in the Victory Parade.

◄To the accompaniment of 200 military drummers, 200 Soviet soldiers fling banners of the defeated Wehrmacht and Hitler's own personal standard at the granite foot of Lenin's Tomb. The Romans would have loved it!

◄The splendid three. Marshal of the Soviet Union Georgi K. Zhukov flanked by the two top air aces of the Red Army: Left – Three Times Hero of the Soviet Union, Colonel (and later Marshal of Aviation) Alexander Pokryshkin with 59 kills in 156 air battles; right – Major (and later Marshal of Aviation) Ivan Kozhedub with 62 kills (including one jet) in 120 air battles.

▼The *éminence grise* of Soviet victory – Dmitry Ustinov, USSR People's Commissar for Armaments, future Marshal of the Soviet Union and USSR Defence Minister (first row left). Ustinov was responsible for the massive outpouring of war *matériel*. Here he poses with some of the military and civilian personnel of the artillery production effort.

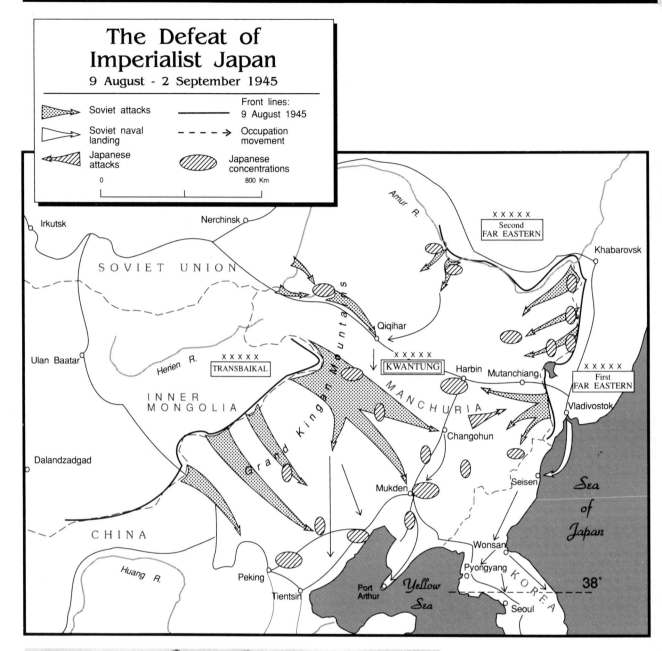

The Defeat of Imperialist Japan
9 August - 2 September 1945

Soviet attacks

Soviet naval landing

Japanese attacks

Front lines: 9 August 1945

Occupation movement

Japanese concentrations

0 — 800 Km

Irkutsk · Nerchinsk · Khabarovsk · Amur R. · Second FAR EASTERN · SOVIET UNION · Qiqihar · KWANTUNG · Harbin · Mutanchiang · First FAR EASTERN · Ulan Baatar · Herien R. · TRANSBAIKAL · MANCHURIA · Vladivostok · INNER MONGOLIA · Grand Kingan Mountains · Changohun · Seisen · Sea of Japan · Dalandzadgad · Mukden · CHINA · Wonsan · Huang R. · Peking · Pyongyang · KOREA · 38° · Tientsin · Port Arthur · Yellow Sea · Seoul

◄The Red Army not only planned thoroughly for the logistics support of the operation but imaginatively and flexibly as well. Where necessary, fuel was delivered by air to deployed forces as shown here on the Transbaykal Front, July 1945. This technique was used later during the fighting to supply 6th Guards Tank Army which had outrun its wheeled supply trains. Every expedient was used to keep the mobile forces moving forward.

AUGUST STORM – THE MANCHURIAN CAMPAIGN

THE PERFECT VICTORY

With Nazi Germany in its death agonies, the Red Army began planning in March the campaign to destroy the Japanese forces in Manchuria, as Stalin had promised the Western Allies at the Yalta Conference the previous month.

Stalin pointedly directed the General Staff to strengthen the staffs and command elements of the armies in the Far East with experienced officers from the campaigns against Germany. He also specified that divisions with combat experience in conditions similar to those found in Manchuria should also be sent to bolster the Red Army forces in the Far East, in particular units with experience in mountain operations and fighting in heavily fortified areas. The combat experience paid for with rivers of blood were not to be wasted. By April the Trans-Siberian Railway was crammed with traffic heading eastwards, bearing massive reinforcements.

To provide the strength necessary to allow the Far East Command to crush the Kwantung Army in Manchuria, the Soviet High Command transferred from the Western Theatre of Operations the following forces: two Front headquarters – Karelian and 2nd Ukrainian; four army headquarters – 5th, 39th, 53rd and 6th Guards Tank; fifteen rifle, artillery, mechanized and tank corps headquarters; 36 rifle, artillery, anti-aircraft divisions; 53 combat arms brigades; and numerous air and air defence units. The redeployment effectively doubled the strength of Soviet forces in the Far East from 40 to 89 divisions. It was an impressive logistics feat, employing 136,000 railway wagons to move more than 500,000 men 9-12,000 kilometres in less than three months and then deploy to launch one of the largest and most difficult mobile operations in military history. When the concentration was complete in early August, 1,500,000 troops in fifteen armies of 89 divisions and 113 brigades, more than 5,200 tanks and 27,000 guns and mortars, and 3,700

▲Tarpaulin-covered T-34 tanks aboard a Soviet train on the Trans-Siberian Railway on the way to the Far East, June 1945. Some 136,000 wagons were used to move almost a million men and their equipment and supplies 9-12,000 kilometres in less than three months, a triumph of logistics.

▼Compounding the logistics problem was the lack of basic infrastructure in the theatre of operations – the vast front from Mongolia to the Pacific Ocean. Here water for the troops quartered in the steppes and deserts of Mongolia had to be delivered from areas hundreds of kilometres away, Transbaykal Front, early August 1945.

combat aircraft had been massed from the Mongolian border to Vladivostok. The Pacific Fleet, Amur River Flotilla and the allied Mongolian Army were also assigned missions to support the operation code-named 'Autumn Storm'.

Command of this vast effort was given to one of the finest Soviet commanders, Marshal of the Soviet Union Alexander Vasilevskiy. His Far East Command consisted of three Fronts. Transbaykal Front (six armies) in Mongolia, commanded by Marshal Malinovskiy would form one of the two great pincers that would meet in south central Manchuria in the vicinity of Mukden, Changchun, Harbin, and Kirin. First Far East Front (five armies) from Primoye commanded by Marshal Meretskov would strike from the east as the other great pincer. A secondary mission of 1st Far East Front was to strike south with two armies to cut off the Japanese escape route into Korea. To the north, 2nd Far East Front (four armies) near Khabarovsk, commanded by General Purkayev, would support the other Fronts by attacking south. Their aim was to break up the concentrations of the Kwangtung Army, isolate them in central and southern Manchuria, and destroy them one by one.

The strategic plan of operations called for the destruction of the Japanese Kwangtung Army in Manchuria and the occupation of Manchuria and Northern Korea. Speed would be the hallmark of this campaign. The Soviet planners did not want to get bogged down in battles of position with Japanese forces conducting a coherent and unbroken defence, whose soldiers would have to be killed one by one. The Kwangtung Army included 31 infantry divisions and twelve brigades and numbered 713,000 men, 1,200 tanks, 6,200 guns and 1,900 combat aircraft. Another 280,000 troops were stationed in Southern Korea, Sakhalin and the Kuriles, and the Japanese could count on another 214,000 auxiliary Manchukuoan Army and Inner Mongolian Forces troops. Numerically, the Japanese had 1,217,000 men in the theatre, almost a one to one ratio with the attacking Soviet Far East Command. That was a deceptive advantage for the Japanese. The Soviets had the mobility to concentrate their combat power; the Japanese did not and could be beaten in detail. Although many of its best divisions had been withdrawn to the Pacific and China and replaced with reserv-

◀In a parallel effort to the operations in Manchuria, the Soviet Pacific Fleet conducted operations to seize ports in Korea, southern Sakhalin Island and the Kurile Islands chain with Japanese garrisons of 280,000 men. Here transports are being loaded in Vladivostok in preparation for these operations, July 1945.

▶A battery of BM-13 multiple rocket-launchers prepares fire support for 1st Far East Front's attack, early August 1945.

◀Confounding the Japanese, Red Army forces of all three Far East Command Fronts attacked over terrain and distances that seemed impossible. In one sector the Japanese had surveyed, they had deemed only two avenues of approach usable. the Red Army used ten.

▶The operation begins! Red Army infantry crossing the Soviet-Manchurian border in the vicinity of Grodekovo, 2nd Far East Front, 9 August 1945.

▶On the first day of the operation, 9 August 1945, Soviet 152mm heavy artillery of the Transbaykal Front, probably 36th Army, attacking Japanese strongpoints across the rain-swollen Argun as infantry battalions make an assault crossing.

227

mass the Japanese did not think possible.

Forces of Transbaykal Front bypassed or overwhelmed Japanese defences in the Khingan mountain range across the Mongolian border. The 6th Guards Tank Army with its 1,000 tanks and self-propelled guns crossed through the mountain passes into the central Manchurian plain in barely three days. By 14 August Transbaykal Front had three armies across the mountain barrier upon which the Japanese had hoped to base their defence. First Far Eastern Front attacked in torrential rain over thickly woooded mountains, bypassing Japanese fortified areas near the border. Two armies converged on Mutanchiang on 13-14 August, completely unhinging Japanese intentions to anchor their defence in that area. By 18 August the Front had exploited its success, pursuing Japanese forces in northern and central Manchuria and threatening to slam shut the Japanese escape route into Korea. Second Far East Front attacked across the border and fulfilled its supporting mission to apply pressure along its sector, advancing 120 kilometres in five days. By 20 August Soviet forces had advanced 400-800 kilometres from the west and 200-300 kilometres from the north and reached the Manchurian plain. The Kwangtung Army found itself dismembered into a number of isolated and ineffective parts, incapable of co-ordinated action. Its encirclement was complete. By 2 September the last pockets of resistance had been mopped up and the whole of Manchuria had been occupied.

Simultaneously with the Manchurian Operation, Soviet troops seized southern Sakhalin Island and the Kurile Islands. In the Kuriles the Japanese put up a bitter fight against the Soviet landings which did not end until 30 August.

The Far Eastern campaign had lasted barely 23 days but was executed with such precision and professionalism, the embodiment of the experiences of the Great Patriotic War, that it became a model for

ists, it would give a good account of itself when its troops were given an opportunity to fight. Nevertheless such a force would have to have the legs knocked out from under it by a grand encirclement. The Red Army had honed such skills in the last two years of the war and was prepared to employ them again in a virtuoso performance.

Repaying the Japanese for their surprise attack on Port Arthur in 1904, the Red Army began its attack ten minutes after midnight on 9 August without warning. Simultaneous air and naval attacks supported the ground forces as Japanese air ases were struck, and the River Amur Flotilla attacked down the River Sungari

and Pacific Fleet torpedo-boats attacked Japanese shipping in the sea of Japan. An airborne landing was made at Harbin. The Japanese were soon to discover three Soviet surprises that confounded their plans for defence. The Red Army had determined to employ avenues of approach the Japanese thought completely unsuitable for the transit or support of large forces. Secondly, they sent mobile groups far in advance of the main body to disrupt Japanese operations and seize key objectives. An Army's mobile group might be a tank brigade; for Transbaykal Front the entire 6th Guards Tank Army served as its mobile group. Thirdly, the Red Army would advance with a speed and

▲Pe-2 bombers of 9th Air Army supporting the attack of 1st Far East Front, 9 August 1945. Each of the three Fronts was supported by its own air army consisting of bomber, fighter and ground-attack air divisions.

▼Infantry of 25th Army, 1st Far East Front, scaling Ryzhaya (Red) Hill. The 39th Rifle Corps were charged with the seizing of the Tungning Fortified Region and the cutting of Japanese communications between Manchuria and Korea.

generations of Red Army (soon to be Soviet Army) strategists on the conduct of mobile operations at the strategic and operational levels of warfare. In this mastepiece of a campaign, the Red Army killed or captured almost 700,000 (84,000 dead and 594,000 prisoners) of its opponents for a loss of barely 8,000 killed and 32,000 wounded. Immense stocks of equipment were captured. The Kwangtung Army, Japan's best field force, was capable of a better performance. The Red Army just never gave it a chance.

Perhaps the most telling summary of the Manchurian Operation is given by Colonel David M. Glantz, US Army, an eminent historian and analyst of Soviet military affairs.

'. . . Confounding Japanese difficulties was the nature of the Soviet offensive. Japanese plans might have succeeded to a greater degree against a lesser foe. Unfortunately, the Japanese High Command faced a highly professional force led by the cream of the Soviet officer corps, blooded and educated in four years of war. Far East Command units were among the best

in the Soviet Army, and their equipment had been tested against the best weaponry European arsenals could produce. For the Soviet Army, this was the last campaign in a long war, quite literally one last opportunity to excel. And excel it did. The Manchurian operation qualified as a postgraduate exercise for Soviet forces, the culmination of a rigorous quality education in combat begun in western Russia in June 1941.'

▲The 46th Guards Tank Brigade, 9th Guards Mechanized Corps, 6th Guards Tank Army, forces a river with their US Lend-Lease M4 Sherman tanks. The 9th Guards Mechanized Corps had initially been the lead formation of the 6th Guards Tank Army's right column of march, but because of its wheeled vehicles and insufficient fuel was replaced by the 5th Guards Tank Corps. Compared to the T-34, the Shermans had higher fuel consumption and less mobility.

◄Tank infantry forces of 1st Far East Front, one of the two great pincers that would close on the heart of Japanese Manchuria, approaching the Manchurian border, early August 1945.

▲A detachment of Red Army signalmen passing a T-34/85 tank to establish wire communications for a rapidly advancing army, a difficult task that can never be accomplished fast enough, 1st Far East Front, August. By 11 August, two days after the beginning of operations, 5th Army had reached objectives planned for the eighth day. Much of the success of that drive was due to signalmen who kept the forces stitched together with wire and radio.

▼Infantry of 63rd Rifle Division, 72nd Corps, who have just taken the city of Muleng on the road to Mutancianga by storm, 5th Army, 1st Far East Front, 10 August 1945.

◄Infantry and 152mm heavy self-propelled guns moving deeper into eastern Manchuria, 1st Far East Front.

▼After crossing the Grand Khinghan Mountains, the columns of 6th Guards Tank Army were separated by as much as 100 kilometres; they kept in contact with one another by using motor-cycle units, such as these shown here, and reconnaissance aircraft, Transbaykal Front, 15-16 August, 1945.

◄One of the élite formations of 6th Guards Tank Army – 20th Tank Brigade of 5th Guards Tank Corps, after crossing the Grand Khinghan Mountains, Transbaykal Front, 13 August 1945. The 6th Guards was chosen for this operation because of its combat experience over similiar terrain in the Carpathian Mountains.

▼Tankers of 6th Guards Tank Army take a well-earned and relaxed view of the Pacific Ocean at the end of their vast and lightning trek from the borders of Outer Mongolia. On 21 August the Army occupied Mukden, two days after its seizure by Soviet airborne forces. Fuel shortages forced 6th Guards to make the rest of the drive to Port Arthur and Dalny by rail.

▲Pacific Fleet torpedo-boat approaching the Korean port of Seisin, escorting the amphibious assault of the naval infantry, 14 August 1945.

The Soviet Navy's Pacific Fleet and river flotillas carried the assault deep into the Japanese rear.

▼Advance elements of 1st Guards Airborne Division in their assault on the Japanese air base at Harbin, 18 August 1945.

▶Soviet airborne forces landed to seize major cities and airfields ahead of the advancing ground forces. Mukden (now Shenyang), 19 August 1945. By this time Japanese resistance was crumbling. Elements of 6th Guards Tank Army completed the last stages of their advance on Mukden as an administrative road march, entering on 21 August.

▼Revenge is sweet! Forty years before the Russian garrison of Port Arthur had surrendered to the Japanese Imperial Army after an epic siege. Here, their grandsons, now Soviet paratroopers, aboard this US Lend-Lease PBY transport, are approaching Port Arthur to take possession of the port and city, 22 August 1945.

◀Naval infantry of 355th Separate Battalion, Pacific Ocean Fleet, capturing the pier in an assault landing in the city of Seisin (now Chongjin), Korea, 14 August 1945 – one of the many supporting landings made by the Soviet Navy in the Manchurian Operation.

▶Marshal of the Soviet Union and Commander of the Far East Command, Alexander Vasilevskiy, and Colonel-General Afanasy Beloborodov, Commander of 1st Red Banner Army, reviewing the Soviet airborne forces that seized the Japanese airfield at Harbin, late August 1945.

◀Naval infantry of 13th Separate Brigade, Pacific Ocean Fleet, continuing the fight to wrest Seisin (now Chongjin) from its 4,000-man Japanese garrison, 15 August 1945.

▶▼War booty – of a sort! Here Colonel-General Afanasy Beloborodov, Commander of 1st Red Banner Army, and Lieutenant-General K. P. Kuznetzov, commander of army artillery, inspect the huge haul of captured *matériel* , 30 August 1945. These light tanks must have seemed like a joke to the men of the Red Army who had had the equal of the best if not the best tanks in the world during the war with the Germans.

▼The bitterness of defeat. Marshal of the Soviet Union Alexander Vasilevskiy, Commander of Soviet forces in the Far East, and Marshal of the Soviet Union, Kirill Meretskov, Commander of 1st Far East Front, instruct General H. Hata, Chief of Staff of the Kwangtung Army, on the articles of surrender, 19 August 1945.

◄Some of the 148 Japanese generals captured by the Red Army being flown to the rear, September 1945 (left). Note that Marshal Vasilevskiy has allowed them to retain their swords as a mark of honour. Samurai swords were no longer a novelty for Stalin by this time. Zhukov had already presented him with bundles of these Japanese swords after his victoy at Khalkin Gol in 1939. The Red Army's chivalry in allowing Japanese generals to retain their swords is in marked contrast to their justifiably hard-hearted attitude towards the Germans.

◄Japanese soldiers surrendering their weapons to troops of 7th Guards Mechanized Corps, 6th Guards Tank Army, Transbaykal Front, Changchun, 21 August 1945. Other elements of 6th Guards Tank Army were accepting more surrenders at Mukden at the same time.

◄▼After the surrender, the Red Army would count 594,000 Japanese prisoners taken in the Manchurian Operation.

►Red Army trumpeters announce the beginning of the march in review of the troops of the victorious Far East Command, at Voroshilov-Ussuriisky (now Ussuriisk), 7 November 1945.

▼Decorated veteran officers of the Far East Command in parade formation to commemorate the victory over Japan, Voroshilov-Ussuriisky (now Ussuriisk), 7 November 1945. The cost of victory for the Red Army in this 23-day campaign was light in comparison to the battles that crushed Germany – 8,000 dead and 32,000 wounded.

The Price of Victory

1. Interview with General M.A. Moiseyev, chief of General Staff, USSR Armed Forces, by Major General V.I. Filatov, chief editor, *Voyenno-istoricheskiy zhurnal*, No. 3, March 1990; on the occasion of the 45th anniversary of victory in the Great Patriotic War: 'The Price of Victory'.

a. The Soviet armed forces lost during the Great Patriotic War: Killed in action, missing in action, taken prisoner and not returned, dead as a result of wounds, illness or accident:

Total Dead	8,668,400
Army and Navy	8,509,300
Internal Troops	97,700
Border Troops	61,400
Wounded, Sick	18,000,000*

*Wounded are counted once despite the number of times wounded.

b. Losses during the first period of the war:

1941: 20% of total losses in the war The Battle of Smolensk, and Kiev and Moscow defensive operations: 1,500,000 casualties

1942: 33⅓% of total losses Battle of Kharkov, Voronezh-Voroshilovgrad, Stalingrad, and North Caucasus defensive operations: 1,000,000

c. Material losses of total of that available at the beginning of the war, and received from all sources to include industry, Lend-Lease:

	Lost	Percent of Total
Small arms:	15,500,000	53.0
Tanks/S Party:	96,500	73.3
Artillery	317,500	50.0
Combat aircraft:	88,300	31.8

Soviet losses of the prewar inventory were 20,500 of 22,600 tanks/SP arty. Of those lost 16,500 were in need of major or medium repair and had a limited range.

Losses stated as a percentage of material available before the war broke out:

Small arms:	67.0
Tanks:	91.0
Artillery/mortars	90.0
Combat aircraft	90.0

After German attack, Soviet industry could replace the following losses in 1941:

Small arms:	30.0
Tanks:	27.0
Artillery/mortars:	58.0
Combat aircraft:	55.0

2. V.N. Shevchenko, 'Military Art of Soviet Forces in Operations of 1945', *Voyennaya mysl*, No. 4, April 1990

a. Warfare of 1945 was characterized by the total forces of opposing forces:

Personnel:	18,000,000
Artillery/mortars:	260,000
Tanks/SP guns:	40,000
Combat aircraft:	38,000

b. Enemy losses inflicted by Soviet armed forces:

Divisions destroyed:	98
Divisions captured:	56
Divisions surrendered:	93
total:	247

c. Soviet personnel losses in Central and Southeastern Europe were more than 1,000,000 dead.

d. Soviet material losses in the concluding operations of the war:

Tanks/SP guns:	12,500
Artillery/mortars:	11,500
Combat aircraft:	11,800

e. Operational Information. Front breakthrough sectors comprised up to 15 per cent of the overall width of zones of advance and were allotted the following resources:

Combined arms large strategic formations:	75.0%
Tank and mechanized large strategic formations:	90.0%

Artillery and main air forces: 75–90.0%

f. Operational densities on breakthrough sectors per kilometre (example: Vistula-Oder Operation):

Tanks/SP guns:	80–115
Artillery/mortars:	230–250
Engineer companies:	13–17

Resulting forces ratios on the Warsaw-Berlin axis:

Personnel:	4:1
Tanks:	5.5:1
Artillery:	6:1
Aircraft:	8:1

EPILOGUE

'With every passing year we draw farther and farther away from those years of war. A new generation of people has grown up. For them war only means our reminiscences of it. And the numbers of us who took part in those historic events are dwindling fast. But I am convinced that time cannot cause the greatness of all that we experienced during the war to fade. Those were extraordinarily difficult, but also truly glorious years. Once a person has undergone great trials and come through victorious, then throughout his life he draws strength from this victory.'

Marshal of the Soviet Union Georgi K. Zhukov, *Reminiscences and Reflections*, 1974

APPENDIXES

SOVIET OPERATIONS AND BATTLES IN THE GREAT PATRIOTIC WAR 1941–5

Operations and Battles Before 1941
(not officially part of The Great Patriotic War)

Date	Operation	Soviet Forces
1936–9	Battle of Madrid	International Brigades
29 July-11 Aug 1938	Battle of Lake Khasan	Far East Command
20 Aug-31 Aug 1939	Battle of Khalkin Gol	1st Army Group of Forces
17 Sept-5 Oct 1939	Invasion of Poland	Belorussian, Kiev Military Districts
30 Nov 1939-13 Mar 1940	Soviet-Finnish War	NW Front

THE GREAT PATRIOTIC WAR 1941–5
First Period of the War
(22 June 1941–18 November 1942)

Date	Operation	Soviet Forces
22–29 June 1941	Frontier Battles	Border Guards, Covering Forces
22–30 June 1941	Tank Battle of 1941	SW
June 1941–Oct 1944	Defence of Arctic Regions	Karelian
June 1941-Oct 1944	Defence of Karelia	Karelian
7 July-26 Sept 1941	Kiev Defensive Operation	SW
10 July-10 Sept 1941	Battle of Smolensk	Western, Reserve, Central, Bryansk
10 July-30 Dec 1941	Leningrad Defensive Operation	Northern, NW, Leningrad
10 July 1941– 9 Aug 1944	The Battle of Leningrad	Northern, NW, Volkov, Karelian, 2nd Baltic
10 July-10 Sept 1941	Battle of Smolensk	Western, Reserve, Central, Bryansk
5 Aug-28 Aug 1941	The Defence of Talinn	Baltic Fleet
5 Aug-16 Oct 1941	The Defence of Odessa	Independent Maritime Army
30 Aug-8 Sept 1941	Yelnya Offensive Operation	Reserve
30 Sept-23 Oct 1941	Orel-Bryansk Defensive Operation	Bryansk
30 Sept-5 Dec 1941	Moscow Defence Operation	Western, Reserve, Bryansk
30 Sept 1941– 20 Apr 1942	Battle of Moscow	Western, Kalinin, Reserve, Bryansk, SW
2 Oct-13 Oct 1941	Vyazma Defensive Operation	Western, Reserve
10 Oct-30 Oct 1941	Mozhaysk-Maloyaroslavets Defensive Operation	Western
10 Oct-4 Dec 1941	Kalinin Defensive Operation	Western, Kalinin
16 Oct-18 Nov 1941	Tikhvin Defensive Operation	4th, 52nd Independent Armies, Leningrad
18 Oct-16 Nov 1941	Crimean Defensive Operation	51st, Maritime Independent Armies
20 Oct-28 Oct 1941	Sinyavino Offensive Operation	Leningrad, Volkhov, 54th Independent Army
24 Oct-5 Dec 1941	Tula Defensive Operation	Bryansk, Western
30 Oct 1941– 4 July 1942	Defence of Sevastopol	Black Sea Fleet
10 Nov-30 Dec 1941	Tikhvin Offensive Operation	Leningrad, 4th, 52nd Independent Armies
5–16 Nov 1941	Rostov Defensive Operation	SW, 56th Independent Army
15 Nov–5 Dec 1941	Klin Solnechnogorsk Defensive Operation	Western, Kalinin
17 Nov-2 Dec 1941	Rostov Offensive Operation	SW, 56th Independent Army
5 Dec 1941– 20 Apr 1942	Moscow Offensive Operation	Western, Kalinin, SW, Bryansk
1–5 Dec 1941	Naro-Fominsk Defensive Operation	Western
5 Dec 1941– 7 Jan 1942	Kalinin Offensive Operation	Kalinin
6–16 Dec 1941	Tula Offensive Operation	Western
6–16 Dec 1941	Yelets Offensive Operation	SW
6–25 Dec 1941	Klin-Solnechnogorsk Offensive Operation	Western, Kalinin
17 Dec 1941– 5 Jan 1942	Kaluga Offensive Operation	Western
25 Dec 1941– 5 Jan 1942	Kerch-Feodosiya Amphibious Operation	Trans-Causasus
7 Jan-20 May 1942	Demyansk Offensive Operation	NW
8 Jan-20 Apr 1942	Rzhev-Vyazma Offensive Operation	Kalinin, Western, Bryansk, NW
9 Jan-6 Feb 1942	Toropets-Kholm Offensive Operation	NW, Kalinin
18–31 Jan 1942	Barvenkovo-Lozovaya Offensive Operation	SW, Southern
18 Jan-24 Feb 1942	Vyazma Airborne Operation	4th Airborne Corps
5 May-8 Jun 1942	Yevpatoriya Amphibious Operation	Black Sea Fleet
12–29 May 1942	Battle of Kharkov	SW, Southern
28 June-24 July 1942	Voronezh-Voroshilograd Defensive Operation	Bryansk, SW, Southern
17 July-18 Nov 1942	Stalingrad Defensive Operation	Stalingrad, SE, Don
17 July 1942–	Battle of Stalingrad	Stalingrad, SE, SW, Don, Voronezh
25 July-31 Dec 1942	Defence of the Caucasus	Southern, North Caucasus, Trans-Caucasus

Date	Operation	Soviet Forces
25 July 1942–9 Oct 1943	Battle of the Caucasus	Southern, North Caucasus, Trans-Caucasus
30 July-23 Aug 1942	Rzhev-Sychevka Offensive Operation	Western, Kalinin
6–17 Aug 1942	Armavir-Maykop Defensive Operation	North Caucasus
19 Aug-10 Oct 1942	Sinyavino Offensive Operation	Leningrad, Volkhov
19 Aug-26 Sept 1942	Novorossiysk Offensive Operation	North Caucasus
1–28 Sept 1942	Mozdok-Malgobek Defensive Operation	Trans-Caucasus
25 Sept-20 Dec 1942	Tuapse Defensive Operation	Trans-Caucasus

Second Period of the War
(19 November 1942–31 December 1943)

Date	Operation	Soviet Forces
19 Nov 1942–2 Feb 1943	Stalingrad Offensive Operation	Stalingrad, SE, Don
24 Nov 1942-30 Jan 1943	Velikiye Luki Offensive Operation	Kalinin
12–30 Dec 1942	Koltel'nikovskiy Defensive Operation	Stalingrad
16–30 Dec 1942	Middle Don Offensive Operation	SW, Voronezh
1 Jan-4 Feb 1943	North Caucasus Offensive Operation	Southern, North Caucasus, Trans-Caucasus
1 Jan–18 Feb 1943	Rostov Offensive Operation	Southern, North Caucasus
12–13 Jan 1943	Breakthrough of the Siege of Leningrad	Leningrad, Volkhov
13–17 Jan 1943	Ostrogozhsk-Rossosh Offensive Operation	Voronezh, SW
24 Jan-2 Feb 1943	Voronezh-Kastornoye Offensive Operation	Voronezh, Bryansk
29 Jan-18 Feb 1943	Voroshilograd Offensive Operation	SW
2 Feb-3 Mar 1943	Kharkov Offensive Operation	Voronezh, SW
4–15 Feb 1943	Malaya Zemlya (beachhead)	18th Army
4–15 Feb 1943	South Ozereysk Amphibious Operation	18th Army
9 Feb-16 Mar 1943	Krasnodar Offensive Operation	North Caucasus
15–28 Feb 1943	Demyansk Offensive Operation	NW
2–31 Mar 1943	Rzhev-Vyazma Offensive Operation	Western, Kalinin
4–25 Mar 1943	Kharkov Defensive Operation	Voronezh, SW
5–23 July 1943	Kursk Defensive Operation	Central, Voronezh, Steppe
5 July-23 Aug 1943	Battle of Kursk	Central, Voronezh, Steppe, SW, Bryansk, Western
12 July-18 Aug 1943	Orel Offensive Operation	Bryansk, Central, Western
12 July-23 Aug 1943	Kursk Offensive Operation	Western, Bryansk, Central, Voronezh, SW
22 July-22 Aug 1943	Mga Offensive Operation	Leningrad, Volkhov
3–23 Aug 1943	Belgorod-Kharkov Offensive Operation	Voronezh, Steppe

Date	Operation	Soviet Forces
7–20 Aug 1943	Spas-Demensk Offensive Operation	Western
7 Aug-2 Oct 1943	Smolensk Offensive Operation	Western, Kalinin
13 Aug-22 Sept 1943	Donbass Offensive Operation	SW, Southern
25 Aug-23 Dec 1943	Battle of the Dnieper	1st Bel, 1st, 2nd Ukr
26 Aug-30 Sept 1943	Chernigov-Pripet Offensive Operation	Central
28 Aug-6 Sept 1943	Yelnya-Dorogobuzh Offensive Operation	Western
1 Sept-3 Oct 1943	Bryansk Offensive Operation	Bryansk
7 Sept-19 Oct 1943	Defence of the Moonzund Islands	NW
9 Sept-9 Oct 1943	Novorossiysk-Taman Offensive Operation	North Caucasus
9–16 Sept 1943	Novorossiysk Offensive Operation	North Caucasus
14 Sept-2 Oct 1943	Dukhovshchina-Demidov Offensive Operation	Kalinin
15 Sept-2 Oct 1943	Smolensk-Roslavl Offensive Operation	Western
24 Sept-13 Nov 1943	Dnieper Airborne Operation	3rd, 5th AB Bdes
26 Sept-5 Nov 1943	Melitopol Offensive Operation	4th Ukr
10–14 Oct 1943	Zaporoshye Offensive Operation	SW
23 Oct-5 Nov 1943	Dnepropetrovsk Offensive Operation	2nd, 3rd Ukr
31 Oct-11 Dec 1943	Kerch-Eltigen Amphibious Operation	North Caucasus
3–13 Nov 1943	Kiev Offensive Operation	1st Ukr
13 Nov–22 Dec 1943	Kiev Defensive Operation	1st Ukr
24 Dec 1943–14 Jan 1944	Zhitomir-Berdichev Offensive Operation	1st Ukr
24 Dec 1943-17 Apr 1944	Offensive by Soviet Forces in the right-bank Ukraine	1st, 2nd, 3rd, 4th Ukr, 2nd Bel

Third Period of the War
(1 January 1944-9 May 1945)

Date	Operation	Soviet Forces
5–17 Jan 1944	Kirovograd Offensive Operation	2nd Ukr
14–30 Jan 1944	Krasnoye Selo-Ropsha Offensive Operation	Leningrad
14 Jan-1 Mar 1944	Leningrad-Novgorod Offensive Operation	Leningrad, Volkhov, 2nd Baltic
14 Jan-15 Feb 1944	Novgorod-Luga Offensive Operation	Volkhov, Leningrad
17–31 Jan 1944	Pskov-Ostrov Offensive Operation	3rd Baltic
24 Jan-17 Feb 1944	Korsun-Shevchenkovsky Offensive Operation	1st, 2nd Ukr
27 Jan-11 Feb 1944	Rovno-Lutsk Offensive Operation	1st Ukr
30 Jan-29 Feb 1944	Nikopol-Krivoy Rog Offensive Operation	3rd, 4th Ukr
21–26 Feb 1944	Rogachev-Zhlobin Offensive Operation	1st Bel
4 Mar-17 Apr 1944	Proskurov-Chernovotsy Offensive Operation	1st Ukr
6–18 Mar 1944	Bereznegovatoye-Snigirevka Offensive Operation	3rd Ukr

Date	Operation	Soviet Forces
5 Mar-17 Apr 1944	Uman-Botosani Offensive Operation	2nd Ukr
26–28 Mar 1944	Nikolayev Amphibious Operation	Black Sea Fleet, 3rd Ukr
26 Mar-14 Apr 1944	Odessa Offensive Operation	3rd Ukr
8 Apr-12 May 1944	Crimean Offensive Operation	4th Ukr, Independent Maritime Army
10–20 June 1944	Vyborg Offensive Operation	Leningrad
21 June-9 Aug 1944	Svir-Petrozavodsk Offensive Operation	Karelian
23–27 June 1944	Tuloksa Amphibious Operation	Ladoga Flotilla
23–28 June 1944	Mogliev Offensive Operation	2nd Bel
23–28 June 1944	Vitebsk-Orsha Offensive Operation	1st Baltic, 2nd Bel
23 June-29 Aug 1944*	Belorussian Offensive Operation	1st, 2nd, 3rd Bel, 1st Baltic
24-29 June 1944	Bobruysk Offensive Operation	1st Bel
28 June 1944	Petrozavodsk Amphibious Operation	Onega Flotilla
29 June-4 Jul 1944	Minsk Offensive Operation	1st, 2nd, 3rd Bel, 1st Baltic
5–20 July 1944	Vilnius Offensive Operation	3rd Bel
5–27 July 1944	Bialystok Offensive Operation	2nd Bel
5–31 July 1944	Shyaulyay Offensive Operation	1st Baltic
13 July-29 Aug 1944	Lvov-Sandomierz Offensive Operation	1st Ukr
28 July-28 Aug 1944	Kaunas Offensive Operation	3rd Bel
10 Aug-6 Sept 1944	Tartu Offensive Operation	3rd Baltic
20–29 Aug 1944	Iasi-Kishinev Offensive Operation	2nd, 3rd Ukr
8 Sept-28 Oct 1944	Eastern Carpathian Offensive Operation	1st, 4th Ukr
8 Sept-28 Oct 1944	Carpathian-Duka Offensive Operation	1st, 4th Ukr
9 Sept-28 Oct 1944	Carpathian-Uzhgorod Offensive Operation	1st, 4th Ukr
14 Sept-22 Oct 1944	Riga Offensive Operation	1st, 2nd, 3rd Baltic
14 Sept-24 Nov 1944	Baltic Offensive Operation	Leningrad, 1st, 2nd, 3rd Baltic
17–26 Sept 1944	Tallin Offensive Operation	Leningrad
27 Sept-24 Nov 1944	Moonzund Amphibious Operation	Leningrad
28 Sept-20 Oct 1944	Belgrade Offensive Operation	3rd Ukr
5–22 Oct 1944	Memel Offensive Operation	1st Baltic, 3rd Bel
6–28 Oct 1944	Debrecen Offensive Operation	2nd Ukr
7–29 Oct 1944	Petsamo-Kirkenes Offensive Operation	Karelian
29 Oct 1944– 13 Feb 1945	Budapest Offensive Operation	2nd, 3rd Ukr
12 Jan-3 Feb 1945	Sandomierz-Silesian Offensive Operation	1st Ukr
12 Jan-18 Feb 1945	Western Carpathian Offensive Operation	2nd, 4th Ukr
12 Jan-3 Feb 1945	Vistula-Oder Offensive Operation	1st, 2nd Bel, 1st, 4th Ukr
13–27 Jan 1945	Isterburg-Königsberg Offensive Operation	3rd Bel
13 Jan-25 Apr 1945	East Prussian Offensive Operation	2nd, 3rd Bel, 1st Baltic
14–26 Jan 1945	Mlawa-Elbing Offensive Operation	2nd Bel
8–24 Feb 1945	Lower Silesian Offensive Operation	1st Ukr
10 Feb-4 Apr 1945	Eastern Pomeranian Offensive Operation	1st, 2nd Bel
6–15 Mar 1945	Balaton Defensive Operation	3rd Ukr
10 Mar-5 May 1945	Moravska Ostrava Offensive Operation	4th Ukr
15–31 Mar 1945	Upper Silesian Offensive Operation	1st Ukr
16 Mar-15 Apr 1945	Vienna Offensive Operation	2nd, 3rd Ukr
25 Mar-5 May 1945	Bratislava-Brno Offensive Operation	2nd Ukr
6–9 Apr 1945	Königsberg Offensive Operation	3rd Bel
13–25 Apr 1945	Zemland Offensive Operation	Zemland Gp
16 Apr-8 May 1945	Berlin Offensive Operation	1st, 2nd Bel, 1st Ukr
6–11 May 1945	Prague Offensive Operation	1st, 2nd, 4th Ukr

The Defeat of Imperialist Japan
(2 August–9 September 1945)

9 Aug-2 Sept 1945	Manchurian Offensive Operation	Transbaykal, 1st, 2nd Far East
9 Aug-2 Sept 1945	Kharbin-Kirin Offensive Operation	1st Far East
9 Aug-2 Sept 1945	Sungari Offensive Operation	2nd Far East
9 Aug-2 Sept 1945	Khinghan-Mukden Offensive Operation	Transbaykal
11–25 Aug 1945	Southern Sakhalin Offensive Operation	2nd Far East
13–16 Aug 1945	Seishin Amphibious Operation	Pacific Fleet
18 Aug-1 Sept 1945	Kuril Amphibious Operation	Pacific Fleet, 2nd Far East

Source: Marshal of the Soviet Union, Nikolai V. Ogarkov, *Military Encyclopedic Dictionary*, Moscow, Voyenizdat, 1983.

* Offensive began on 22 June, but Soviet historians always cite 23 June.

GENERAL OFFICER RANK EQUIVALENTS

German	Soviet	US	British
Reichsmarschall	none	none	none
Generalfeldmarschall	Marshal of the Soviet Union	General of the Army	Field Marshal
none	Chief Marshal	none	none
none	Marshal	none	none
Generaloberst	Army General	General	General
General der Infanterie, der Artillerie, etc.	Colonel General	Lieutenant General	Lieutenant General
Generalleutnant	Lieutenant General	Major General	Major General
Generalmajor	Major General	Brigadier General	none

RED ARMY AND NAVY UNITS AWARDED GUARDS APPELLATION 1941–1945

Red Army
11 Combined Arms Armies Brigades
6 Tank Armies
1 Cavalry Mechanized Gp
40 Rifle Corps
7 Cavalry Corps
12 Tank Corps
9 Mechanized Corps
14 Aviation Corps
117 Rifle Divisions Brigades
9 Airborne Divisions
17 Cavalry Divisions
6 Artillery Divisions
7 Rocket Artillery Divisions
6 Anti-aircraft Artillery Divisions
53 Aviation Divisions
13 Motorized Rifle
3 Airborne Brigades
66 Tank Brigades
28 Mechanized Brigades
3 SP Artillery Brigades
64 Artillery Brigades
1 Mortar Brigade
11 Tank Destroyer Brigades
40 Rocket Artillery Brigades
1 Railway Brigade
6 Engineer Brigades
1 Fortified Area

Red Navy
18 Surface Combatants
16 Submarines
13 Combat Patrol Craft Divisions
2 Air Divisions
2 AA Regiments
1 Naval Infantry Brigade
1 Naval Railway Artillery Brigade

Source: Marshal of the Soviet Union, Nikolai V. Ogarkov, *Military Encyclopedic Dictionary* (Moscow: Voyenizdat, 1983).

SOVIET GUARDS TANK ARMIES

During the war, large operational–strategic ground forces formations were awarded the appelation of Guards for the heroism, courage, and high degree of combat skill of their men. The 3rd and 5th Guards Tank Armies were formed directly from guards combined units and immediately received the Guards appellation.

1st Guards Tank Army
Formed as 1st Tank Army in July 42 based on 38th Army of Stalingrad Front
Deactivated Aug 42; HQ becomes nucleus of Southeastern Front HQ
Reactivated Jan-Feb 43 on Southwestern Front
Designated as Guards Tank Army 25 Apr 44
Operations: Kursk, Right Bank Ukraine, SE Poland, Lvov-Sandomierz, Vistula-Oder, East Pomeranian, Berlin
Commanders: K.S. Moskalenko, M. Ye. Katukov

2nd Guards Tank Army
Formed as 2nd Tank Army in Jan-Feb 43 based on 3rd Reserve Army of Bryansk Front
Designated Guards Tank Army 20 Nov 44
Operations: Sevsk Sector, Kursk, Chernigov-Pripet, Vinnitsa Sector, Korsun-Shevchenkovsky, Uman-Botosani, Belorussian, Vistula-Oder, East Pomeranian, Berlin
Commanders: P.L. Romanenko, A.G. Rodin, S.I. Bogdanov, A.I. Radziyevskiy

3rd Guards Tank Army
Formed in May 43 in the HQ SHC Reserve
Operations: Kursk, Dnieper, Kiev, Right Bank Ukraine, Poland, Berlin, Prague
Commander: P.S. Rybalko

4th Guards Tank Army
Formed as 4th Tank Army in July 42 on the Stalingrad Front
Reorganized and redesignated 65th Army in Oct 42
Reconstituted and reactivated as 2nd Tank Army in July 43
Redesignated as Guards Tank Army on 17 Mar 45
Operations: Kursk, Right Bank Ukraine, Lvov-Sandomierz, Vistula-Oder, Lower Silesian, Upper Sileasian, Berlin, Prague
Commanders: V.D. Kryuchenkin, V.M. Badanov, D.D. Lelyusenko

5th Guards Tank Army
Formed in Feb-Mar 43 in the HQ SHC Reserve
Operations: Kursk, Dnieper Bridgehead, Kirovogarad, Korsun-Shevchenkovsky, Uman-Botosani, Belorussian, Baltic, and East Prussian
Commanders: P.A. Rotmistrov, M.D. Solomatin, V.T. Vol'skiy, M.D. Sinenko

6th Guards Tank Army
Formed as 6th Tank Army in Jan 44 on the 1st Ukrainian Front
Operations: Korsun-Shevchenkovsky, Uman-Botosani, Iasi-Kishinev, Debrecen, Budapest, Vienna, Bratislava-Brno, Prague, Manchurian
Commanders: A.G. Kravchenko

Source: Marshal of the Soviet Union Nikolai V. Ogarkov, *Military Encyclopedic Dictionary* (Moscow: Voyenizdat, 1983).

PERSONNEL AND EQUIPMENT IN TANK ARMIES AT THE BEGINNING OF OFFENSIVE OPERATIONS

Tank Army	Personnel	Tanks/SPs	Guns/ Mortars	Rocket Launchers*	AAA
1st Guards	30,626–48,958	257–752	266–558	25–64	80–133
2nd Guards	28,000–58,299	101–840	107–667	8–78	33–132
3rd Guards	31,660–66,674	309–924	266–690	32–98	57–112
4th Guards	30,003–49,992	276–732	390–580	8–44	34–126
5th Guards	26,704–43,904	146–585	126–755	20–55	44–131
6th Guards	25,363–75,000	86–984	126–611	8–46	20–165

*M-8 & M-13.

Source: I.M. Ananyev, *Tank Armies in the Offensive*, (Moscow: Voyenisdat, 1988).

SOVIET MATERIAL LOSSES* 1941–1945

	No. Lost	%Total
Small Arms:	15,500,000	53.0
Tanks/SP Arty:	96,500	73.3
Artillery:	317,500	50.0
Combat Aircraft:	88,300	31.8

*Material losses of total available at the beginning of the war and received from all sources to include industry and Lend-Lease.

Source: Army General M.A. Moiseyev, Chief of the General Staff, *Voyenno-istoricheskiy zhurnal*, No. 3, March 1990.

SOVIET AND GERMAN COMBAT EQUIPMENT AT THE END OF 1941

	Soviet Dec 41	German Dec 41	Soviet Jan 45
Tanks:	1,954	1,940	15,700
Artillery and Mortars:	22,000	26,800	144,200
Combat Aircraft:	2,238	2,830	22,600

Sources: 'Heroism or Tragedy? Historians Take Close Look at the Initial Period of War', *Sovetskiy voin*, No. 2, Feb 1989; Lt.-Gen. A.I. Yevseyev, 'The Influence of the Experience of the Great Patriotic War in the Organizational Development of the Armed Forces', *Voyenno-istoricheskiy zhurnal*, No. 5, May 1988.

LEND-LEASE AFVS/TRUCKS PROVIDED TO THE RED ARMY (1941–1945)

British Tanks

Valentine (British)	2,394
Valentine (Canadian)	1,388
Valentine Bridgelayer	25
Matilda	1,084
Churchill	301
Cromwell	6
Tetarch	20

US Tanks

M3A1 Light Tank	1,676
M5 Light Tank	5
M24 Light Tank	2
M3A3 Medium Tank	1,386
M4A2 (75mm) Medium Tank	2,007
M4A2 (76mm) Medium Tank	2,095
M26 Heavy Tank	1
M31 ARV	115

British Armoured Troop Carriers

Universal Carrier (Brit)	1,212
Universal Carrier (Can)	1,348

US Armoured Troop Carriers

M2 Halftrack	342
M3 Halftrack	2
M5 Halftrack	421
M9 Halftrack	413
Universal Carrier T16	96
M2A1 Scout Car	3,340
LVT	5

US Trucks and Jeeps

1½ Ton Trucks	200,662
2½ Ton Trucks	151,053
Jeeps	77,972

US Self-Propelled Artillery

M15A1 MGMC	100
M17 MGMC	1,000
T48 Tank Destroyer	650
M18 Tank Destroyer	5
M10 Tank Destroyer	52

LEND-LEASE AND SOVIET TANKS IN SOVIET TANK BRIGADES – 1943

Brigades Equipped	%
Solely with Lend-Lease tanks:	10–17
With mix of Soviet/Lend-Lease tanks:	19–22
Soley with Soviet tanks:	61–68

Source: Steven Zaloga and James Grandsen, *Soviet Tanks and Combat Vehicles of World War Two* (London: Arms and Armour Press, 1984).

Note: The Western Allies shipped 22,800 armoured fighting vehicles (AFVs) to the Soviet Union between 1941 and 1945, of which 1,981 were lost to German submarines. The total amounted to 20 per cent of Soviet tank production and 16 per cent of SP artillery production. In contrast to the 429,687 trucks and jeeps sent by the United States from its production of 2,382,311, the Soviet Union produced only 197,100 such vehicles from 1943 to 1945.

Source: Steven Zaloga and James Grandsen, *Soviet Tanks and Combat Vehicles of World War Two* (London: Arms and Armour Press, 1984).

SOVIET LOSSES 1941–1945

Dead*

Army and Navy	8,509,000
Internal Troops	97,700
Border Troops	61,400
Total	8,668,400

Wounded   18,000,000

*Killed in action, missing in action, taken prisoner and not returned, dead as a result of wounds, illness, or accident.

**Includes men that suffered one, two, or more wounds.

Source: Army General M.A. Moiseyev, Chief of the General Staff, *Voyenno-istoricheskiy zhurnal*, No. 3, March 1990.

SOVIET IRRECOVERABLE LOSSES 1941–1945
(First Period of the War)
(22 June 1941–18 November 1942)

1941: 1,733,680 (20.0%)
   of which 1,500,000 lost in Battles of Smolensk, Kiev, and Moscow Defensive Operations
1942: 2,859,472 (33.0%)
   of which 1,000,000 lost in Battles of Kharkov, Voroshilograd-Voronezh, Stalingrad, and North Caucasus Defensive Operations
Total: 4,593,152 (53.0%)
   of which 2,200,000 lost in Battle of Moscow (30 Sept 41–20 Apr 42) to include Vyazma/Bryansk Pockets*

Second Period of the War
(19 November 1942–31 December 1943)

1943: 2,958,248 (34.0%)

Third Period of the War
(1 January 1944–9 May 1945)

1944–5: 1,085,000 (12.5%)**
   of which the following were killed in the liberation of these countries:

Poland	600,000
Czechoslovakia	140,000
Hungary	140,000
Berlin Operation	102,000
Roumania	69,000
Austria	26,000
Yugoslavia	8,000

Defeat of Imperialist Japan
(2 August–9 September 1945)

1945: 32,000 (.4%)

Sources: Army General M.A. Moiseyev, Chief of the General Staff, *Voyenno-istorichesky zhurnal*, No. 3. March 1990.
*Colonel V. Yelishev, department chief in the USSR Ministry of Defence, Military Historical Institute, *Argumenty I Fakty*, No. 49, December 1991.
**S. Pshennikov, ed., *The Liberating Mission of the Soviet Union in the Second World War*, Moscow, 1985.
Note: Wounded are roughly three times the number of dead where figures are available. For example, total casualties for the Berlin Operation were 304,887; for the liberation of Roumania, 286,000.

SOVIET AND GERMAN TANK AND ARTILLERY PRODUCTION 1939–1945

	Tanks/SP Artillery		Artillery/AT/AAA	
	Soviet	German	Soviet	German
1939	2,950	247	17,348	1,214
1940	2,794	1,643	15,300	6,730
1941	6,590	3,790	42,300	11,200
1942	24,446	6,180	127,000	23,200
1943	24,089	12,063	130,300	46,100
1944	28,963	19,002	122,400	70,700
1945	15,419	3,923	62,000	?
Totals	105,251	46,857	516,648	159,144

Source: John Ellis, *Brute Force: Allied Strategy and Tactics in the Second World War* (New York: Viking, 1990).

ALLIED AND GERMAN MILITARY TRUCK PRODUCTION (1939 – 1945)

	US	UK	Soviet	German
1939	32,604	?	?	32,558
1940		89,582	?	53,348
1941	183,614	88,161	?	51,085
1942	619,735	87,449	30,400	58,049
1943	621,502	113,912	45,600	74,181
1944	596,963	54,615	52,600	67,375
1945	327,893	47,174	68,500	9,318
Totals	2,382,311	480,943	197,100	345,914

Source: John Ellis, *Brute Force: Allied Strategy and Tactics in the Second World War* (New York: Viking, 1990).

GERMAN CLAIMS OF SOVIET LOSSES IN ENCIRCLEMENTS 1941–2

1941	Date	POWs	Tanks	Guns	Armies	Opponent Army Gp
Belostok/Minsk	27 Jun	328,000	2,500	1,500	5	Centre
Smolensk	5 Aug	138,000	2,000	1,900	2	Centre
Uman	7 Aug	103,000	317	850	3	South
Roslavl/Krichev	14 Aug	54,000	200+	?	1	Centre
Kiev	26 Sep	665,000	886	3,718	5	South
Mariupol	10 Oct	65,000	212	672	1	South
Vyazma/Bryansk	17 Oct	663,000	1,242	5,412	9	Centre
1942						
Kerch	16 May	170,000	258	1,133	3	South
Izyum	28 May	239,000	1,250	2,026	3	South
Volkhov	28 May	33,000	?	?	1	North
Sevastopol	3 Jul	90,000	—	467	2	South
Kalach	8 Aug	50,000	1,000	750	2	South

Source: Paul Carrell, *Hitler Moves East* (Boston: Little, Brown & Co., 1964).

Although these German figures give the scale of the battles and captures of the first two years of the war, they should be taken with some reservation. For example, the Soviet forces of the Southwestern Front had a strength of 667,085 before the Battle of Kiev and 150,541 afterwards, though the Germans claimed 665,000 POWs. The former Soviet military press is still wrestling with the issue of exactly how many Soviet troops were taken prisoner. They do shed some light on German figures by stating that the Germans counted, in addition to captured military personnel, all males 16–60 years of age also caught with the pocket (see A. G. Khorkov, *Voyennaya Mysl*, No. 6, June, 1991)

COMPARATIVE SIZES OF MAJOR COMMANDS, NOVEMBER 1941 TO JANUARY 1943

German

1. Army Groups
   On the Eastern Front 4 to 5 plus the Twentieth Mountain Army and the Finnish Army to September 1944
2. Armies
   2 to 4 in any army group
3. Corps (including Panzer Corps)
   2 to 7 in an army
4. Divisions
   2 to 7 in a corps

Authorized Strengths, Divisions:

Panzer Division	14,000
(103 to 125 tanks)	to
	17,000
Motorized Division	14,000
(48 tanks)	
Infantry Division, 9 battalions	15,000
Infantry Division, 6 battalions	12,700
Artillery Division	3,380
(113 guns)	

Soviet

1. *Fronts* (Soviet army groups)
   10 to 12
2. Armies
   3 to 9 in a *Front*. Probable average 5 to 7
3. Rifle Corps
   Disbanded August 1941, reactivated late 1942 with 3 to 9 divisions
4. Divisions
   2 to 3 in a corps

Authorized Strengths, Armoured Corps and Divisions:

Tank Corps (189 tanks)	10,500
Mechanized Corps	16,000
(186 tanks)	
Rifle Division	9,375
Guards Rifle Division	10,585
Artillery Division	6,550
(210 guns)	

GERMAN AND SOVIET EASTERN FRONT ALLIES

German Allies Strength 1 May 1942

Finland	300,000	(55,000)*
Roumania	330,000	(350,000)*
Hungary	70,000	
Italy	68,000	
Slovakia	28,000	
Italy	227,000	
Spain	14,000	
Total	1,037,000	

Soviet Allies Strength 9 May 1945

Poland	440,000
Czechoslovakia	21,000
Roumania**	
Yugoslavia	
Hungary	
France***	
Total	550,000

Soviet Support to Allies

Formations Raised/Equipped
2 Field Armies
3 Army Corps
1 Tank Corps
1 Aviation Corps
30 Inf, Arty, Avn Divisions
31 Brigades
182 Regiments
9 Military Schools
19 Officer Schools

Equipment
16,502 guns and mortars
1,124 tanks
2,346 aircraft
900,000 rifles/submachine-guns
40,627 machine-guns

Soviet Personnel

20,000 Soviet military personnel trained allies.
13,000 Soviet military specialists supported the Polish Army.
20,000 Soviet military personnel served with Polish Army in combat.
900 Soviet officers and generals fell in combat serving with the Polish Army.

* Killed.
** Roumania changed sides in 1944 and lost a further 170,000 men killed against the Germans and Hungarians.
*** Represents the Free French Normandie fighter squadron sent by De Gaulle.

BIBLIOGRAPHY

This bibliography provides the reader with a comprehensive review of the most important literature in English of the epic Russo-German campaigns of World War II – with an emphasis on Soviet operations and, where possible, from the Soviet perspective. German accounts have been much more widely read in the West and are only included here where they are primary sources, general histories, or fill in the gaps. The heading 'Campaigns, Operations, and Battles' is subdivided by Soviet reckoning into the three periods of the war against Germany and a fourth on the defeat of Japan. Although some campaigns fall into several periods, they are referenced only in the section in which the primary effort fell.

Prelude to the Great Patriotic War

Alexandrov, V. *The Tukachevsky Affair.* New York, 1968.

Cecil, Robert. *Hitler's Decision to Invade Russia 1941.* New York, 1976.

Condon, R. W. *The Winter War: Russia versus Finland.* London, 1972.

Conquest, Robert. *The Great Terror: A Reassessment.* Oxford and New York, 1990.

Coox, Alvin D. *The Anatomy of a Small War: The Soviet-Japanese Struggle for Changkufeng/Khasan 1938.* Westport, Connecticut, 1977.

Creveld, Martin Van. *Hitler's Strategy 1940-41.* New York, 1973.

Department of the Army. *The German Campaign in the Balkans (Spring 1941).* Pamphlet No. 260. Washington, 1953.

Drea, Edward J. *Nomonhan: Japanese-Soviet Tactical Combat, 1939,* Leavenworth Paper No. 2. Fort Leavenworth, Kansas, 1981.

Engle, Eloise and Paananen, Lauri. *The Winter War: The Soviet Attack on Finland 1939-1940.* New York, 1973.

Erickson, John. *The Soviet High Command: A Military-Political History 1918-41.* London and New York, 1962.

Kennedy, Robert M. *The German Campaign in Poland (1939),* Department of the Army Pamphlet No. 20-255. Washington, 1956.

Leach, Barry. *German Strategy Against Russia 1937-41.* London and New York, 1973.

Simpkin, Richard. *Deep Battle: The Brainchild of Marshal Tukhachevskii.* London, 1987.

Thomas, Hugh. *The Spanish Civil War.* New York, 1961.

Warner, Oliver. *Marshal Mannerheim and the Finns.* London, 1967.

Wollenberg, Erich. *Red Army.* Secker and Warburg, 1940.

Zaloga, Steven J. and Madej, W. Victor. *The Polish Campaign 1939.* London and New York, 1985.

The Soviet Armed Forces

Boyd, Alexander. *The Soviet Air Force Since 1918.* London, 1977.

Garder, Michael. *A History of the Soviet Army.* New York, 1966.

Leites, Nathan. *The Soviet Style in War.* New York, 1982.

Liddell Hart, Basil H. *The Soviet Army.* London, 1956; US title: *The Red Army.* New York, 1956.

Mackintosh, Malcolm. *Juggernaut: A History of the Soviet Armed Forces.* New York, 1967.

O'Ballance, Edgar. *The Red Army.* London and New York, 1964.

Poierier, Robert B. and Albert Z. Conner. *The Red Army Order of Battle in the Great Patriotic War.* Novato, California, 1985.

Seaton, Albert. *The Horsemen of the Steppes (Cossacks).* London, 1985.

—. *The Soviet Army, 1918 – Present.* London and New York, 1986.

Zaloga, Steven J. *The Red Army of the Great Patriotic War 1941-5.* London, 1989.

Soviet Equipment and Combat Arms

Alexander, Jean. *Russian Aircraft since 1945.* London, 1975.

Barker, A. J. and John Walter. *Russian Infantry Weapons of World War 2.* London and New York, 1971.

Bellamy, Chris. *Red God of War: Soviet Artillery and Rocket Forces.* London, 1986.

Brereton, John M. and Feist, Uwe. *Russian Tanks 1915-1968.* Berkeley, California, 1970.

Chamberlain, P. and Ellis, C. *Soviet Combat Tanks 1939-1945.* London, 1970.

Green, William and Swanborough, Gordon. *Soviet Air Force Fighters.* New York, 1978.

Grove, Eric. *Russian Armour 1941-1943.* London, 1976.

Higham, Robin and Kipp, J. W. *Soviet Aviation and Air Power: A Historical View.* New York, 1977, and Boulder, Colorado, 1977.

Meister, J. Soviet *Warships of the Second World War.* London, 1977.

Milsom, John. *Russian Tanks 1900-1970.* London and Harrisburg, Pennsylvania, 1970.

Zaloga, Steven J. and Magnuski, J. *Soviet Mechanized Firepower 1941-1945.* London, 1989.

Zaloga, Steven J. and Grandsen, James. *Soviet Heavy Tanks.* London, 1981.

—. *Soviet Tanks and Combat Vehicles of World War Two.* London, 1984.

—. *The T-34 Tank.* London, 1980.

—. *The T-34 in Action.* London, 1981.

Soviet Command and Control

Bialer, Seweryn (ed.). *Stalin and His Generals: Soviet Military Memoirs of World War II.* London, 1965, 1970, and New York, 1969.

Chaney, Otto P. *Zhukov.* Norman, Oklahoma, 1971.

Erickson, John. *The Russian Imperial/Soviet General Staff.* College Station, Texas, 1981.

Kozhevnikov, M. N. *The Command and Staff of the Soviet Army Air Force in the Great Patriotic War 1941-1945.* Moscow, 1977 (translated and published under the auspices of the U.S. Air Force, Washington).

Seaton, Albert. *Stalin as Warlord.* London, 1976; US title: *Stalin As Military Commander.* New York, 1976.

Shtemenko, Sergei M. *The Soviet General Staff at War, 1941-1945*. Moscow, 1970, 1986.

Campaigns, Operations, and Battles

First Period of the War (22 June 1941-18 November 1942)

Bethell, Nicholas. *Russia Besieged*. Alexandria, Virginia, 1977.

Blau, George E. *The German Campaign in Russia – Planning and Operations (1940-1942)*. Department of the Army Pamphlet No. 20-261a. Washington, 1955.

Carell, Paul. *Hitler Moves East 1941-1943*. Boston, 1964; UK title: *Hitler's War on Russia*. London, 1964.

Craig, W. *Enemy at the Gates: The Battle for Stalingrad*. New York, 1973.

Chuikov, Vasili I. *The Beginning of the Road*. London, 1963; US title: *The Battle for Stalingrad*. New York, 1964.

Eremenko (also spelled Yeremenko), A. I. *Stalingrad*. Moscow, 1961.

Erickson, John. *The Road to Stalingrad: Stalin's War With Germany*. London and New York, 1975; and Boulder, Colorado, 1984.

Fugate, Bryan I. *Operation Barbarossa: Strategy and Tactics on the Eastern Front, 1941*. Novato, California, 1984.

Goure, Leon. *The Siege of Leningrad*. Stanford, California, 1962.

Grechko, Andrei. *Battle for the Caucasus*. Moscow, 1971.

Guderian, Heinz. *Panzer Leader*. London and New York, 1952.

Halder, Franz. *The Halder War Diary 1939-1942*. Novato, California, and London, 1988.

Jukes, Geoffrey. *The Defence of Moscow*. London, 1970.

—. *Stalingrad: The Turning Point*. London, 1968.

Keegan, John. *Barbarossa: Invasion of Russia 1941*. London, 1970.

Luck, Hans von. *Panzer Commander: The Memoirs of Colonel Hans von Luck*. New York, 1989.

Madeja, W. Victor, (ed.). *Russo-German War: Summer-Autumn 1942*. Allentown, Pennsylvania, 1989.

—. *Russo-German War: Summer 1941*. Allentown, Pennsylvania, 1989.

—. *Russo-German War: Winter-Spring 1942*. Allentown, Pennsylvania, 1989.

Nekrich, A. M. *June 22, 1941*. Columbia, South Carolina, 1968.

Pavlov, D. V. *Leningrad 1941: The Blockade*. Chicago, 1965.

Parrish, Michael (ed.). *Battle for Moscow: The 1942 Soviet General Staff Study*. Washington, New York, London, 1989.

Piekalkiewicz, Janusz. *Moscow: 1941 – The Frozen Offensive*. Novato, California, and London, 1985.

Rotundo, Louis (ed.). *Battle for Stalingrad: The 1943 Soviet General Staff Study*. Washington, New York, London, 1989.

Salisbury, Harrison E. *The 900 Days: The Siege of Leningrad*. New York, 1969; UK title: *The Siege of Leningrad*, London, 1969.

Seaton, Albert. *The Battle for Moscow, 1941-1945*. London, 1971.

Senger und Etterlin, Frido von. *Neither Hope Nor Fear*. London, 1963, and Novato, California, and London, 1989.

Turney, Alfred. *Disaster at Moscow: von Bock's Campaigns, 1941-1942*. London, 1971.

Werth, Alexander. *The Year of Stalingrad*. London, 1946.

Whaley, B. *Codeword: BARBAROSSA*. Cambridge, Massachusetts, 1973.

Wray, Timothy A. *Standing Fast: German Defensive Doctrine on the Russian Front During World War II: Prewar to March 1943*, Combat Studies Institute Research Survey No. 5. Fort Leavenworth, Kansas, 1986.

Wykes, Alan. *The Siege of Leningrad: Epic of Survival*. New York, 1968.

Yeremenko (also spelled Eremenko as above), A. I. *An Arduous Beginning*. Moscow, 1966.

Ziemke, Earl F. *Moscow to Stalingrad: Decision in the East*. Washington, 1987.

Second Period of the War (19 November-End of 1943)

Caidin, Martin. *The Tigers Are Burning*. New York, 1974.

Carell, Paul. *Scorched Earth*. London and Boston, 1970.

Chant, Christopher. *Kursk*. London, 1975.

Glantz, David. *From the Don to the Dnepr: Soviet Offensive Operations December 1942 – August 1943*. New York, 1991.

Jukes, Geoffrey. *Kursk: the Clash of Armour*. London, 1969.

Madeja, W. Victor, (ed.). *Russo-German War: Summer-Autumn 1943*. Allentown, Pennsylvania, 1987.

—. *Russo-German War: Summer 1943*. Allentown, Pennsylvania, 1989.

—. *Russo-German War: Winter-Spring 1943*. Allentown, Pennsylvania, 1989.

Pertotkin, I. (ed.). *The Battle of Kursk*. Moscow, 1974.

Piekalkiewicz, Janusz. *Operation Citadel: Kursk and Orel, the Greatest Tank Battle of the Second World War*. Novato, California, 1987.

Sadarananda, Dana V. *Beyond Stalingrad: Manstein and the Operations of Army Group Don*. London, New York, and Westport, Connecticut, 1990.

Shaw, John. *The Red Army Resurgent*. Alexandria, Virginia, 1979.

Solovyov, Boris. *The Battle of Kursk*. Moscow, 1973.

Third Period of the War (1 January 1944-9 May 1945)

Adelman, Jonathan. *The Soviet & American Destruction of the Third Reich, June 1944-May 1945*. Boulder, Colorado, 1985.

Buchner, Alex. *Ostfront 1944: The German Defensive Battle on the Russian Front*. New York, 1991.

Chuikov, Vasili I. *The End of the Third Reich*. London, 1964; US title: *The Fall of Berlin*. New York, 1967.

Duffy, Christopher. *Red Storm on the Reich: The Soviet March on Germany, 1945*. London and New York, 1991.

Erickson, John. *The Road to Berlin: Continuing the History of Stalin's War With Germany*. Boulder, Colorado, 1983.

Gebhardt, James F. *The Petsamo-Kirkenes Operation: Soviet Breakthrough in the Arctic, October 1944*, Leavenworth Papers No. 17. Fort Leavenworth, Kansas, 1989.

Grechko, Andrei A. *Liberation Mission of the Soviet Armed Forces in the Second World War*. Moscow, 1975.

Konev, Ivan S. *The Great March of Liberation: Poland Achieves Freedom*. Moscow, 1972.

—. *Year of Victory*. Moscow, 1969.

Kuby, E. *The Russians and Berlin, 1945*. London, 1968.

Madeja, W. Victor, (ed.). *Russo-German War: Autumn 1944 to January 25 1945*. Allentown, Pennsylvania, 1987.

—. *Russo-German War: January 25 Through Spring 1945: The Last 100 Days*. Allentown, Pennsylvania, 1987.

—. *Russo-German War: Summer 1944*. Allentown, Pennsylvania, 1987.

Ryan, Cornelius. *The Last Battle*. New York and London, 1966.

Schultz-Naumann, Joachim. *The Last Thirty Days: The War Diary of the Wehrmacht High Command from April to May 1945*. New York, 1991.

Seruk, V. (ed.) *How Wars End: Eye Witness Accounts of the Fall of Berlin.* Moscow, 1969.

Shtemenko, Sergei M. *The Last Six Months.* London and New York, 1977.

Slater, Lisa. *The Rape of Berlin.* Brooklyn, New York, 1972.

Smith, Jean. *The Defense of Berlin.* Baltimore, Maryland, 1974.

Thorwald, Juergen. *Defeat in the East: Russia Conquers – January to May 1945.* New York, 1959. (formerly *Flight in the Winter.* London and New York, 1951).

Toland, John. *The Last 100 Days.* New York and London, 1966.

Tully, Andrew. *Berlin, Story of a Battle.* New York, 1963, and Westport, Connecticut, 1977.

Zaloga, Steven J. and Grandsen, James. *The Road to Berlin.* London, 1990.

Zawodny, J. K. *Nothing But Honor: The Story of the Warsaw Uprising, 1944.* Stanford, California, 1978.

Ziemke, Earl F. *Stalingrad to Berlin: The German Defeat in the East.* Washington, 1968.

—. *The Soviet Juggernaut.* Alexandria, Virginia, 1980.

Defeat of Imperialist Japan (9 August-2 September 1945)

Coox, Alvin. D. *Soviet Armor in Action Against the Japanese Kwangtung Army.* Baltimore, 1952.

Dzirkals, Liita I. *"Lighting War" in Manchuria: Soviet Military Analysis of the 1945 Far East Campaign.* Santa Monica, California, 1976.

—. *August Storm: The Soviet 1945 Strategic Offensive in Manchuria,* Leavenworth Papers No. 7. (by David M. Glantz). Fort Leavenworth, Kansas, 1983.

—. *August Storm: Soviet Tactical and Operational Combat in Manchuria, 1945,* Leavenworth Papers No. 8. (by David M. Glantz). Fort Leavenworth, Kansas, 1983.

Meretskov, Kirill A. *Serving the Soviet People.* Moscow, 1971.

Zakharov, M. V. *Finale.* Moscow, 1972.

General Works on Operations

Beaumont, J. *Comrades in Arms: British Aid to Russia 1941-45.* London, 1980.

Chew, Allen F. *Fighting the Russians in the Winter: Three Case Studies,* Leavenworth Paper No. 5. Fort Leavenworth, Kansas, 1981.

Clark, Alan. *Barbarossa: the Russian-German Conflict 1941-45.* New York and

London, 1965.

Collet's Holdings, Ltd. Staff, (ed.). *The Great Patriotic War of the Soviet People & Our Time.* (History of the USSR: New Research No. 3). London, 1985.

Department of the Army. *Military Improvisations During the Russian Campaign,* Pamphlet No. 20-201. Washington, 1951.

—. *Russian Combat Methods in World War II.* Pamphlet No. 20-230. Washington, 1950.

—. *Combat in Russian Forests and Swamps,* Pamphlet No. 20-231. Washington, 1951.

—. *Airborne Operations: A German Appraisal,* Pamphlet No. 20-232. Washington, 1951.

—. Pamphlet No. 20-233. *German Defense Tactics Against Russian Breakthroughs,* Pamphlet No. 20-233. Washington, 1951.

—. *Operations of Encircled Forces: German Experiences in Russia,* Pamphlet 20-234. Washington, 1952.

—. *Night Combat,* Pamphlet No. 20-236. Washington, 1953.

—. *German Armored Traffic Control During the Russian Campaign.* Pamphlet No. 20-242. Washington, 1952.

—. *Small Unit Actions During the German Campaign in Russia,* Pamphlet No. 20-269. Washington, 1953.

—. *Terrain Factors in the Russian Campaign.* Pamphlet No. 20-270. Washington, 1951.

—. *Effects of Climate on Combat in European Russia,* Pamphlet No. 20-291. Washington, 1952.

—. *Warfare in the Far North,* Pamphlet No. 20-292. Washington, 1951.

Dunnigan, J. F. (Ed.). *The Russian Front: Germany's War in the East 1941-45.* London, 1978. US Title: *War in the East: The Russo-German Conflict 1941-45.* New York, 1977.

Dupuy, T. N. and Martell, P. *Great Battles on the Eastern Front.* New York, 1982.

Glantz, David M. *The Role of Intelligence in Soviet Military Strategy in World War II.* Novato, California, 1991.

—. *The Soviet Airborne Experience.* Combat Studies Institute Research Survey No. 4. Fort Leavenworth, Kansas, 1984.

—. *Soviet Military Deception in the Second World War.* London and Totowa, New Jersey, 1990.

Gorbatov, A. V. *Years Off My Life.* New York, 1958.

Grigorenko, Petro G. *Memoirs.* London and New York, 1981.

Khrushchev, Nikita S. *Khrushchev Remembers.* London and New York, 1971.

Jones, Robert Huhn. *The Road to Russia: United States Lend-Lease to the Soviet Union.* Norman, Oklahoma, 1969.

Karpov, Vladimir. *Russia At War 1941-45.* New York, 1987, and London, 1988.

Larionov, V., et. al. *World War II Decisive Battles of the Red Army.* Moscow, 1984.

Mannerheim, Gustav. *The Memoirs of Marshal Mannerheim.* New York, 1953.

Manstein, Erich von. *Lost Victories.* London, 1958, and Novato, California, 1982.

Mellenthin, F. W. von. *German Generals of World War II As I Saw Them.* Norman, Oklahoma, 1977,

—. *Panzer Battles: A Study of the Employment of Armor in the Second World War.* Norman, Oklahoma, 1956, 1971.

Rokossovsky, Konstantin K. *A Soldier's Duty.* Moscow, 1985.

Sajer, Guy. *The Forgotten Soldier.* London and New York, 1971.

Salisbury, Harrison. *The Unknown War.* New York, 1978.

Sasso, Claude R. *Soviet Night Operations in World War II,* Leavenworth Paper No. 6. Fort Leavenworth, Kansas, 1982.

Seaton, Albert. *The Russo-German War, 1941-45.* New York, 1971, Novato, California, 1991.

Sokolov, Sergei, ed. *Main Front: Soviet Leaders Look Back on World War II.* London, 1987.

Werth, Alexander. *Russia at War, 1941-45.* London and New York: 1964.

Zaloga, Steven J. and Grandsen, James. *The Eastern Front 1941-45.* London, 1983.

Ziemke, Earl F. *The German Northern Theater of Operations 1940-1945,* Department of the Army Pamphlet No. 20-271. Washington, 1959.

Zhukov, Georgi K., et. al. *Battles Hitler Lost: And the Marshals Who Won Them.* New York, 1986.

—. *Marshal Zhukov's Greatest Battles.* New York and London, 1969.

—. *Reminiscences and Reflections.* Moscow, 1974. US title: *The Memoirs of Marshal Zhukov.* New York, 1971.

Air and Naval Operations

Achkasov, A. I. and Pavlovich, N. B. *Soviet Naval Operations in the Great Patriotic War 1941-1945.* Annapolis, 1973.

Deichmann, Paul. *German Air Force Operations in Support of the Army*. New York, 1962.

Golovko, A. G. *With the Red Fleet: Memoirs of the Late Admiral Arseni G. Golovko*. London, 1965.

Hardesty, Von. *Red Phoenix: The Rise of Soviet Air Power 1941-1945*. Washington and London, 1982.

Jackson, Robert. *The Red Falcons: The Soviet Air Force in Action 1919-1969*. New York, 1970.

Kolyshkin, I. *Submarines in Arctic Waters*. Moscow, 1966.

Mitchell, Donald W. *A History of Russian and Soviet Sea Power*. New York, 1974.

Morzik, Fritz. *German Air Force Airlift Operations*, USAF Historical Studies No. 167. Maxwell AFB, AL, 1961.

Murray, W. *Luftwaffe: Strategy for Defeat 1933-45*. London, 1985.

Plocher, Hermann. *The German Air Force Versus Russia 1941*. New York, 1965 (originally USAF Historical Division GAF 153).

—. *The German Air Force Versus Russia 1942*. New York, 1966 (originally USAF Historical Division GAF 154).

—. *The German Air Force Versus Russia 1943*. New York, 1967 (originally USAF Historical Division GAF 155).

Ruge, Friedrich. *The Soviets As Naval Opponents*. Annapolis, Maryland, 1979.

Schwabedissen, Walter. *The Russian Air Force in the Eyes of German Commanders*. New York, 1968 (originally USAF Historical Division GAF 175).

Uebe, D. K. *Russian Reactions to German Airpower in World War II*. New York, 1968 (originally USAF Historical Division GAF 176).

Wagner, Ray (Ed.) *The Soviet Air Force in World War II: The Official History*. New York, 1973.

German Occupation, Partisan Operations, and the Anti-Soviet Opposition

Armstrong, John A. (Ed.). *Soviet Partisans in World War II*. Madison, Wisconsin, 1964.

Cooper, Mathew. *The Nazi War Against Soviet Partisans, 1941-1944*. London, 1979.

Dallin, Alexander. *German Rule in Russia, 1941-45*. London, 1957.

—. *Rear Area Security in Russia: The Soviet Second Front Behind German Lines*, Pamphlet No. 20-240. Washington, 1951.

Fisher, George. *Soviet Opposition to Stalin: A Case Study in World War II*. Cambridge, Massachusetts, 1952.

Gordon, G. *Soviet Partisan Warfare: The German Perspective*. Iowa, 1972.

Howell, Edgar M. *The Soviet Partisan Movement 1941-1944*. Department of the Army Pamphlet 20-244. Washington, 1956.

Sodol, Petro R. *UPA: They Fought Hitler and Stalin: A Brief Overview of Military Aspects from the History of the Ukrainian Insurgent Army, 1942-1949*. New York, 1987.

Steenberg, Sven. *Vlasov*. New York, 1970.

Strik-Strikfeldt, Wilfried. *Against Hitler and Stalin: Memoir of the Russian Liberation Movement 1941-1945*. London, 1970, and New York, 1971.

The German Armed Forces

Cooper, Mathew. *The German Army 1933-45: Its Political and Military Failure*. London, 1978.

Dupuy, T. N. *A Genius for War: The German Army and the General Staff*. Englewood Cliffs, New Jersey, 1977.

Keegan, John. *Waffen SS: The Asphalt Soldiers*. London and New York, 1970.

Lucas, James. *Alpine Elite: German Mountain Troops of World War II*. London 1980.

Madej, W. Victor. *German Army Order of Battle, 1939-1945*. Allentown, Pennsylvania, 1981.

Mason, H. M. *The Rise of the Luftwaffe 1918-1940*. New York, 1976.

Newland, Samuel J. *Cossacks in the German Army 1941-1945*. New York, 1991.

Seaton, Albert. *The German Army 1933-1945*. London and New York, 1985.

Stein, George H. *The Waffen SS: Hitler's Elite Guard at war, 1939-1945*. Ithaca, New York, 1966.

Sydnor, Chalres W. *Soldiers of Destruction: The SS Death's Head Division, 1933-1945*. Princeton, New Jersey, 1977.

German Equipment and Combat Arms

Chamberlain, P. and Doyle, H., and Jenz, T. *Encyclopedia of German Tanks of World War Two*. London and New York, 1978.

Cooper, Mathew and James, Lucas. *Panzer: The Armoured Force of the Third Reich*. London, 1976, and New York, 1978.

Edwards, Roger. *Panzer: A Revolution in Warfare, 1939-1945*. London, 1989.

Shepherd, Christopher. *German Aircraft of World War II*. London, 1975.

German Command and Control

Addington, Larry H. *The Blitzkrieg Era and the German General Staff, 1865-1941*. New Brunswick, New Jersey, 1971.

Gilbert, Felix, ed. *Hitler Directs His War*. New York, 1950.

Goerlitz, Walter. *History of the German General Staff 1657-1945*. New York, 1953; UK title: *The German General Staff: Its History and Structure, 1657-1945*. London, 1953.

Schultz-Naumann, Joachim. *The Last Thirty Days: The War Diary of the Wehrmacht High Command from April to May 1945*. New York, 1991.

Strawson, J. *Hitler As Military Commander*. London, 1971.

Warlimont, W. *Inside Hitler's Headquarters*. London, 1964, and Novato, California, 1991.

The German Commanders and Allies

Barnett, Correlli. *Hitler's Generals*. London and New York, 1989.

Blummentritt, Guenther. *Von Rundstedt: The Soldier and the Man*. London, 1952.

Davis, C. R. *Von Kleist: From Hussar to Panzer Marshal*. Houston, Texas, 1979.

Doenitz, Karl. *Memoirs: 10 Years and 20 Days*. Cleveland, Ohio, 1959.

Gehlen, Reinhard. *The Service: The Memoirs of General Reinhard Gehlen*. London and New York, 1972.

Halder, Franz. *Hitler as War Lord*. London, 1950.

Keitel, Wilhelm. *The Memoirs of Field Marshal Keitel*. New York, 1965.

Liddell Hart, Basil H. *The Other Side of the Hill*. London, 1948. US title: *The German Generals Talk*, New York, 1948.

Macksey, Kennneth. *Guderian, Creater of the Blitzkrieg*. London, 1975, 1992, and New York, 1976.

—. *Kesselring: The Making of the Luftwaffe*. Batsford, UK, 1978.

Messenger, Charles. *Hitler's Gladiator: The Life and Times of Oberstgruppenfuerher and Panzergeneral-Oberst der Waffen-SS Sepp Dietrich*. London and New York, 1987.

Rudel, Hans Ulrich. *Stuka Pilot*. Dublin, 1952, and New York, 1958.

Schramm, Percy Ernst. *Hitler: The Man and the Military Leader*. New York, 1971.

Strawson, J. *Hitler As Military Commander*. London, 1971.

INDEX